Practical Android 4
Games Development

J. F. DiMarzio

Apress®

Practical Android 4 Games Development

ISBN-13 (pbk): 978-1-4302-4029-7

ISBN-13 (electronic): 978-1-4302-4030-3

President and Publisher: Paul Manning
Lead Editor: James Markham
Technical Reviewers: Yosun Chang, Tony Hillerson
Editorial Board: Steve Anglin, Mark Beckner, Ewan Buckingham, Gary Cornell,
    Morgan Ertel, Jonathan Gennick, Jonathan Hassell, Robert Hutchinson,
    Michelle Lowman, James Markham, Matthew Moodie, Jeff Olson, Jeffrey Pepper,
    Douglas Pundick, Ben Renow-Clarke, Dominic Shakeshaft, Gwenan Spearing,
    Matt Wade, Tom Welsh
Coordinating Editor: Corbin Collins
Copy Editor: Heather Lang
Compositor: MacPS, LLC
Indexer: SPi Global
Artist: SPi Global
Cover Designer: Anna Ishchenko

Distributed to the book trade worldwide by Springer Science+Business Media, LLC., 233 Spring Street, 6th Floor, New York, NY 10013. Phone 1-800-SPRINGER, fax (201) 348-4505, e-mail orders-ny@springer-sbm.com, or visit www.springeronline.com.

For information on translations, please e-mail rights@apress.com, or visit www.apress.com.

Apress and friends of ED books may be purchased in bulk for academic, corporate, or promotional use. eBook versions and licenses are also available for most titles. For more information, reference our Special Bulk Sales–eBook Licensing web page at www.apress.com/bulk-sales.

The source code for this book is available to readers at www.apress.com. You will need to answer questions pertaining to this book in order to successfully download the code.

This book is dedicated to my wife Suzannah and our three children, Christian, Sophia, and Giovanni; for putting up with the late nights and long weekends while I created this book.

Contents at a Glance

Contents

Foreword

I dreamed of making video games when I was young, like nearly every other boy my age, but had no idea where to even begin. Everyone has the capability for a great game idea, but having the tools to create it is a much different story. The internet was in its infancy and there were precious few resources on game development, since even those in the industry were still figuring things out. For me, things changed as I got into my early 20s and found that universities were now starting to teach game design and development.

Even after finishing my degree, I remember realizing that there was very little opportunity for me to showcase my skills to potential employers. I was good at programming, but there wasn't much in the way of game development software that would allow me to focus on creating gameplay. It really took a team then to create anything more than the most simplistic games. There was certainly no way for a single developer to make a living working on their own unless they were skilled in all types of programming, art, and design and could sustain themselves for years while working on it.

Things started changing rapidly as the social gaming market began to explode and mobile devices became powerful enough to run truly fun game experiences. Things have continued to evolve so much that I'm blown away to see that games that I played on a console a decade ago are now fully functional in the palm of my hand. Along with this came game development software environments that allowed game developers to easily create games and focus on fun and functionality, no longer having to worry about just getting the nuts and bolts going.

Now there are so many choices out there for game developers that the decision just becomes which one to focus your time on? If flexibility is your goal, then Android is the clear winner with its open environment that encourages the developer and gives options for how and where to make their content available to consumers. It's also simple to create content that is usable on both Android tablets and mobile devices, making your chance for profit much higher with the same work involved.

If you are jumping into Android development as a springboard for other things, the good news is that Java is a widely used language, so, you will be able to use the knowledge gained in the future. Plus Java is one of the easier languages to start with as a beginner. I wish I had had such tools and platforms available when I began my career! Now is a great time to jump in and make that dream of making games happen.

Jameson Durall
Game Designer
@siawnhy on Twitter
www.jamesondurall.com

About the Author

J. F. DiMarzio is a seasoned Android developer and author. He began developing games in Basic on the TRS-80 Color Computer II in 1984. Since then, DiMarzio has worked in the technology departments of companies such as the U.S. Department of Defense and the Walt Disney Company. He has been developing on the Android platform since the beta release of version .03, and he has published two professional applications and one game on the Android Market.

About the Technical Reviewers

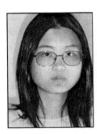 **Yosun Chang** has been creating apps for iOS and Android since early 2009, and is currently working on a next generation 3D and augmented reality mobile games startup called nusoy. Prior to that, since 1999 she did web development on the LAMP stack and Flash. She has also spoken at several virtual world, theater, and augmented reality conferences under her artist name of Ina Centaur. She has a graduate level background in physics and philosophy from UC San Diego and UC Berkeley. An avid reader who learned much of her coding chops from technical books like the current volume, she has taken care to read every single word of the chapters she reviewed — and vet the source. Contact her @yosunchang on Twitter.

 **Tony Hillerson** is a software architect at EffectiveUI. He graduated from Ambassador University with a B.A. in Management Information Systems. On any given day, Tony might be working with Android, Rails, Objective-C, Java, Flex, or shell scripts. He has been interested in developing for Android since the early betas. Hillerson has created Android screencasts, has spoken about Android at conferences, and has served as technical reviewer on Android books. He also sometimes gets to write Android code. He is interested in all levels of usability and experience design, from the database to the server to the glass. In his free time, Hillerson enjoys playing the bass, playing World of Warcraft, and making electronic music. Tony lives outside Denver, Colorado, with his wife and two sons.

About the Game Graphics Designer

Ben Eagle has been working with computer graphics and web development for 14 years, which he learned while serving in the Marine Corps. While working with various companies, Ben has designed hundreds of sites, company signs, logos, commercials, and marketing graphics. Currently he works as a senior programmer, living in Davenport Florida. At the age of 34 he continues to pursue his career and teaches graphics to students on the side. He has acquired two associate's degrees in digital media and web development. Ben also has his MCP and C++/Java certification. In his leisure he continues his passion in computer arts and programming and performs in a band.

Acknowledgments

I would like to thank everyone who made this book possible: my agent Neil Salkind and everyone at Studio B; Steve Anglin, Corbin Collins, James Markham, Yosun Chang, Tony Hillerson, and the gang at Apress books; Ben Eagle for the *in-game* graphics; MD, JS, CL, DL, MB, JK, CH, BB, DB, and KK at DWSS; and everyone else who helped me along the way who I may have forgotten.

Preface

Welcome to *Practical Android 4 Games Development*. This book takes you step by step through the evolution of two different mobile games; from concept through code. You will learn how to conceive a game from a root idea and carry through to the complex task of coding an engine to turn your idea into a playable game.

I decided to write this book to teach the skills needed to create your own 2D and 3D games for the Android 4 platform. Android 4 unites the operating systems of Android-based mobile phones and tablets under one common SDK. This means that the games you develop can be played on the latest tablets and phones, and on the best possible hardware. The same game is now playable on either kind of device; you just need to take the first step and create a compelling game.

When the first Android SDK with full OpenGL ES 2D and 3D support was released, I immediately found myself looking for ways to create games that were compelling and fun to play. That's when I realized that the skills needed to create these games, though not hard to master, were definitely not easy to discover on one's own. In fact, unless you had previous experience in OpenGL and specifically OpenGL ES, it was very hard to just dive right in to casual Android game development.

I decided to take what I had learned in developing casual games on Android and break that knowledge into a core set of basic skills that could be easily mastered and expanded on as you progress in your game development. These basic skills might not see you creating the next *Red Faction: Armageddon* right after you complete this book, but they will give you the knowledge necessary to understand how such games are made and possibly create them with the right dedication and practice.

No doubt you have your first Android game already mapped out in your head. You know exactly the way you want it to look, and exactly the way you want it to play. What you don't know is how to get that idea out of your head and on to your phone or tablet. While it is great to have an idea for a game, it is getting that game from the idea stage to the "playable on a mobile device" stage that is the tricky part.

My advice to you as you read through this book is to keep your ideas simple. Do not try to overcomplicate a good game just to because you can. What I mean by that is, some of the most "addictive" games are not necessarily the most complex. They tend to be the games that are easy to pick up and play but hard to put down. Keep this in mind as you begin to conceptualize the kind of games you want to make. In this book you will make a simple engine that will power a scrolling shooter. The scrolling shooter is a simple game type that can encompass very difficult and challenging games. It has long been considered one of the more addicting arcade style games because it offers fast action and a nearly unlimited amount of game play. It is very easy to go back to a scrolling shooter time and time again and have a rewording gaming experience. This is why I chose this style of game to start you off. In the end, if you try to make games that you would like to play as a gamer, then your experience will be rewarding. I hope you enjoy your journey into the wonderful world of Android game development.

Part I

Planning and Creating 2D Games

The first part of this book, Chapter 1-9, will take you through the processes of planning and creating a playable 2D Android game – Star Fighter. The creation of this game will follow a distinct and logical path. First you will plan and write the story behind your game. Next, you will create the background for the game. Then you will create the playable and non-playable characters. Finally you will create the weapons systems and collision detection. Before following the steps needed to deploy your game to a mobile device in Chapter 9, at the end of Chapter 8, I provide the complete code listings of the most important 2D files that you either created or modified in Part 1. Use these listings to compare your code and ensure that each game runs properly. This will prepare you for the 3D development phase that follows in Part 2: "Creating 3D Games" (Chapters 10-12).

Chapter 1

Welcome to Android Gaming

I began developing on Android in early 2008 on the beta platform. At the time, no phones were announced for the new operating system and we developers genuinely felt as though we were at the beginning of something exciting. Android captured all of the energy and excitement of the early days of open source development. Developing for the platform was very reminiscent of sitting around an empty student lounge at 2:00 a.m. with a Jolt cola waiting for VAX time to run our latest code. It was an exciting platform to see materialize, and I am glad I was there to see it.

As Android began to grow and Google released more updates to solidify the final architecture, one thing became apparent: Android, being based on Java and including many well known Java packages, would be an easy transition for the casual game developer. Most of the knowledge that a Java developer already had could be recycled on this new platform. The very large base of Java game developers could use that knowledge to move fairly smoothly onto the Android platform.

So how does a Java developer begin developing games on Android and what tools are required? This chapter aims to answer these questions and more. Here, you will learn how to block out your game's story into chunks that can be fully realized as parts of your game. We'll explore some of the essential tools required to carry out the tasks in future chapters

This chapter is very important, because it gives you something that not many other gaming books have—a true focus on the genesis of a game. While knowing how to write the code that will bring a game to life is very important, great code will not help if you do not have a game to bring to life. Knowing how to get the idea for your game out of your head in a clean and clear way will make the difference between a good game and a game that the player can't put down.

Programming Android Games

Developing games on Android has its pros and cons, which you should be aware of before you begin. First, Android games are developed in Java, but Android is not a complete Java implementation. Many of the packages that you may have used for OpenGL and other graphic embellishments are included in the Android software development kit (SDK). "Many" does not mean "all" though, and some very helpful packages for game developers, especially 3-D game developers, are not included. Not every package that you may have relied on to build your previous games will be available to you in Android.

With each release of new Android SDK, more and more packages become available, and older ones may be deprecated. You will need to be aware of just which packages you have to work with, and we'll cover these are we progress through the chapters.

Another pro is Android's familiarity, and a con is its lack of power. What Android may offer in familiarity and ease of programming, it lacks in speed and power. Most video games, like those written for PCs or consoles, are developed in low-level languages such as C and even assembly languages. This gives the developers the most control over how the code is executed by the processor and the environment in which the code is run. Processors run very low-level code, and the closer you can get to the native language of the processor, the fewer interpreters you need to jump through to get your game running. Android, while it does offer some limited ability to code at a low level, interprets and threads your Java code through its own execution system. This gives the developer less control over the environment the game is run in.

This book is not going to take you though the low-level approaches to game development. Why? Because Java, especially as it is presented for general Android development, is widely known, easy to use, and can create some very fun, rewarding games.

In essence, if you are already an experienced Java developer, you will find that your skills are not lost in translation when applied to Android. If you are not already a seasoned Java developer, do not fear. Java is a great language to start learning on. For this reason, I have chosen to stick with Android's native Java development environment to write our games.

We have discussed a couple of pros and cons to developing games on Android. However, one of the biggest pros to independent and casual game developers to create and publish games on the Android platform is the freedom that you are granted in releasing your games. While some online application stores have very stringent rules for what can be sold in them and for how much, the Android Market does not. Anyone is free to list and sell just about anything they want. This allows for a much greater amount of creative freedom for developers.

In Chapter 2, you'll create your first Android-based game, albeit a very simple one. First, however, it's important look behind the scenes to see what inspires any worthwhile game, the *story*.

Starting with a Good Story

Every game, from the simplest arcade game to the most complex role-playing game (RPG), starts with a story. The story does not have to be anything more than a sentence, like this: Imagine if we had a giant spaceship that shot things.

However, the story can be as long as a book and describe every land, person, and animal in the environment of a game. It could even describe every weapon, challenge, and achievement.

> **NOTE:** The story outlines the action, purpose, and flow of a game. The more detail that you can put into it, the easier your job developing the code will be.

Take a look at the game in Figure 1–1, what does it tell you? This is a screen shot from *Star Fighter*; the game that you will be developing through the beginning chapters of this book. There is a story behind this game as well.

Figure 1–1. Star Fighter *screen shot*

Most of us never get to read the stories that helped create some of our favorite games, because the stories are really only important to the people who are creating the game. And assuming the developers and creators do their jobs well, the gamer will absorb the story playing the game.

In small, independent development shops, the stories might never be read by anyone other than the lead developer. In larger game-development companies, the story could be passed around and worked on by a number of designers, writers, and engineers before it ends up in the hands of the lead developers.

Everyone has a different way to write and handle the creation of the story for the games that they want to make. There is no right or wrong way to handle a game's story other than to say that it needs to exist before you begin to write any code. The next section will explain why the story is so important.

Why Story Matters

Admittedly, in the early days of video gaming, stories may not have been looked upon as importantly as they are now. It was much easier to market a game that offered quick enjoyment without needing to get very deep into its purpose.

This is definitely not the case anymore. People, whether they are playing *Angry Birds* or *World of Warcraft*, expect a defined purpose to the action. This expectation may even be on a subconscious level, but your game needs to hook the players so that they want to keep playing. This hook is the driving purpose of the story.

The story behind your game is important for a few different reasons. Let's take a look at exactly why you should spend the time to develop your story before you begin to write any code for your game.

The first reason why the story behind your game is important is because it gives you a chance to fully realize your game, from beginning to end, before you begin coding. No matter what you do for a living, whether you are a full-time game developer or are just doing this as a hobby, your time is worth something.

In the case of a full-time game developer, there will be an absolute dollar value assigned to each hour you spend coding and create a game. If you are creating independent games in your spare time, your time can be measured in the things you could be doing otherwise: fishing, spending time with others, and so on. No matter how you look at it, your time has a definite and concrete worth, and the more time you spend coding your game, the more it costs.

If your game is not fully realized before you begin working on your code, you will inevitably run into problems that can force you to go back to tweak or completely rewrite code that was already finished. This will cost you in time, money, or sanity.

> **NOTE:** To be fully realized an idea must be complete. Every aspect of the idea has been though out and carefully considered.

As a game developer, the last thing that you want is to be forced to go back and change code that is finished and possibly even tested. Ideally, your code should be extensible enough that you can manipulate it without much effort—especially if you want to add levels or bosses onto your game later. However, you may have to recode something relatively minor, like the name of a character or environment, or you might have to change something more drastic. For example, maybe you realized you never gave your main character the weapon needed to finish the game because you didn't know how it was going to end when you started building it.

Having a fully developed story arc for your game will give you a linear map to follow when writing your code. Mapping out your game and its details like this will save you from many of the problems that could cause you to recode already-finished parts of your game. This leads us to the next reason why you should have a story before you begin coding.

The story that your game is based on will also serve as reference material as you write your code. Whether you need to look back on the correct spelling of the name of a character name or group of villains or to refresh your memory as to the layout of a city street, you should be able to pull your information from your.

Being able to refer to the story for details is especially key if multiple people are going to be working on the game together. There may be sections of the story that you did not write. If you are coding something that refers to one of those sections, the fully realized story document is an invaluable piece of reference material for you.

Having a story developed to this scale and magnitude means that multiple people can refer to the same source and they will all get the same picture of what needs to be done. If you have multiple people working together in a collaborative environment, it is critical that every person be moving in the same direction. If everyone starts coding what they *think* the game should be, each person will code something different. A well-written story, one that can be referred to by every developer working on the game, will help keep the team moving toward the same goal.

But how do you get the story out of your head and prepare it to be referenced by either yourself or others? This question will be answered in the following section.

Writing Your Story

There is no trick to writing out your story. You can be as elaborate or rudimentary as you feel is necessary. Anything from a few quick sentences on the scratch pad near your PC to a few pages in a well-formatted Microsoft Word document will suffice. The point is not to try to publish the story as a book; rather, you just need to get the story out of your head and into a legible format that can be referenced and hopefully not changed.

The longer the story stays in your head, the more time you will have to change the details. When you change any details at all in the story, you risk having to rewrite code (and we have already discussed the dangers of this). Therefore, even if you are a one-person, casual-development machine, and you think that it is not necessary to write down a story just for you, think again. Writing down the story ensures that you will not forget or accidentally change any of the details.

No doubt you have a game in mind that you want to develop as soon as you learn the skills in this book. However, you may not have ever really considered what the story for that game would be. Give some thought to that story.

> **TIP:** Take some time now to write down a quick draft of your game, if you have one in mind. When you finish, compare it to the mock story that follows.

Let's look at a quick example of a story that can be used to develop a game.

> *John Black steals a somewhat-fast but strong car from a local impound. The bad guys catch up to him quickly. Now, he has to make it out of Villiansburg with the money, avoid the police, and fight off the gang he stole the money from. The gang's cars are faster, but luckily for John, he can shoot and drive at the same time. Hopefully, the lights are still on at the safe house.*

In that quick story, even though there are few details, you still have enough for one casual developer to start working on fairly simple game. What can you get out of this paragraph?

The first concept that comes to mind from this short story would be a top-down, arcade-style driving game; think original *Spy Hunter*. The driver, or the car, could have a gun to fire at enemy vehicles. The game could end when the player reaches the edge of the town, or possibly a safe house or garage of some sort.

This short story even has enough details to make the game a bit more enjoyable to play. The main character has a name, John Black. There are two sets of enemies to avoid: the police and the gang. The environment is made up of the streets of Villiansburg, and the majority of the enemy vehicles travel faster than the main character's. There is definitely enough good material here to make a quick, casual game.

Already the metaphoric wheels in your brain should be turning out ideas for this game. A fair amount of good, arcade-style action is described in this one short paragraph. If you can describe the game that you want to make in a short paragraph like this, than as a single, casual developer, you are well on your way to making a fairly enjoyable game.

Where one short paragraph might have enough detail for a fairly convincing casual game, imagine what a longer story could provide. The more detail that you can put into your story now, the easier your job will be as you are coding, and the better your game will be.

Take some extra time with your story to get the details just right. Sure a short paragraph, like the one in this section, is enough to go on, but more details could definitely help you as you are coding. Here is a list of questions that you should already be asking yourself after reading this story:

- What kind of car does John steal and drive?

- Why did he steal the money?

- What kind of weapon does he have?

- What kind of weapons, if any, are on the car?

- Is Villiansburg a city or country environment?

- Is there a boss battle at the end?

- How is scoring accumulated, if at all?

If we go back and answer some of these questions, the story may look like this.

John Black, framed for a crime he didn't commit, seizes an opportunity to get back at the gang that set him up. He intercepts $8 million that was on its way to Big Boss, the leader of the Bad Boys. He knows he can't get away on foot, so he steals a somewhat-fast but strong black sedan from a local impound.

This car has everything: twin mounted machine guns, oil slick, and mini missiles.

The bad guys catch up to him quickly. Now, he has to make it out of the crowded city streets of Villiansburg with the money. Dilapidated and boarded up buildings line the streets. The faster John can drive, the better his chances are of making it out alive. All he has to do is avoid the police and fight off the gang he stole the money from.

The gang's cars might be faster, but luckily for John, he can shoot and drive at the same time. He will need these skills when Big Boss catches up to him at the edge of town in his re-commissioned U.S. Army tank.

If John can defeat Big Boss, he will keep the money, but if he gets hit along the way, Big Boss's henchmen will take what they can get away with until John has nothing. John better be careful, because Big Boss's henchmen will be coming at him with everything they have: sports cars, motorcycles, machine guns, and even helicopters.

Hopefully, the lights are still on at the safe house.

Now, let's take a look at the story again. We have a lot more to go on now, and clearly, the more detailed story would make for more interesting game play. Anyone coding this game would now be able to discern the following game play details.

- The main character's car is a black sedan.

- The car has two machine guns, missiles, and oil slicks as weapons.

- The environment is a crowded city street lined with rundown, boarded up buildings.

■ The player will start with $8,000,000 (8,000,000 points).

■ The player will lose money (points) if an enemy catches or hits him.

■ The enemy vehicles will be sports cars, motorcycles, and helicopters.

■ At the end of the city is a boss battle against a tank.

■ The game ends when the play is out of money (points).

As you can see, the picture of what needs to be done is much clearer. There would be no confusion over this game play. This is why it is important to put as much detail as possible into the story that your game will be based on. You will definitely benefit from all of the time you put in before you begin coding.

Now that we've addressed some of the reasons why you might want to develop games on the Android platform and reviewed the philosophy behind making your game matter, let's look at the approach I'll be taking and what tools you will need to be a successful Android game developer. These will serve as the basis for all projects in the remaining chapters.

The Road You'll Travel

In this book, you will learn both 2-D and 3-D development. If you start from the beginning of this book and work through the basic examples, building the sample 2-D game as you go, the chapters on 3D graphics should be easier to pick up. Conversely, if you try to jump straight to the chapters on 3-D development, and you are not a seasoned OpenGL developer, you may have a harder time understanding what is going on.

As with any lesson, class, or path of learning, you will be best served by following this book from the beginning to the end. However, if you find that some of the earlier examples are too basic for your experience level, feel free to move between chapters.

Gathering Your Android Development Tools

At this point, you are probably eager to dive right into developing your Android game. So what tools do you need to begin your journey?

First, you will need a good, full-featured integrated development environment (IDE). I write all of my Android code in Eclipse Indigo (which is a free download). All of the examples from this book will be presented using Eclipse. While you can use almost any Java IDE or text editor to write Android code, I prefer Eclipse because of the well-crafted plug-ins, which tightly integrate many of the more tedious manual operations of compiling and debugging Android code.

If you do not already have Eclipse and want to give it a try, it is a free download from the Eclipse.org site (http://eclipse.org), shown in Figure 1–2:

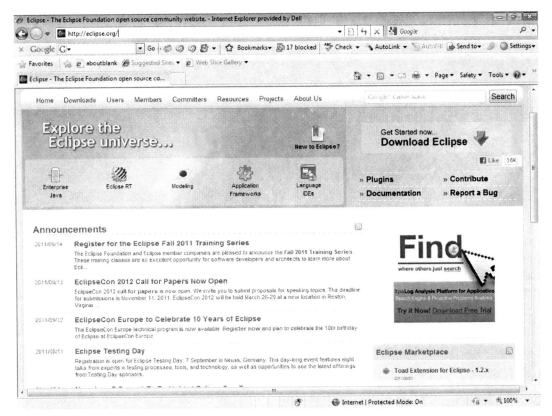

Figure 1–2. *Eclipse.org*

This book will not dive into the download or setup of Eclipse. There are many resources, including those on Eclipse's own site and the Android Developer's Forum, that can help you set up your environment should you require assistance.

> **TIP:** If you have never installed Eclipse, or a similar IDE, follow the installation directions carefully. The last thing you want is an incorrectly installed IDE impeding your ability to write great games.

You will also need the latest Android SDK. As with all of the Android SDKs, the latest can be found at the Android developer site (http://developer.android.com/sdk/index.html), as shown in Figure 1–3:

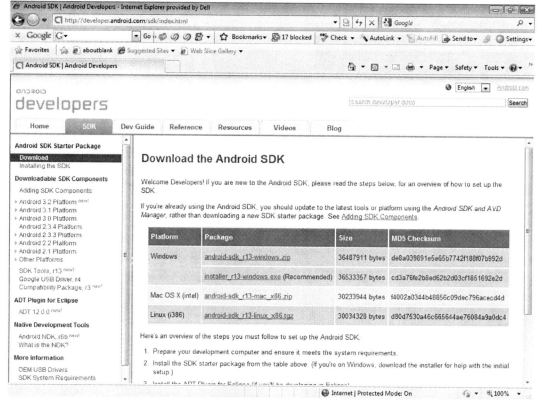

Figure 1–3. *The Android developer site*

As with the IDE, many resources are available to help you download and install the SDK (and the corresponding Java components that you may need) if you need help doing so.

Finally, you should possess at least a basic understanding of development, specifically in Java. While I do my best to explain many of the concepts and practices used in creating the code for this book, I will not be able to explain the more basic development concepts. In short, my explanations alone should be enough to get you through the code in this book if you are a novice, but a more advanced Java developer will be able to easily take my examples and expand on them.

Installing OpenGL ES

Arguably one of the most important items you'll be using is OpenGL ES, a graphics library that was developed by Silicon Graphics in 1992 for use in computer-aided design (CAD). It has since been managed by the Khronos Group and can be found on most platforms. It is very powerful and an invaluable tool to anyone who wants to create games.

NOTE: It does bear mention that the version of OpenGL that is provided with, and supported by, Android is actually OpenGL ES (OpenGL for Embedded Systems). OpenGL ES is not as fully featured as standard OpenGL. However, it is still an outstanding tool for developing on Android. Throughout this book, for ease of discussion, I will refer to the OpenGL ES functions and libraries as OpenGL; just be warned that we are actually using OpenGL ES

When most people think of OpenGL, the first things that come to mind are 3-D graphics. It's true that OpenGL is very good at rendering 3-D graphics and can be used to create some convincing 3-D games. However OpenGL is also very good at rendering 2-D graphics. In fact, OpenGL can render and manipulate 2-D graphics much faster than the native Android calls. The native Android calls are good enough for most application developers, but for games, which require as much optimization as possible, OpenGL is the best way to go.

For those of you who may not have the most OpenGL experience, fear not. In the chapters that deal with heavy OpenGL graphics rendering, I will do my best to fully explain every call you need to make. Therefore, if the following OpenGL code looks like a foreign language to you, don't worry; it will make sense by the end of this book:

```
gl.glViewport(0, 0, width, height);
gl.glMatrixMode(GL10.GL_PROJECTION);
gl.glLoadIdentity();
GLU.gluOrtho2D(gl, 0.0f, 0.0f, (float)width,(float)height);
```

OpenGL is a perfect tool for you to use and learn in this book, because it is a cross-platform development library. That is, you can use OpenGL and the OpenGL knowledge that you learn here across many environments and disciplines. From the iPad and iPhone to Microsoft Windows and Linux, many of the same OpenGL calls can be used across all of these systems.

Using OpenGL for your 2-D game graphics throughout this book has an added benefit.

OpenGL, for all intents and purposes, does not care if you are working with 2-D or 3-D graphics. Many of the same calls are used for both. The only difference is in how OpenGL will render the polygons when it comes time to draw to the screen. This being said, your transition from 2-D to 3-D graphics will be a lot smoother and a lot easier using OpenGL. Keep in mind that this book is not intended to be a complete desk reference on OpenGL ES, nor is it going to show you complex matrix math and other optimization tricks that you would otherwise be using in a profession game house. The truth is, as a casual game developer, the OpenGL methods provided for things like matrix math, while they come with some overhead, are good enough for learning the lessons this book.

In this book, you are going to use OpenGL ES 1.0. There are three versions of OpenGL available to Android users: OpenGL ES 1.0, 1.1, and 2.0. Why use version 1.0? First, there is already a lot of reference material available on the Internet about OpenGL ES 1.0. Therefore if you get stuck, or want to expand your knowledge, you will have a lot of places to turn for help. Second, it is tried and tested. Being the oldest of the OpenGL ES platforms, it will be available to the most devices and will have been extensively tested. Finally, it is just plain easy to pick up and learn. Also, picking up 1.1 and maybe even 2.0 after you already know 1.0 will be a lot easier.

Choosing an Android Version

One of the appeals of developing for Android is that it is so widely used across many different devices, such as mobile phones, tablets, and MP3 players. The games that you develop have a chance to run one dozens of different cell phones, tables, and even e-readers. From different wireless carriers to different manufacturers, the hardware exposure that your game could get is quite varied.

Unfortunately, this ubiquity can also be a tough hurdle for you to jump through. At any given time, there could be up to 12 different versions of Android running on dozens of different pieces of hardware. The latest tablets and phones will be running version 2.3.3, 3.0, 3.1, or 4.0—the most recent versions, which are run on the most powerful devices. Therefore, these will be the versions that we are going to target in this book.

> **NOTE:** If you do not have an Android device to test on you can use the PC emulator. However, I highly recommend that you try to use an actual Android phone or tablet to test your code. In my testing, I have noticed some minor discrepancies when running my code in an emulator versus running it on my phone or tablet.

Most importantly, have fun as you work through the process of creating games. Games, after all, are fun, and you should have fun making them!

Summary

In this chapter, we discussed what you should expect to get out of this book. You learned the importance of story to the creation of a game and how sticking to that story can help you create better code. You also learned about the process of creating games on the Android platform, the versions of Android, and Android's development environment. Finally, you discovered the key to creating games on the Android platform, OpenGL ES, and we covered a few pertinent details about Android version releases.

Chapter **2**

Star Fighter:
A 2-D Shooter

The game you will be creating as you work your way through this book is *Star Fighter*.
Star Fighter is a 2-D, top-down, scrolling shooter. Even though the action is fairly limited,
the story is surprisingly detailed. In this chapter, you'll get a sneak preview of the game
and the story behind it. You will also learn about the different parts of the game engine
and what the game engine does.

Telling the *Star Fighter* Story

The story for *Star Fighter* is as follows; we will be referring to it periodically as we
progress through this book:

*Captain John Starke is a grizzled galactic war veteran. He fought his way out of every
battle the Planetary Coalition has been involved in. Now, on his way back to earth and
ready to retire from years of service to a quiet little farm in western Massachusetts, he
finds himself caught in the middle of a surprise enemy invasion force.*

*Captain Starke prepares for battle. But this is no ordinary Kordark invasion fleet;
something is different.*

*Starke cranks up the thrusters on his AF-718 and sets his guns to automatically fire.
Luckily, the AF-718 is light and nimble. As long as he can avoid enemy guns and the
occasional collision, the autofire cannons should make short work of the smaller Kordark
fighters.*

*Unfortunately, what the AF-718 has in agility and autofire capabilities, it lacks in shields.
Captain Starke is best served by avoiding the enemy craft altogether. If he does sustain
any damage, after three strikes, he is out. The AF-718 can't take very many direct blaster
hits without good shields. As for a direct collision from an enemy, unfortunately, it is "one
and done" for Captain Starke.*

While Captain Starke is navigating his way through wave after wave of enemy ships, he may be lucky enough to come across some debris of other destroyed AF-718s—casualties of the last group to be surprised by the invasion force. As long as he is not destroyed along the way, Captain Starke may find a use for these parts.

The AF-718 has a very helpful feature that will aid Captain Starke in his fight. The latest versions of the AF-718, specially made for the last Centelum Prime Rebellion, are equipped with a self-repair mode. If Captain Starke gets into trouble and he is losing his shields, or finds that he needs even more firepower, all he needs to do is navigate his ship up to some of the AF-718 parts that are drifting around the battle space. He should be able to obtain anything from stronger shields, which could double or triple the amount of damage that his ship can take, to more powerful guns that are faster and require fewer hits to destroy the enemy.

Captain Starke and his AF-718 are not the only ones with tricks up their sleeves. The Kordark invasion fleet is made up of three different ships:

- Kordark Scout
- Kordark Interceptor
- Larash War Ship

Kordark Scouts are the most numerous of all of the ships in the invasion fleet. They are fast—just as fast as Captain Starke's AF-718. The Scout flies in a swift but predictable pattern. This should make them easy to recognize and even easier to anticipate. Good thing for Starke, in diverting all of the Scout's power to their thrust engines, the Kordarks gave them very weak shields. One good blast from the AF-718 should be all that is needed to take down a Kordark Scout. They do have a single blast cannon mounted on the front of the ship that fires slow, single-round bursts. Some rapid fire and quick navigation should get the AF-718 out of harm's way and give Captain Starke the leverage he needs to destroy a Scout.

Kordark Interceptors, on the other hand, are very direct and deliberate enemies. They will fly slowly but directly at Captain Starke's AF-718. An Interceptor is unmanned and is used as a computer-guided battering ram. They are programmed to take out all enemies as soon as they can lock on to an enemy's position.

The Interceptor was built to penetrate the strong hulls of the massive Planetary Coalition's battle cruisers. Therefore their shields are very strong. It would easily take four direct hits from the AF-718 best weapon to stop this craft. Captain Starke's best offense, in this case, is a good defense. The Kordark Interceptor locks on to its target very early, and it is programmed not to break its path once it has locked on. If Captain Starke is in a clear area, he should have no problem moving out of the way before the quick Interceptor makes contact. If he is lucky, he might destroy one or two with his cannons, but that would take some definite skill.

The final type on enemy that Captain Starke will face is the Larash War Ship.

The presence of the Larash War Ships is what makes this invasion fleet unlike any other Captain Starke as ever seen. The Larash War Ships are as strong as the Kordark

Interceptors, but they also have forward facing guns, like the Scouts. They can maneuver in a random pattern and should give Captain Starke his greatest challenge. Luckily for him, there are relatively few of these War Ships, giving him time to recoup between appearances.

The computer of the AF-718 will track how many ships are in the invasion force. It will notify Captain Starke when he has eliminated all of the potential enemies. These statistics will be sent to the forward command on Earth to let them know how he is ranking against the invasion.

Help Captain Starke eliminate as many invasion force waves as possible and reach Earth alive.

So there it is, the story that you will be referring to as you code Star Fighter. What game details can you get out of this story? Let's list them, in the same way we did for the sample story in Chapter 1:

- The main character Captain John Starke will be piloting an AF-718 spaceship.
- The player will not have to operating any firing mechanism, because the ship has an autofire feature.
- The player can power up by obtaining more shields and guns.
- If the player sustains three hits from an enemy cannon without repair, the game will end.
- If the play sustains a direct hit from an enemy craft, the game will end.
- There are three different types of enemy ships:
    - Scouts move quickly in a predictable pattern and fire a single cannon.
    - Interceptors have no cannons but can take four direct blaster hits from the player. They cannot change their course once they have locked on to the player's position
    - The War Ships have cannons and can take four direct blaster hits. They move in a random pattern
- The game will track the number of enemies in each wave. Every time the player destroys one, the counter will be decreased by one until the wave is finished.
- The scores will be uploaded to a central area.

This sounds like it is going to be a very fun, exciting, and detailed game to play. The best part is that the code needed to create this game will not be that complicated, or at least not as complicated as you might expect.

In the next section, you will learn about the game engine for *Star Fighter*. You will learn what the different parts of the game engine are, and what the engine as a whole does for your game. Finally, you will begin to stub out some basic engine functionality and begin to build your game.

What Makes a Game?

Now that you know what *Star Fighter* is going to be about, we can begin to look at the different pieces necessary to build the game. Many pieces will all have to fit together in a very tight and cohesive way to create the end product that is a playable, enjoyable Android game.

When you think about everything a game has to do to deliver a truly enjoyable experience, you will begin to appreciate the time and effort it takes to create even the simplest of games. A typical game will do the following:

- Draw a background.
- Move the background as needed.
- Draw any number of characters.
- Draw weapons, bullets, and similar items.
- Move the characters independently.
- Play sound effects and background music.
- Interpret the commands of an input device.
- Track the characters and the background to make sure none move where they should not be able to move.
- Draw any predefined animation.
- Make sure that when things move (like a ball bouncing), they do so in a believable way.
- Track the player's score.
- Track and manage networked or multiple players.
- Build a menu system for the player to select to play or quit the game.

This may not be a comprehensive list, but it is a fairly good list of all of the things that most games do. How does a game accomplish all of the things in this list?

For the purposes of this book, we can divide all of the code in a game into two categories: the game engine and the game-specific code. Everything in the previous list is handled in one or both of these categories of code. Knowing which is handled where is critical to understanding the skills in this book. Let's begin examining these two categories of code with a look at the game engine.

Understanding the Game Engine

At the core of every video game is the game engine. Just as the name suggests, the game engine is the code that powers the game. Every game, regardless of its type—

RPG, first-person shooter (FPS), platformer, or even real-time strategy (RTS)—requires an engine to run.

> **NOTE:** The engine of any game is purposely built to be generic, allowing it to be used in multiple situations and possibly for multiple different games. This is in direct opposition to the game-specific code, which, as the name suggests, is code that is specific to one game and only one game.

One very popular game engine is the Unreal engine. The Unreal engine, first developed around 1998 by Epic for its FPS called Unreal, has been used in hundreds of games. The Unreal engine is easily adaptable and works with a variety of game types, not just first-person shooters. This generic structure and flexibility make the Unreal engine popular with not only professions but casual developers as well.

In general terms, the game engine handles all of the grunt work of the game code. This can mean anything from playing the sound to rendering the graphics onto the screen. Here is a short list of the functions that a typical game engine will perform.

- Graphics rendering
- Animation
- Sound
- Collision detection
- Artificial intelligence (AI)
- Physics (noncollision)
- Threading and memory management
- Networking
- Command interpreter (I/O)

Why do you need a game engine to do all of this work? The short answer is that for a game run efficiently, it cannot rely on the OS of the host system to do this kind of heavy-duty work. Yes, most operating systems have built-in features to take care of every item on this list. However, those rendering, sound, and memory management systems of an OS are built to run the operating system and adapt to any number of unpredictable uses, without specializing in any one. This is great if you are writing business applications but not so great if you are writing games. Games require something with a little more power.

For a game to run smoothly and quickly, the code will need to bypass the overhead that the standard OS systems create and run directly against the hardware required for the specific process. That is, a game should communicate directly with the graphics hardware to perform graphics function, communicate directly with the sound card to play effects, and so on. If you were to use the standard memory, graphics, and sound systems that are available to you through most OSs, your game could be threaded with all of the other OS functions and applications that are running on the system. Your internal messages could also be queued up with every other system message. This would make for a choppy looking game that would run very slowly.

For this reason, game engines are almost always coded in low-level languages. As we touched on earlier, low-level languages offer a more direct path to the hardware of the system. A game engine needs to be able to take code and commands from the game-specific code and pass them directly to the hardware. This allows the game to run quickly and with all of the control that it needs to be able to provide a rewarding experience.

Figure 2–1 shows a simplified version of the relationship among the game engine, the device hardware, and the game-specific code.

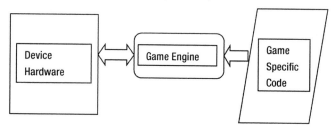

Figure 2–1. *The relationship among the game engine, the game-specific code, and the device hardware*

A game engine will not do anything specifically for the game. That is to say, a game engine will not draw a kitten to the screen. A game engine will draw *something* to the screen because it handles graphic rendering, but it will not draw anything specific. It is the job of the game-specific code to give the engine a kitten to draw, and it is the job of the engine to draw whatever is passed to it.

Therefore, you will never see the following function in a game engine:

```
DrawFunnyKitten();
```

Rather, you would have a function that is more like this:

```
DrawCharacter(funnyKitten);
```

Admittedly the final graphic rendering functions that you create in this book will require a few more parameters than just the name of the image that needs to be rendered, but you should be able to understand the point that I am making; the engine is very general, the game-specific code is not.

Now that you have a good overview of what an engine does, let's contrast that with the game-specific code, so you will have the full picture of what makes a game.

Understanding Game-Specific Code

Let's examine the role of the game-specific code. As we discussed earlier, the game-specific code is the code that is run by one game and only one game, unlike a game engine, which can be shared and adapted among multiple games.

> **NOTE:** When creating small, casual games—like the ones in this book—the game engine and the game-specific code may be so tightly coupled to its engine that it may be hard to tell the two apart at times. It is still very important to understand the conceptual difference between the two.

The game-specific code is composed of all of the code that makes the characters in your game (the A-718, the Scout, and the Interceptor, etc.), whereas the game engine just draws a character. The game-specific code knows the main character fired a cannon shot and not a missile, whereas the game engine draws an item. The game-specific code is the code that will destroy the main character if he hits a Scout, but not if he hits a power-up; the game engine will just test for the collision of two onscreen objects.

For example, in simplified stub code, the collision of the A-718 and a Scout might look like this:

```
GameCharacter goodGuy;
GameCharacter scout;
GameCharacter arrayOfScouts[] = new GameCharacter[1];
arrayOfScouts[0] = scout;
/**Move characters***/
Move(goodGuy);
Move(arrayOfScouts);
/***Test for collisions***/
If (TestForCollision(goodGuy,arrayOfScouts))
{
        Destroy(goodGuy);
}
```

Although this is only a simplified version of what a section of the game routine might look like, it shows that we created the A-718 and Scout, moved them on the screen, and tested to see if they collided. If the characters did collide, goodGuy is destroyed.

In this example, goodGuy, arrayOfScouts, and the Destroy() function are all game-specific code. The Move() and TestForCollision() functions are parts of the game engine. From this short sample, it is easy to see that you could interchange goodGuy and arrayOfScouts for any characters in almost any other game, and the Move() and TestForCollision() functions would still work. This illustrates that the goodGuy and arrayOfScout objects are game specific and not part of the engine, and the engine functions Move() and TestForCollision() work for any game.

On a larger project, like a game that tens or hundreds of people are working on, the engine will be developed first and then the game-specific code will be created to work with that engine. In the case of small casual games like those in this book, the game engine and game-specific code can be developed simultaneously. This is going to give you the unique chance to see the relationship between the two blocks of code as you are creating them.

You will learn as you progress through this book that some of the functions of the game engine for small games can almost be indistinguishable from game-specific code. In small games, you may not be overly worried about the line between engine and game-specific code as long as the game works the way you want. However, I urge you to keep the line between the two as clear as possible to help promote the reusability of your own code and to help keep your development skills sharp. In other words, try to avoid lazy code and lazy coding practices.

In Chapter 1, you were presented with a list of items that compose almost any game. Let's take a look at the list again and determine which of those items are handled in the game engine and which in the game-specific code; see Table 2–1.

Table 2–1. *The Elements of a Game*

Game Element	Engine Element	Game-Specific Code
Draw a background.	Graphics rendering	Create a star field.
Move a background.	Graphics rendering	Scroll the background from top to bottom.
Draw characters.	Graphics rendering	Put the A-718 on the screen.
Draw weapons, bullets, etc.	Graphics rendering	Draw A-718 debris and cannon blasts.
Move the characters independently.	Graphics rendering and AI	Move an Interceptor toward the A-718. Move a Scout in a slow predictable pattern.
Play sound effects and background music.	Sound	Create an explosion when an enemy is hit. Play background music.
Interpret input device commands.	Command interpreter	
Track the characters and background to make sure no one moves where they should not be able to move.	Collision detection	If the A-718 runs into a Scout, it will explode. But if two Scouts clip each other, that is OK.
Draw any predefined animation.	Animation	When the player wins, draw a victory animation.
Make sure that when things move (like a ball bouncing), they do so in a believable way.	Physics	
Track the player's score.	Graphics rendering and memory management	For each enemy that is hit, subtract one from the total number of enemies left to eliminate.

Game Element	Engine Element	Game-Specific Code
Track and manage networked or multiple players.	Networking	
Build a menu system for the player to select to play or quit the game.	Graphics rendering and command interpreter	Start a new game, quit a game, or upload a score.

As Table 2–1 shows, even the smallest games contain a lot of pieces. All of the elements of a game are handled by the game engine in some capacity; some of the elements are exclusive to the engine. This should give you a much better idea of the importance of the game engine and the line between the engine and the game-specific code.

Now that you know what game engines do in general, what will *our* game engine do for *Star Fighter*?

Exploring the *Star Fighter* Engine

The game engine for *Star Fighter* is going to be slightly different from the general game engine you may use. Keep in mind that Android is built on a Linux kernel, and the development is done using a slightly modified version of Java. This means that Android, as it is, is actually quick enough to run some casual games with ease. We are going to take advantage of this in *Star Fighter* and keep our coding efforts down.

We are not going to build a true, low-level, game engine in this book simply because it is not necessary for the games that we are building. Let's face it; the more time you spend writing your game, the less time you have to enjoy playing it. Android has systems that we can take advantage of and, while they may not be optimal to running high-end games, they are easy to learn and well suited for the kind of games we will make.

The game engine for *Star Fighter* will utilize the Android SDK (and its related Java packages) to do the following:

- Redner graphics
- Play back sound and effects
- Interpret commands
- Detect collisions
- Handle the enemy AI

After reading the discussion earlier in this chapter, you may notice that some functions are missing from our game engine, such as noncollision physics, animation, and networking/social media. This is because the game we are building will not need to utilize those features, so we don't need to build them.

To keep this book flowing smoothly and logically, we are going to build the engine and the game-specific code simultaneously. For example, you will learn to create the graphics renderer while you are creating the background and the characters. This will give you fully functional pieces of engine and game-specific code at the end of every chapter.

Creating the Star Fighter Project

As an initial task to get you up and running, in this section, you are going to quickly create the project that will be used for the *Star Fighter* game. We will use the project through this entire book.

First, open Eclipse, and click the menu button to open new Android project wizard; see Figure –2.

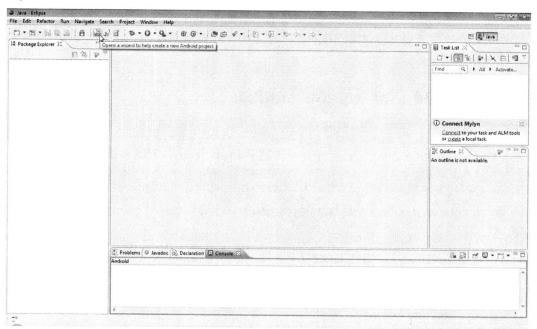

Figure 2–2. *Starting the new Android project wizard*

Once you open the wizard, you will be able to create the project. If you have experience with creating Android projects, this should be a breeze for you.

> **TIP:** If you are using NetBeans, or any other Java IDE to create your Android applications, this short tutorial will not help you. There are many resources that you should be able to leverage to get a project created in those IDEs if you need assistance.

Figure 2–3 illustrates the options that you should select when creating your project. The project name is `planetfighter`. Since all of the code for the `planetfighter` game will be created in the same project, it makes sense to name the project **planet fighter**. This will also result in all of the code being put into a `planetfighter` package.

> **TIP:** If you have never created an Android (or Java) project or package before, there are some naming conventions that you should be made aware of. When naming your package, think of it as though it is a URL, only written in reverse. Therefore, it should start with the designation, such as `com` or `net`, and end with your entity name. In this case, I am using `com.proandroidgames`.

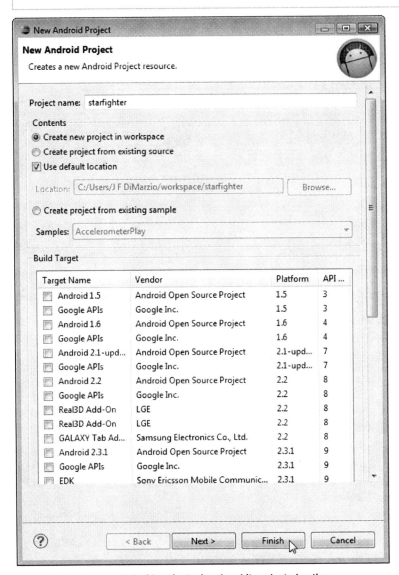

Figure 2–3. *The new Android project wizard and its selected options*

Now, you can select the "Create new project in workspace" option. This will ensure that you project is created in the standard Eclipse workspace that you should have set for yourself when you installed Eclipse. The "Use default location" check box is marked by default. Unless you want to change the location of your workspace for your project, you should leave it as it is.

Your next step is to select the latest version of the Android SDK, and click the Finish button. Figure 2–4 illustrates the finished project. We will begin modifying this project in the next chapter.

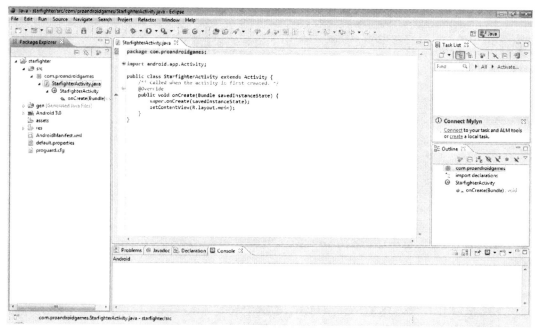

Figure 2–4. *The project is correctly set up.*

Summary

In this chapter, you learned about the story behind *Star Fighter*. You also explored not only the different parts to a generic game engine but also those that will be included in the game engine of *Star Fighter*. Finally, you created the project that will hold the code for your game.

In the next five chapters, you will put together the code that will make up the *Star Fighter* game. You will begin to build up your skill set as a casual game developer, and you will learn more about the Android platform.

Press Start: Making a Menu

In this chapter, you are going to begin developing the *Star Fighter* 2D arcade shooter. You will create the first lines of code in your engine and develop the first two screens that the user will see in your game: the game splash screen and the game menu with two game options. Throughout this chapter, you'll learn several essential skills in game development on the Android platform.

You will learn

- Displaying graphics
- Creating activities and intents
- Creating an Android service
- Starting and stopping Android threads
- Playing music files

In addition to the splash screen and game menu, you'll create some background music to play behind the menu.

There is a lot to cover, so let's begin with the very first screen that the player will see in your game, the splash screen.

Building the Splash Screen

The splash screen is the first part of the game that the user is going to see. Think of the splash screen as the opening credits or title card of your game. It should display the name of the game, some game images, and maybe some information about who made the game. The splash screen for *Star Fighter* is depicted in Figure 3–1.

Figure 3–1. Star Fighter *splash screen*

For games that are built by multiple people at multiple development shops, you may see more than one splash screen before a game begins. This is not uncommon as each development shop, distributer, and producer could have its own splash screens that it wants posted before the game. However, for our game, we are going to create one splash screen because you will be the only developer.

If you play any typical game, you will see that the splash screen will generally transition automatically to the game's main menu. In *Star Fighter*, you are going to create a splash screen that fades in and out to the main menu. Therefore, to create the splash screen, you will also need to create the activity that will hold the main menu, so that you can properly set up the fading effect of the splash screen without any errors.

Creating an Activity

To begin, open the Star Fighter project that you created in the preceding chapter. If you have not created the Star Fighter project, please go back now and do so before continuing; the remainder of this chapter assumes you are working in the Star Fighter project.

Your Star Fighter project, in its current state, should contain one activity—StarfighterActivity. StarfighterActivity was created automatically by Android and is the automatic entry point to the project. Were you to run your project now, StarfighterActivity would launch. However, you will actually need two activities for this chapter: one for the splash screen and one for the game's main menu. Android has already provided you an activity for the splash screen, so in the next section, you will create a new activity for the main menu.

Even though the activity for the main menu will be empty right now, it will allow you to fully implement the splash screen's fade transition, a task you'll tackle in just a bit.

Creating a New Class

To create a new activity, first create a new Java class in your main package. If you are using the same package name as outlined in the preceding chapter, your main package is com.proandroidgames. Right-click the package name, and select New ➤ Class to bring up the New Java Class window shown in Figure 3–2.

Figure 3–2. *The New Java Class creation window*

Keep most of the default options as they are. All you need to do at this point is provide a class name. The name for your class should be SFMainMenu. Click the Finish button to create the class.

Right now, the new class that you created is a simple Java class with the following code.

```
package com.proandroidgames;

public class SFMainMenu {

}
```

However, the class is not yet an activity. For that, you need to add some code to the class. Once this class is an activity, you can begin to create the splash screen and its effects.

Transforming the Class to an Activity

Import the `Activity` package, and extend your `SFMainMenu` class to turn this Java class into an Android activity. Your class code should now appear as follows:

```
package com.proandroidgames;

import android.app.Activity;

public class SFMainMenu extends Activity {

}
```

Now, let's associate this activity with the Star Fighter project so that we can create a splash screen. Open the `AndroidManifest.xml` file to associate the `SFMainMenu` activity with your project, as shown in Figure 3–3.

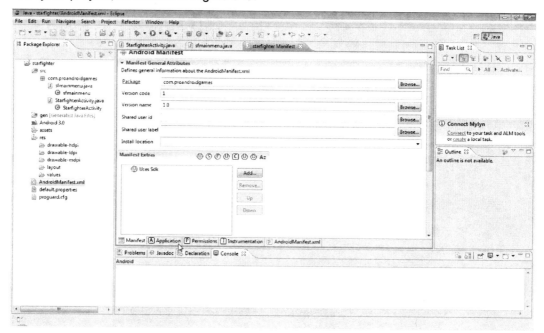

Figure 3–3. *The AndroidManifest.xml*

Scroll to the bottom of the AndroidManifest Application tab, and locate the area labeled Application Nodes. This area of the manifest lists all of the application nodes that are associated with your project. Right now, the only application node listed should be .StarfighterActivity. Because you want to add a new activity, click the Add button, and select Activity from the screen pictured in Figure 3–4.

Figure 3–4. *Creating a new Activity element*

This creates an empty Activity element. The empty element that you see in the GUI of AndroidManifest is a representation of an XML element in the AndroidManifest.xml file. Click the AndroidManifest.xml view at the bottom of the tab, and you should see the following snippet of XML code:

```
<activity></activity>
```

Obviously, this empty element is not going to do you much good. You need to somehow tell the AndroidManifest that this activity element represents the SFMainMenu Activity. This can be done manually of course. However, let's take a look at doing it the automated way.

Once you have created the new Activity element, you need to associate that new element with the actual SFMainMenu activity you created earlier. Click the Activity element in the Application Nodes section of the AndroidManifest to highlight it. To the right of the Application Nodes section of the AndroidManifest is a section that is now labeled Attributes for Activity, as pictured in Figure 3–5.

> **NOTE:** Were you to click .StarfighterActivity, this section would then be labeled Attributes for .StarfighterActivity.

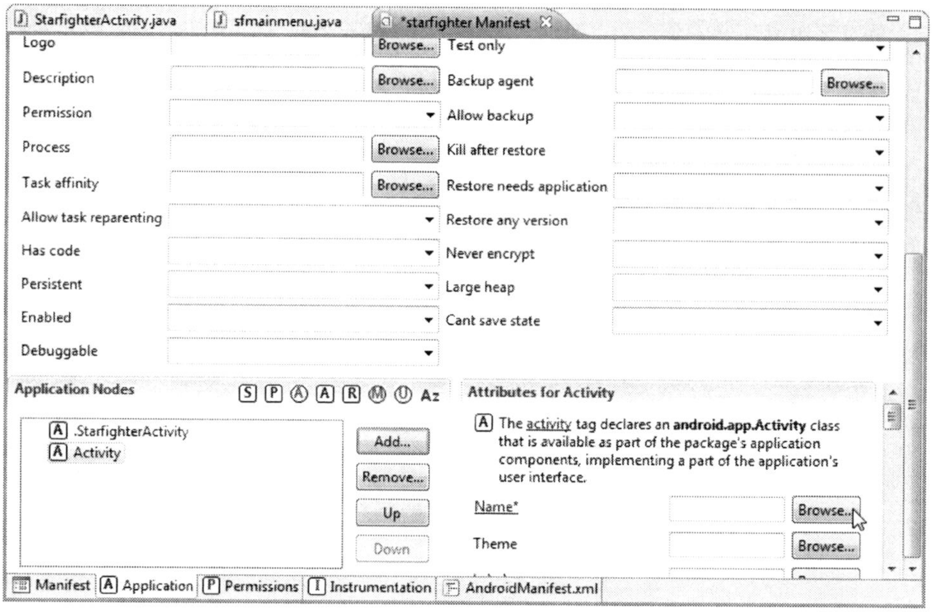

Figure 3–5. *Attributes for an activity*

Click the Browse button that is next to the Name attribute to bring up a browsing tool that shows you all of the available `Activity` classes from your project. Your browsing tool options should look like Figure 3–6.

Notice that the `SFMainMenu` activity is listed in the "Matching items" box. Select the `SFMainMenu` activity, and click OK.

> **TIP:** If you do not see the `SFMainMenu` activity as an option in your "Matching items" box, try going back to the SFMainMenu tab in Eclipse. If the tab label has an asterisk before the `SFMainMenu` name, the file has not been saved. Save the file, and then reopen the Name attribute browser.
>
> If you still do not see the `SFMainMenu`, confirm that your `SFMainMenu` class is extending `Activity`. In the event that you are extending `Activity` in your class and you still do not have an option to select the `SFMainMenu Activity`, you can edit the `AndroidManifest` manually by filling in the needed element attributes (these are provided later in this chapter).

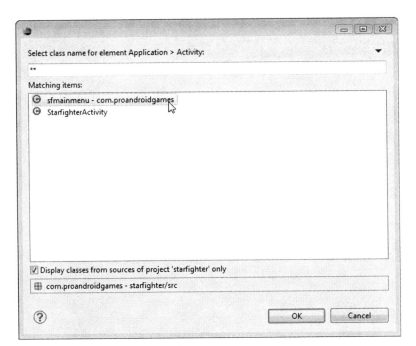

Figure 3–6. *The Name attribute selector*

After you have selected the SFMainMenu as the name attribute for this activity, set the screen orientation for both the .StarfighterActivity and SFMainMenu activities to portrait, as shown in Figure 3–7.

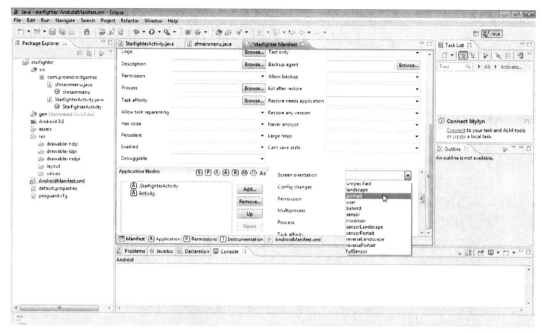

Figure 3–7. *Setting "Screen orientation" to portrait*

Setting the screen orientation for .StarfighterActivity (your splash screen) and SFMainMenu (the game's main menu) will lock in the orientation of the screen to portrait. Given the style of this game, you want the player to be able to use the game only in portrait mode. Therefore, even if the player tries to rotate a device into landscape mode, the screens for your game will remain portrait.

The finished XML code of your new SFMainMenu activity should appear like this:

```
<activity android:name="SFMainMenu" android:screenOrientation="portrait"></activity>
```

The main menu activity is now associated with the Star Fighter project, and you can create the splash screen. Keep in mind that all of the code for the main menu will be added in the following section of the chapter; you just need the activity created now to properly set up your fading effect.

> **CAUTION:** One of the most common causes of Android application crashes and failures is an incorrect setting in the AndroidManifest file, which is easily one of the most important files in your project.

Let's just quickly review where we are at this point and why. The splash screen that you are creating for *Star Fighter* is going to fade into the main menu. You have created the activity that will hold the main menu, and it is now time to create the splash screen and the fade effect.

Creating Your Splash Screen Image

Now, you need to import the graphic that you will use for your splash screen image into your project. Android is capable of working with most common image formats. However, you are going to stick to two for this game: .png and .9.png. For all of the sprites and other game images, you are going to use standard .png images, and for the splash screen and main menu, you are going to use .9.png files.

A .9.png image is also known as a nine-patch image. A nine-patch image is a special kind of format that allows Android to stretch the image as needed, because it contains a 1-pixel black border around the left and top of the image.

> **NOTE:** Most of the images that you include in your game will *not* be nine-patch images, because you will want to controls the manipulation of most images yourself. However, for the splash screen and main menu, it is fully appropriate to use nine-patch.

The difference between nine-patch and other image resizing processes is that you can control how Android is allowed to stretch the image by manipulating the black boarder. Figure 3–8 represents our splash screen image in nine-patch format.

Figure 3–8. *Nine-patch splash screen*

If you look closely at the left-hand side of the picture in Figure 3–8, you will notice the thin line of black dots. This black line is what differentiates nine-patch images from other image formats.

NOTE: The nine-patch image that I have used in this example is meant to stretch freely in all directions. If there are parts of your images that you do not want to stretch, do not draw a border at those areas. The `draw9patch` tool can help you visualize how your image will stretch depending on how you draw your border.

Unfortunately, applications developed for Android could be run on many different screen sizes on many different devices, from small mobile phones to larger tablets. Therefore, your project has to be able to adjust to all of the different screen sizes. If you're using the nine-patch image as your splash screen, Android can resize the image (with the help of some XML) to fit nicely on any screen size.

TIP: If you have never worked with nine-patch graphics, the Android SDK includes a tool that can help you. In the `\tools` folder of the SDK, you will find the `draw9patch` tool. Launch this tool and you will be able to import any image, draw your nine-patch border, and save the image back out with the `.9.png` extension.

Importing the Image

Now that you have your nine-patch image ready, drag the image from wherever you saved it into the `\res\drawable-hdpi` folder in your Eclipse project, as shown in Figure 3–9.

You may have noticed that there are three folders to choose from: `drawable-hdpi`, `drawable-ldpi`, and `drawable-mdpi`. These folders contain the drawables, or images, for three different types of Android devices: high density (hdpi), medium density (mdpi), and low desity (ldpi).

Why are we using nine-patch graphics to scale the image to fit any screen if Android provides a mechanism to include different images for different screen sizes? The short answer is that the two scenarios are really mutually exclusive. Yes, nine-patch allows for the scaling of an image to fit a device's screen, but that has little to do with the screen density in pixels of the device. The images that you are using (if you use the image from this project) are high-density images and will display as such. However even as large as the images are, they are still not the size of a 10.1-inch Motorola Xoom screen. Therefore, the nine-patch format allows it to be stretched properly.

Figure 3–9. *Dragging an image to the drawable-hdpi folder*

The true benefit of the high-, medium-, and low-density folder separation comes into play when you want to use different layouts and image densities to take advantage of greater screen area or, conversely, to make concessions for screens having less area. If you want to create a menu screen that has four buttons on it, each stacked on top of the other for tablet screens but grouped in side-by-side pairs on smaller devices, these folders will help you achieve that with minimal effort.

For the purposes of our current project, drop your splash screen nine-patch image into the drawable-hdpi folder. You will not address the use of these folders for this game. However, feel free to experiment with them on your own to create different experiences on different devices.

Working with the R.java File

After you drop the image into the folder, Android will create a resource pointer for it. This pointer is placed in the R.java file, which is automatically generated and should not be manually edited. It resides in the gen folder under your package name. If you open the R.java file after adding your image, it should have code similar to the following:

```
package com.proandroidgames;

public final class R {
...
    public static final class drawable {
        public static final int starfighter=0x7f020002;
    }
...
}
```

The R.java file is going to manage all of the images, IDs, layouts, and other resources used by your project. Because this file now contains a pointer to your image, you can refer to this image anywhere in your project with the following line of code:

```
R.drawable.starfighter
```

> **CAUTION:** Be very careful not to delete or manually modify the R.java file in any way. For example, the hexadecimal (hex) value for the starfighter image pointer may be different on your system than in the sample code in this section. Your file will work on your machine because it was generated in your IDE. If you were to modify your hex value to match the one in the sample, your file would no longer work as expected.

Now that you have an image in your project that you want to display as the splash screen, you'll need to tell Android to display this image to the screen. There are many ways this can be accomplished. However, because you want to apply a fade effect to the image, you are going to use a layout.

A layout is an XML file that is used to tell Android how to position resources on a screen. Let's create the layout for the splash screen.

Creating a Layout File

You are going to use a simple layout file to display the splash screen image, starfighter, onto the screen when the player first loads your game. Your splash screen is going to be straight and to the point—an image of an intriguing space setting and the name of the game.

Now you have to get this image to the screen so that the player can appreciate it. First, right-click the res\layout folder, and select **New ➤ Other**. From the New wizard, select **Android ➤ Android XML File**, as shown in Figure 3–10.

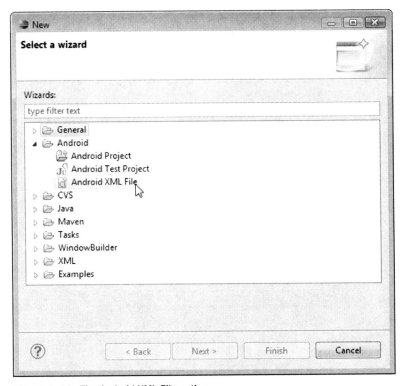

Figure 3–10. *The Android XML File option*

Name your new xml file `splashscreen.xml`, and finish the wizard. This process will place a new XML layout file in your layout folder and create a pointer to this file in the `R.java` file.

At this point, you can attack the layout in on of two ways. You can use a GUI designer or directly edit the XML file. We are going to edit the XML file directly so you'll get a better understanding of exactly what is going into the layout and why.

Editing the XML File

Double-click the `splashscreen.xml` file in your `res\layout` folder to actually open the GUI designer. However, if you look at the bottom of the designer window in Eclipse, you will notice two subtabs. One tab, the current tab, is labeled Graphical Layout. The second tab is labeled splashscreen.xml. This tab is the text editor for the XML file. Click the splashscreen.xml tab to enter the text editor.

You XML file should look like this:

```
<?xml version="1.0" encoding="utf-8"?>
```

This is an empty XML file. Let's add a layout to this file.

A few different types of layouts can be used in general Android development. Since you are developing a game, you do not really need to worry about 75 percent of these layouts because you simply will not come across them in the course of creating *Star Fighter*. However, there are two that you could use for this splash screen: `LinearLayout` and the `FrameLayout`. You will use the `FrameLayout` for *Star Fighter*, because it is great at centering elements and pinning them to a border.

`LinearLayout` is used to display multiple items on a screen and position them one after the other in either a vertical or horizontal orientation. Think of the `LinearLayout` as either a single-column or single-row table. It can be used to place any number of items to the screen, including other layouts, in an organized and linear fashion.

`FrameLayout` is used to hold one item. The one item can be gravitationally set so that it is centered, fills the entire space, or is against any border. The `FrameLayout` layout seems almost purposely made to display a splash screen that is composed of a single image.

Using FrameLayout

You are going to use `FrameLayout` to display the splash screen image *and* a box of text that will identify you as the developer. I know I just went through explaining that `FrameLayout` was built for displaying one item, and it is. However, if you tell a `FrameLayout` to display two items, it will display them overlapping each other with much less fussing and code than would be required with any other type of layout.

Return to your `splashscreen.xml` file, and create the `FrameLayout` as follows:

```
<?xml version="1.0" encoding="utf-8"?>
<FrameLayout
   xmlns:android="http://schemas.android.com/apk/res/android"

</FrameLayout>
```

A `FrameLayout` layout only take two properties that you need to worry about right now: `layout_width` and `layout_height`. These two properties are going to tell Android how to fit the layout onto the activity that you created.

In this situation, you are going to set the `layout_width` and the `layout_height` properties to `match_parent`. The `match_parent` constant tells Android that the width and height of the view should match the width and the height of the parent of that view, in this case, the activity itself.

> **TIP:** If you have developed on Android before, you may remember a constant called `fill_parent`. `Fill_parent` was replaced with `match_parent`, but the two constants function the same way.

Set the `FrameLayout` properties as show here:

```
<?xml version="1.0" encoding="utf-8"?>
<FrameLayout
   xmlns:android="http://schemas.android.com/apk/res/android"
```

```
    android:layout_width="match_parent"
    android:layout_height="match_parent">
</FrameLayout>
```

You now have a functioning `FrameLayout`, but you have nothing for it to work with. Let's add the image and the text.

Adding an Image and Text

Create an `ImageView` inside your `FrameLayout`, and give it the ID `"splashScreenImage"`.

```
<?xml version="1.0" encoding="utf-8"?>
<FrameLayout
    xmlns:android="http://schemas.android.com/apk/res/android"
    android:layout_width="match_parent"
    android:layout_height="match_parent">
    <ImageView android:id="@+id/splashScreenImage"
    >
    </ImageView>
</FrameLayout>
```

You have created the `ImageView` that will hold your splash screen image. Now, you have to set the `src` property to point to the image that you want to display, in this case, the starfighter image in the `res\drawable-hdpi` folder. You also need to set the `layout_width` and `layout_height` properties just as you did for the `FrameLayout`.

```
<?xml version="1.0" encoding="utf-8"?>
<FrameLayout
    xmlns:android="http://schemas.android.com/apk/res/android"
    android:layout_width="match_parent"
    android:layout_height="match_parent">
    <ImageView android:id="@+id/splashScreenImage"
        android:src="@drawable/starfighter"
        android:layout_width="match_parent"
        android:layout_height="match_parent">
    </ImageView>
</FrameLayout>
```

Notice that the `src` property is pointing to "@drawable/starfighter"; this tells Android to display the `starfighter` image from the `drawable` folder. Now for something that is a little less obvious. If you think back to our discussion on nine-patch images, I mentioned that we needed some code to make use of the scaling abilities of nine-patch. Setting the `layout_width` and/or the `layout_height` to `match_parent` will make use of the nine-patch format to correct scale your image the way you have specified.

Create a `TextView` now in your layout. This `TextView` will be used to display whatever credits or text you want to display on your splash screen.

```
<?xml version="1.0" encoding="utf-8"?>
<FrameLayout
    xmlns:android="http://schemas.android.com/apk/res/android"
    android:layout_width="match_parent"
    android:layout_height="match_parent">
    <ImageView android:id="@+id/splashScreenImage"
        android:src="@drawable/starfighter"
```

```
            android:layout_width="match_parent"
            android:layout_height="match_parent">
    </ImageView>
    <TextView
        android:text="game by: j.f.dimarzio - graphics by: ben eagel"
        android:id="@+id/creditsText"
    </TextView>
</FrameLayout>
```

There is no voodoo to creating this view, and it should seem fairly straightforward. Once again, you need to tell Android the `layout_width` and `layout_height` of the `TextView`. However, if we set the properties to `match_parent` file as we did on the `ImageView` and the `FrameLayout`, your text would cover the image in a very undesirable way.

Rather, you are going to set the `layout_width` and `layout_height` to `wrap_content`, as shown below. The `wrap_content` constant is going to let Android know that you want the size of the `TextView` to be determined by the size of the text within it. Therefore, the more text that you add, the larger the `TextView` will be.

```
<?xml version="1.0" encoding="utf-8"?>
<FrameLayout
  xmlns:android="http://schemas.android.com/apk/res/android"
  android:layout_width="match_parent"
  android:layout_height="match_parent">
    <ImageView android:id="@+id/splashScreenImage"
        android:src="@drawable/starfighter"
        android:layout_width="match_parent"
        android:layout_height="match_parent">
    </ImageView>
    <TextView
        android:text="game by: j.f.dimarzio graphics by: ben eagel"
        android:id="@+id/creditsText"
        android:layout_height="wrap_content"
        android:layout_width="wrap_content">
    </TextView>
</FrameLayout>
```

Finally, you want to the text that is displaying the credits not to be too distracting, so you are going to set the gravity of the `TextView` to pull the text to the bottom center of the `FrameView`, as shown here.

```
<?xml version="1.0" encoding="utf-8"?>
<FrameLayout
  xmlns:android="http://schemas.android.com/apk/res/android"
  android:layout_width="match_parent"
  android:layout_height="match_parent">
    <ImageView android:id="@+id/splashScreenImage"
        android:src="@drawable/starfighter"
        android:layout_width="match_parent"
        android:layout_height="match_parent">
    </ImageView>
    <TextView
        android:text="game by: j.f.dimarzio graphics by: ben eagel"
        android:id="@+id/creditsText"
        android:layout_gravity="center_horizontal|bottom"
```

```
            android:layout_height="wrap_content"
            android:layout_width="wrap_content">
    </TextView>
</FrameLayout>
```

You have successfully created the layout that will display your splash screen. Now, you just have to tell StarfighterActivity to use this layout.

Connecting StarfighterActivity with the Layout

Connecting StarfighterActivity with the layout is very easy to do and requires only one line of code.

Save the splashscreen.xml file. Saving the file will create another entry in the R.java file so that you can reference the layout in your other code.

Open the StarfighterActivity.java file in the root of your project's source. This file was created for you automatically when you created the project.

> **TIP:** If you do not have a file named StarfighterActivity.java, check that you following the directions for creating a project in the previous chapter. If you named your project anything other than starfighter, your StarfighterActivity will have a different name.

When you open the StarfighterActivity.java file, you are going to see some automatically generated code that displays a premade layout named main.

```
package com.proandroidgames;

import android.app.Activity;
import android.os.Bundle;

public class StarfighterActivity extends Activity {
    /** Called when the activity is first created. */
    @Override
    public void onCreate(Bundle savedInstanceState) {
        super.onCreate(savedInstanceState);
        setContentView(R.layout.main);
    }
}
```

Change the setContentView() from displaying the main layout to displaying the starfighter layout that you just created. The finished activity should look like this.

```
package com.proandroidgames;

import android.app.Activity;
import android.os.Bundle;

public class StarfighterActivity extends Activity {
    /** Called when the activity is first created. */
    @Override
```

```
public void onCreate(Bundle savedInstanceState) {
    super.onCreate(savedInstanceState);

    /*display the splash screen image from a layout*/
    setContentView(R.layout.splashscreen);
}
}
```

Compile and run your code by clicking the green circle with the white arrow in it on the menu bar. You can also press Ctrl + F11 or click **Run ➤ Run** from the menu.

If you have never compiled or debugged an Android application before, you may see a screen that asks you if you want to run your application as a JUnit test or an Android application. You will want to run your application as an Android application. You can then choose which version of the emulator, or any attached Android debug mode device, to run your application on.

> **CAUTION:** If you choose to run your code in the Android emulator rather than on an actual Android phone, you may experience some unexpected results. Keep in mind that the emulator is exactly that, an emulator, and it is not an exact representation of what your game will look like on a device. This is not to say that you shouldn't use the emulator at all; just be cautious until you see your work on an actual device.

Launch your game, and you should see the splash screen as it appears in Figure 3–11. This is big accomplishment and the first hurdle in creating the entry point of your game. However, right now , the screen really doesn't do much. In fact, it really doesn't do anything except display. You need to create the fade in and fade out effects that will lead from your splash screen to your main menu.

Figure 3–11. *The Star Fighter splash screen*

Exit StarfighterActivity, and go back to your code. It is time to create the fade in and fade out effects.

Creating Fade Effects

You are going to use animation to create the effect of fading into the splash screen and then fading out the splash screen to the main menu. Android has some built-in animation effects that are very easy to use and very easy to implement.

Why use animation to fade in and fade out? The simple answer is that it is an easy way to make your game look better. If you just had a static screen that flipped from your splash screen to your main menu, you would still accomplish the same goal, but by fading into and out of your screens, you give your game an extra look of professionalism.

Create two more layout files in the res\layout folder: one named fadein.xml and the other fadeout.xml. As the names suggest, the fadein.xml file will control the animation that fades the splash screen onto your device. The fadeout.xml file will control the animation that fades the splash screen out to the main menu.

The type of animation that you are going to create is called an alpha. "Alpha" refers to the alpha value of an image, or its transparency. An alpha value of 1 is opaque, and an alpha value of 0 is transparent. Therefore, to make an image appear as though it is fading in, you need to create an animation that adjusts the alpha value of your image from 0 to 1 over a set amount of time. Conversely, if you want to fade out an image, you need an animation that adjusts the alpha value of your image from 1 to 0 over a set duration of time. For this reason, you will create two different alpha animations to control the fade in and fade out of your splash screen.

After you have created the `fadein.xml` and `fadeout.xml` files in your `res\layout` folder, double-click the `fadein.xml` file to open it in the editor. The file should be empty except for the following line; if it is not, delete the contents of the file will with exception of this line:

```
<?xml version="1.0" encoding="utf-8"?>
```

Now, create an alpha animation thusly:

```
<?xml version="1.0" encoding="utf-8"?>
<alpha xmlns:android="http://schemas.android.com/apk/res/android"
/>
```

You need to define four properties for this animation to complete it: the type of interpolator to use, the starting and ending alpha values, and the total duration of the animation in time.

First, let's define the interpolator. The interpolator tells the animation how to progress. That is, the animation can just run normally; it can start off slow and build up speed; it can start off fast and get slower; or it can repeat. For the fade in effect, we are going to start the animation slowly and then let it build up over the course of a second.

Use the `accelerate_interpolator` to tell the animation that you want to start off slow and then accelerate over time. The code that follows illustrates how to implement the `accelerate_interpolator` in `fadein.xml`:

```
<?xml version="1.0" encoding="utf-8"?>
<alpha xmlns:android="http://schemas.android.com/apk/res/android"
        android:interpolator="@android:anim/accelerate_interpolator" />
```

Your fade in animation will now start off slow and gradually speed up until the fade is complete. But how long will it run?

Use the `android:duration` property to tell the alpha animation how long to run. The `android:duration` property takes a value in milliseconds. You are going to tell the animation to run for 1 second by setting the `android:duration` to 1000.

```
<?xml version="1.0" encoding="utf-8"?>
<alpha xmlns:android="http://schemas.android.com/apk/res/android"
        android:interpolator="@android:anim/accelerate_interpolator"
        android:duration="1000" />
```

The final step in creating the fade in animation is to set the properties for the starting and ending alpha values of your animation. In this case, you are fading from fully transparent to fully opaque. However, that doesn't mean that these are your only options. You can choose to start and end at any values in between. You could have an animation that started are 25 percent opaque and faded to 100 percent opaque if you wanted to.

Set the android:fromAlpha and android:toAlpha properties to indicate what alpha values you want to start and finish at.

```xml
<?xml version="1.0" encoding="utf-8"?>
<alpha xmlns:android="http://schemas.android.com/apk/res/android"
        android:interpolator="@android:anim/accelerate_interpolator"
        android:duration="1000"
        android:fromAlpha="0.0"
        android:toAlpha="1.0"/>
```

> **CAUTION:** The values for fromAlpha and toAlpha are floats and not ints. This is important because the alpha value only ranges from 0 to 1.

Here, you have set the fromAlpha property to 0.0. This indicates that the animation begins with the view fully transparent. The toAlpha property has been set to 1.0 indicating that the animation is to end with the view fully opaque. This animation will provide you with a smooth fade in.

It is now time to create the fade out.

Think about how the fade out should work in relationship to the fade in. The fade out should work just like the fade in only in reverse. That means that the animation should use an interpolator that starts off fast and gets slower until it finishes. The animation should also start with a fully opaque object and transition to a fully transparent one.

Save the fadein.xml file, and open the fadeout.xml. Here too, you should only have one line of code in fadeout.xml:

```xml
<?xml version="1.0" encoding="utf-8"?>
```

You need to set the android:interpolator, android:duration, android:fromAlpha, and android:toAlpha for fadeout.xml.

You used the accelerate_interpolator in the fade-in animation to start off at a slow rate of fade and gradually move to a greater rate. Therefore, to reverse the animation for a fade out, you are going to use the decelerate_interpolator. The decelerate_interpolator will start the animation off at a faster rate and slowly decrease that rate until the animation finishes.

Once again, you will set up an animation duration of 1 second (1000 milliseconds) for the fade out.

```xml
<?xml version="1.0" encoding="utf-8"?>
<alpha xmlns:android="http://schemas.android.com/apk/res/android"
        android:interpolator="@android:anim/decelerate_interpolator"
        android:duration="1000" />
```

Set the properties android:fromAlpha and android:toAlpha to complete the animation. Because you are fading out from a solid image to nothing, you will be setting the android:fromAlpha to fully opaque and the android:toAlpha to fully transparent. This will start the animation at a solid image and fade it to a transparency.

```xml
<?xml version="1.0" encoding="utf-8"?>
<alpha xmlns:android="http://schemas.android.com/apk/res/android"
        android:interpolator="@android:anim/decelerate_interpolator"
        android:duration="1000"
        android:fromAlpha="1.0"
        android:toAlpha="0.0"/>
```

You can now save your finished `fadeout.xml` file.

At this point, you have a layout and two animations to control and define your splash screen. Now, you need some way to tell the three of them to interact and create an animation splash screen.

To understand how you are going to create and run the animation, you need to understand how threading works in relationship to your game.

Threading Your Game

One of the biggest obstacles that you, as a game developer, need to overcome is how your game runs on any given platform. At its most basic root element, an Android game is still just a basic Android activity. Every other "application" that is written for Android is also written as an activity. The only difference between your activity and any other is that yours will contain a game, whereas others might be business, mapping, or social media tools.

The problem with this architecture is that, because all Android activities are the same, they are all treated the same. This means that every Android activity that you write will run in the main execution thread of the system. This is bad for games.

Running your game in the main execution thread of the system means that your game has to compete for resources with every other activity running in that thread. This will lead to a choppy or slow game at best and a game that halts or freezes the device at worst.

But fear not, there is a way to get around this singly threaded nightmare. You have to ability to spawn off any number of threads and run anything you want to run within them. Ideally, you will want your game to run in a thread that is separate everything else that runs on the device to ensure that your game runs as smoothly as possible and has access to the resources it needs.

In the remainder of this chapter, you are actually going to spawn two separate threads for the execution of your game. The first thread, discussed in this section, will be for the game to run in, and the second thread (which you will create a little later in this chapter) will be to run any background music that you want to play behind your game.

Why two separate threads? With the exception of animation and game logic, one of the most processor-intensive things you can do on a device is play media, such as music. You will ensure that the game and music will run smoothly and concurrently without interfering with each other. By running the music in a separate thread from the game, you will also be able to kill the music without interfering with the game play should your find that the device's resources are running low.

Now that you understand why you need to spawn different threads for your game, let's create one for the main game and splash screen. This game thread will tie together the splash screen that you created, the fade in and fade out animations, and the main menu.

Creating the Game Thread

Open StarfighterActivity.java once again. Just as a reminder, your file should currently be able to launch the splash screen and should contain the following code.

```java
package com.proandroidgames;

import android.app.Activity;
import android.os.Bundle;

public class StarfighterActivity extends Activity {
    /** Called when the activity is first created. */
    @Override
    public void onCreate(Bundle savedInstanceState) {
        super.onCreate(savedInstanceState);

        /*display the splash screen image from a layout*/
        setContentView(R.layout.splashscreen);
    }
}
```

Since StarfighterActivity is the activity that is launched by default and the one that launches the splash screen, it is the perfect place to spawn your game thread. The thread that you create now is going to be the one that game will eventually run in.

Instantiate a new Thread(), and override the run() method to spawn a new thread. Within the run() method, call the main menu to run the game in the new thread. This is the basic roadmap for what you are going to do here.

> **NOTE:** As you progress through building the game, the code in this thread will be modified and even moved to accommodate more complex processes.

The following code shows where to spawn the new thread within the StarfighterActivity code.

```java
package com.proandroidgames;

import android.app.Activity;
import android.os.Bundle;

public class StarfighterActivity extends Activity {
    /** Called when the activity is first created. */
    @Override
    public void onCreate(Bundle savedInstanceState) {
        super.onCreate(savedInstanceState);

        /*display the splash screen image*/
        setContentView(R.layout.splashscreen);
```

```
                /* Start a new game thread */
                new Thread() {
                    @Override
                    public void run() {

                    }
                }
            }
        }
```

There is one problem with this code though. As it is written, the code will spawn the new game thread within milliseconds of the splash screen being displayed. This would barely be enough time to render the splash screen. Therefore, you need to delay spawning of the game thread until the splash screen has had enough time to display.

The answer is to use a time-delayed Handler(). Android has handlers that can manage threads and activities. The postDelay() method of the Handler() takes two parameters: the thread that is to be delayed and the amount of time to delay.

You are going to create a new constant to hold the amount of time that you want to delay your thread. This constant, GAME_THREAD_DELAY, is going to be the first line of code in your game engine. Placing it there will allow you to adjust the delay on the thread from a single location without hunting through your code for it.

Create a new class file in your game package called SFEngine.java. This is an empty class file that will eventually hold the majority of your game engine. Add the following constant to the class:

```
package com.proandroidgames;

public class SFEngine {
        /*Constants that will be used in the game*/
        public static final int GAME_THREAD_DELAY = 4000;
}
```

You are setting the GAME_THREAD_DELAY to 4 seconds; this should be a good amount of time for the splash screen to display before the main menu fades in.

Save SFEngine.java, and reopen the StarfighterActivity. Let's wrap the new game thread in a Handler() and postDelay() it, as shown here.

TIP: Pay close attention to the packages that need to be imported as well; you will receive errors from your code if you try to call a method that lives in a package you have not yet imported. You can also use the Ctrl + Shift + O shortcut to automatically import any referenced packages that you may have missed.

```
package com.proandroidgames;

import android.app.Activity;
import android.os.Bundle;
import android.os.Handler;
```

```
public class StarfighterActivity extends Activity {
    /** Called when the activity is first created. */
    @Override
    public void onCreate(Bundle savedInstanceState) {
        super.onCreate(savedInstanceState);

        /*display the splash screen image*/
        setContentView(R.layout.splashscreen);

        /*start up the splash screen and main menu in a time delayed thread*/
        new Handler().postDelayed(new Thread() {
            @Override
            public void run() {

            }
    }, SFEngine.GAME_THREAD_DELAY);

    }
}
```

Now, you have created the new thread and set a time delay to pause the spawning of the thread for 4 seconds. Finally, it is time to tell the thread what to do.

Setting a New Intent

In the new thread, you are going to start the main menu activity, kill the splash screen activity, and set the fading animation. To start a new activity, you have to create an Intent() method.

Think of Intent() as an operation that you are telling Android to perform. In this case, you are telling Android to start up your main menu activity. The following code shows you how to create a new Intent() method for starting the main menu.

```
package com.proandroidgames;

import android.app.Activity;
import android.content.Intent;
import android.os.Bundle;
import android.os.Handler;

public class StarfighterActivity extends Activity {
    /** Called when the activity is first created. */
    @Override
    public void onCreate(Bundle savedInstanceState) {
        super.onCreate(savedInstanceState);
        /*display the splash screen image*/
        setContentView(R.layout.splashscreen);
        /*start up the splash screen and main menu in a time delayed thread*/
        new Handler().postDelayed(new Thread() {
            @Override
            public void run() {
                    Intent mainMenu = new Intent(StarfighterActivity.this,
SFMainMenu.class);
                    StarfighterActivity.this.startActivity(mainMenu);
```

```
            }
    }, SFEngine.GAME_THREAD_DELAY);

    }
}
```

Let's discuss what this code does before moving on. The first line creates the new `Intent()` named `mainMenu` within the context of `StarfighterActivity`, and the activity is `SFMainMenu`. The second line uses the `StarfighterActivity` context to start the `mainMenu` activity. Keep in mind all of this is happening within a separate thread from the splash screen.

Killing the Activity

Now that the main menu is started, you want to kill the splash screen activity. The code will navigate the play to the main menu regardless, so why kill the splash screen? Think of it as a bit of housekeeping. By killing the splash screen, you ensure that the play cannot inadvertently navigate back to using the back button on the device. If the players were able to navigate back to the splash screen, they could in theory spawn off any number of concurrent game threads and clog up their devices. Therefore, just to be safe, you are going to kill the splash screen as shown here.

```
package com.proandroidgames;

import android.app.Activity;
import android.content.Intent;
import android.os.Bundle;
import android.os.Handler;

public class StarfighterActivity extends Activity {
    /** Called when the activity is first created. */
    @Override
    public void onCreate(Bundle savedInstanceState) {
        super.onCreate(savedInstanceState);

        /*display the splash screen image*/
        setContentView(R.layout.splashscreen);

        /*start up the splash screen and main menu in a time delayed thread*/
        new Handler().postDelayed(new Thread() {
            @Override
            public void run() {
                Intent mainMenu = new Intent(StarfighterActivity.this,
SFMainMenu.class);
                StarfighterActivity.this.startActivity(mainMenu);
                StarfighterActivity.this.finish();

            }
    }, SFEngine.GAME_THREAD_DELAY);

    }
}
```

Finally, your new thread needs the animation that will fade the splash screen into the main menu. You will use the overridePendingTransition() method to tell Android that you want to use the two fade animations that you created as the transition from one activity to the other.

```
package com.proandroidgames;

import android.app.Activity;
import android.content.Intent;
import android.os.Bundle;
import android.os.Handler;

public class StarfighterActivity extends Activity {
    /** Called when the activity is first created. */
    @Override
    public void onCreate(Bundle savedInstanceState) {
        super.onCreate(savedInstanceState);
        /*display the splash screen image*/
        setContentView(R.layout.splashscreen);
        /*start up the splash screen and main menu in a time delayed thread*/
        new Handler().postDelayed(new Thread() {
            @Override
            public void run() {
                Intent mainMenu= new Intent(StarfighterActivity.this,
SFMainMenu.class);
                StarfighterActivity.this.startActivity(mainMenu);
                StarfighterActivity.this.finish();
                overridePendingTransition(R.layout.fadein,R.layout.fadeout);
            }
        }, SFEngine.GAME_THREAD_DELAY);

    }
}
```

You need to do one last thing before you run your splash screen. In the layout directory, you should see an automatically generated file named main.xml. Let's tell the SFMainMenu activity to use this layout. Since the layout is empty, the activity will not display anything, but it will help you as you move into the next section of the chapter.

Open SFMainMenu.java, and make sure it has the following code, which should be the same code that was in the StarfighterActivity before you started modifying it:

```
package com.proandroidgames;

import android.app.Activity;
import android.os.Bundle;

public class SFMainMenu extends Activity {
    /** Called when the activity is first created. */
    @Override
    public void onCreate(Bundle savedInstanceState) {
        super.onCreate(savedInstanceState);
        setContentView(R.layout.main);
    }
}
```

Save SFMainMenu.java.

That is all of the code you need to create the splash screen. You should compile and run this code to see how it works. When you do, your splash screen should be brought to the screen and then fade to a black screen after 4 seconds.

Your next task is to replace the default 'Hello World' screen with the game's main menu. In the following section of this chapter, you will create the main menu for the game. Then, in the final section, you will use your experience creating threads to spawn another thread for the game music.

Creating the Main Menu

In this section, you are going to create the main menu for the game. The main menu is going to consist of a background image and two buttons. One button will start the game; the other will exit the game.

Adding the Button Images

Using the same drag-and-drop process you used earlier, add the images for the buttons to your res\drawable-hdpi folder. In the project created for this book, there are two images for the Start button and two images for the Exit button. One image for each button will be its resting state, and the other image will represent the pressed state. Figures 3–12 and 3–13 show the two images of the resting states of the Start and Exit buttons respectively.

> **NOTE:** Notice the black border around the left and top edges of the button images. These button images are nine-patch.

Figure 3–12. *The Start button's rest state, starfighterstartbtn*

Figure 3–13. *The Exit button's rest state, starfighterexitbtn*

Figures 3–14 and 3–15 represent the pressed states of the Start and Exit buttons respectively.

Figure 3–14. *The Start button's pressed state, starfighterstartbtndown*

Figure 3–15. *The Exit button's pressed state, starfighterexitbtndown*

> **NOTE:** The code that is list in this section is going to assume that you have named the images corresponding to the names in the figure captions above. If you name your images differently, be sure to adjust the code samples as needed.

For the background image of your main menu, in an effort to keep things simple, we are going to use the same image as your splash screen. Of course, you should feel free to change this however you like and use whatever image you want to use for your main menu. However, for the purposes of this book, you are going to use the splash screen image behind the main menu as well.

Open the main.xml that is located in the layout folder. This file should have been created automatically when you created your project.

> **CAUTION:** If you find that you do not have a main.xml file, create one now using the same instructions for creating splashscreen.xml in the preceding section of this chapter. Make sure you have a main.xml file and it is empty before proceeding in this section.

Once again, your main.xml should be empty except for the following line of code. If it is not, clear whatever text is in it with the exception of the following:

```
<?xml version="1.0" encoding="utf-8"?>
```

You are going to use a RelativeLayout layout to hold the background image and the buttons. Using RelativeLayout gives you control over the precise locations of the views that you place within the layout.

Create RelativeLayout as follows:

```
<?xml version="1.0" encoding="utf-8"?>
<RelativeLayout xmlns:android="http://schemas.android.com/apk/res/android"
    android:orientation="vertical"
    android:layout_width="match_parent"
    android:layout_height="match_parent"
    >

</RelativeLayout>
```

Here, you have created a RelativeLayout layout with layout_width and layout_height properties set to match_parent.

Next, add the ImageView that will hold the background image. This code is very close to code you wrote in the last section for the splash screen, so I will go light on the explanations. If you need a refresher on what any of these views do, please refer to the previous section.

```xml
<?xml version="1.0" encoding="utf-8"?>
<RelativeLayout xmlns:android="http://schemas.android.com/apk/res/android"
    android:orientation="vertical"
    android:layout_width="match_parent"
    android:layout_height="match_parent"
    >
    <ImageView android:id="@+id/mainMenuImage"
        android:src="@drawable/starfighter"
        android:layout_width="match_parent"
        android:layout_height="match_parent">
    </ImageView>

</RelativeLayout>
```

Next, you have to place the buttons on the screen, but before that, you have to work a little magic.

Setting the Layouts

Right-click the `res\drawable-hdpi` folder, and add two new XML files: `startselector.xml` and `exitselector.xml`. These files are going to hold a selector that tells your button images to change based on the state of the button. This is what is going to allow your change the image of the button when the player presses it.

Add the following code to `startselector.xml`:

```xml
<?xml version="1.0" encoding="utf-8"?>
<selector
  xmlns:android="http://schemas.android.com/apk/res/android">
  <item android:state_pressed="true"
android:drawable="@drawable/starfighterstartbtndown" />
  <item android:drawable="@drawable/starfighterstartbtn" />
</selector>
```

Notice that the selector has two item properties, one represents the state of the button if it is pressed (android:state_pressed="true") and the other represents the button in its normal at rest state (no designation other than the image). The property for the pressed state has an image set to the `starfighterstartbtndown` image, and the rest state image is the `starfighterstartbtn` image.

Setting the `src` property of an `ImageButton` to this selector will have the result of changing the image of the button as the player presses it.

Set the `exitselector.xml` code as follows to accomplish the same result for the Exit button:

```xml
<?xml version="1.0" encoding="utf-8"?>
<selector
  xmlns:android="http://schemas.android.com/apk/res/android">
  <item android:state_pressed="true" android:drawable="@drawable/starfighterexitbtndown"
/>
  <item android:drawable="@drawable/starfighterexitbtn" />
</selector>
```

With the selectors created to change your button images, you can add the ImageButtons to the layout in main.xml.

Because you want the buttons aligned to the bottom of the screen, you are going to set the alignParentBottom property to true on the RelativeLayout that holds the buttons. Then, setting the height to wrap_content and the width to match_parent will make the layout only as high as the buttons within it and as wide as the screen.

The Start button will be aligned with the left edge of the screen, and the Exit button will be aligned with the right. This will place the buttons to the lower corners of the screen.

```xml
<?xml version="1.0" encoding="utf-8"?>
<RelativeLayout xmlns:android="http://schemas.android.com/apk/res/android"
    android:orientation="vertical"
    android:layout_width="match_parent"
    android:layout_height="match_parent"
    >
    <ImageView android:id="@+id/mainMenuImage"
        android:src="@drawable/starfighter"
        android:layout_width="match_parent"
        android:layout_height="match_parent">
    </ImageView>
    <RelativeLayout
        android:id="@+id/buttons"
        android:layout_width="match_parent"
        android:layout_height="wrap_content"
        android:orientation="horizontal"
        android:layout_alignParentBottom="true"
        android:layout_marginBottom="20dp">
        <ImageButton
            android:id="@+id/btnStart"
            android:clickable="true"
            android:layout_alignParentLeft="true"
            android:layout_width="wrap_content"
            android:src="@drawable/startselector"
            android:layout_height="wrap_content" >
        </ImageButton>
        <ImageButton
            android:id="@+id/btnExit"
            android:layout_width="wrap_content"
            android:src="@drawable/exitselector"
            android:layout_height="wrap_content"
            android:layout_alignParentRight="true"
            android:clickable="true" >
        </ImageButton>

    </RelativeLayout>
</RelativeLayout>
```

Notice that the src properties of the Start and Exit buttons are set to the start and exit selectors that you created to change the image of the button.

If you run your game now, you should see your splash screen fade into the main menu. The main menu should look something like Figure 3–16. Notice the placement of the buttons and the button images. Try pressing a button and see if the image changes.

> **NOTE:** You may notice that your image buttons have a gray background to them instead of the transparent background in Figure 3–16. You are going to set the ImageButton backgrounds to transparent in the SFMainMenu.java code later in this chapter, and doing so will remove the gray.

Figure 3–16. *The main menu*

Wiring the Buttons

The only thing left to do on the main menu is to wire up the buttons so that they actually perform a function. The Exit button will be set up to exit the game and kill all threads. The Start button will start the first level of the game. Since you have not created the first level of the game yet, you are just going to stub out the Start button.

Open the SFEngine.java game engine code. You need to create a few more constants that will be used in the main menu and a function that will do the exit cleanup work. Right now, the engine should look like this:

```
package com.proandroidgames;

public class SFEngine {
        /*Constants that will be used in the game*/
        public static final int GAME_THREAD_DELAY = 4000;
}
```

You need to add two constants: one for setting the transparency of the Start and Exit buttons and one for setting the haptic feedback of the buttons.

> **NOTE:** The haptic feedback is the tactile response the certain devices can give when you touch buttons.

Add the following constants to SFEngine:

```
package com.proandroidgames;

public class SFEngine {
        /*Constants that will be used in the game*/
        public static final int GAME_THREAD_DELAY = 4000;
        public static final int MENU_BUTTON_ALPHA = 0;
        public static final boolean HAPTIC_BUTTON_FEEDBACK = true;
}
```

Next, create a new method that returns a Boolean value. This method will be called when the Exit button is pressed to perform any housekeeping that is needed in the game before it can exit cleanly.

```
package com.proandroidgames;

import android.view.View;

public class SFEngine {
        /*Constants that will be used in the game*/
        public static final int GAME_THREAD_DELAY = 4000;
        public static final int MENU_BUTTON_ALPHA = 0;
        public static final boolean HAPTIC_BUTTON_FEEDBACK = true;

        /*Kill game and exit*/
        public boolean onExit(View v) {
        try
        {
                return true;
        }catch(Exception e){
                return false;
        }

        }
}
```

Now, there is no housekeeping for this method to perform, so it is just going to return true and let the game proceed with its exit routine.

Save the game engine, and open the SFMainMenu.java file.

The first thing you are going to do in the main menu code is to set the background transparency of the image buttons and set up the haptic feedback.

```
package com.proandroidgames;

import android.app.Activity;
```

```
import android.widget.ImageButton;
import android.os.Bundle;


public class SFMainMenu extends Activity {
    /** Called when the activity is first created. */
    @Override
    public void onCreate(Bundle savedInstanceState) {
        super.onCreate(savedInstanceState);
        setContentView(R.layout.main);

        /** Set menu button options */
        ImageButton start = (ImageButton)findViewById(R.id.btnStart);
        ImageButton exit = (ImageButton)findViewById(R.id.btnExit);

        start.getBackground().setAlpha(SFEngine.MENU_BUTTON_ALPHA);
        start.setHapticFeedbackEnabled(SFEngine.HAPTIC_BUTTON_FEEDBACK);

        exit.getBackground().setAlpha(SFEngine.MENU_BUTTON_ALPHA);
        exit.setHapticFeedbackEnabled(SFEngine.HAPTIC_BUTTON_FEEDBACK);
    }
}
```

Here, you are creating two more ImageButtons in memory. Then, using the
findViewById() method, you set those in memory buttons to the actual buttons on the
main menu. Finally, you set the background transparency and the haptic feedback of
each button.

Adding onClickListeners

Next, you need to establish two onClickListeners for the buttons: one for the Start
button and one for the Exit. The onClickListener() method will be executed when the
player presses (or clicks) the respective button. Any code that you want executed when
either button is pressed needs to be called from that button's onClickListener().

For now, onClickListener() for the Start button is not going to do anything. You are just
going to stub it out in preparation for the next chapter where the game play will begin.
The onClickListener() for the exit button will call the onExit() function in the game
engine, and if the function returns true, the game will be exited.

```
package com.proandroidgames;

import android.app.Activity;
import android.os.Bundle;
import android.view.View;
import android.view.View.OnClickListener;
import android.widget.ImageButton;


public class SFMainMenu extends Activity {
    /** Called when the activity is first created. */
    @Override
    public void onCreate(Bundle savedInstanceState) {
        super.onCreate(savedInstanceState);
```

```
        setContentView(R.layout.main);

        final SFEngine engine = new SFEngine();

        /** Set menu button options */
        ImageButton start = (ImageButton)findViewById(R.id.btnStart);
        ImageButton exit = (ImageButton)findViewById(R.id.btnExit);

        start.getBackground().setAlpha(SFEngine.MENU_BUTTON_ALPHA);
        start.setHapticFeedbackEnabled(SFEngine.HAPTIC_BUTTON_FEEDBACK);

        exit.getBackground().setAlpha(SFEngine.MENU_BUTTON_ALPHA);
        exit.setHapticFeedbackEnabled(SFEngine.HAPTIC_BUTTON_FEEDBACK);

        start.setOnClickListener(new OnClickListener(){
                @Override
                public void onClick(View v) {
                        /** Start Game!!!! */
                }

        });

        exit.setOnClickListener(new OnClickListener(){
                @Override
                public void onClick(View v) {
                        boolean clean = false;
                        clean = engine.onExit(v);
                        if (clean)
                        {
                                int pid= android.os.Process.myPid();
                                android.os.Process.killProcess(pid);
                        }
                }
        });
    }

}
```

Save SFMainMenu.java, and run your code. You should now be able to click the Exit button to close the game. The buttons should also have transparent backgrounds, and the splash screen should fade smoothly into the main menu.

The final step in creating a pretty professional splash screen and main menu is adding some background music.

Adding Music

In this section, you will learn how to spawn a second thread from your game. This thread will be used to run the background music that will play behind your main menu. You will spawn a thread, create a service that will play the music, and then kill the music and the thread in the housekeeping function of the engine.

CAUTION: If you have never worked with music files and Android before, be cautious about the size of your files. If your media files are too large, you may consume all of the available memory for your activity and crash it. I try to keep things like background music to a small 10 or 15 second loop that can be repeated.

The first thing that you will need to do is add a res\raw folder. All music files are stored in the raw folder, but unfortunately, this folder is not created for you when you create the project. Right-click the res folder and select **New ➤ Folder**. Name the folder raw, as shown in Figure 3–17.

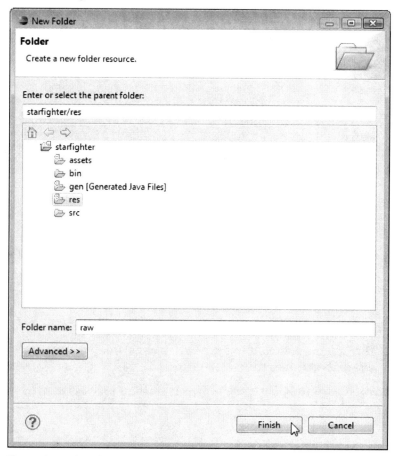

Figure 3–17. *Creating the raw folder*

The next step is to copy your media files into the res\raw folder.

> **NOTE:** The music that is distributed with this code is royalty free music through the Creative Commons licensing agreement from Matt McFarland at www.mattmcfarland.com. I have taken 15-second samples from his songs to loop during parts of this book's game.

If you are using the files from this project, the music for the main menu is warfieldedit.ogg. Once again, feel free to use whatever music you want to for the main menu; just try to mind the size.

Next, let's add some more constants to the engine that will be used in the music service. Open SFEngine.java, and add the following constants:

```java
package com.proandroidgames;

import android.content.Context;
import android.view.View;

public class SFEngine {
        /*Constants that will be used in the game*/
        public static final int GAME_THREAD_DELAY = 4000;
        public static final int MENU_BUTTON_ALPHA = 0;
        public static final boolean HAPTIC_BUTTON_FEEDBACK = true;
        public static final int SPLASH_SCREEN_MUSIC = R.raw.warfieldedit;
        public static final int R_VOLUME = 100;
        public static final int L_VOLUME = 100;
        public static final boolean LOOP_BACKGROUND_MUSIC = true;
        public static Context context;

        /*Kill game and exit*/
        public boolean onExit(View v) {
        try
        {
                return true;
        }catch(Exception e){
                return false;
        }

        }

}
```

SPLASH_SCREEN_MUSIC is a constant pointer to the actual music file that you will be playing, in this case, warfieldedit.ogg. The R_VOLUME and L_VOLUME variables will set the initial volume for the music, and LOOP_BACKGROUND_MUSIC is a Boolean value that tells the service whether or not to loop. Finally, the context variable will hold the current context of the thread that the music is playing in so that we can kill it during the game's housekeeping. All of these new constants and variables will be called from the service.

Now, let's create a service that will play this music file. You can then launch this service in a thread from the main menu.

Creating a Music Service

Add a new class file named SFMusic.java to the game package. You should have a blank class as follows:

```
package com.proandroidgames;

public class SFMusic {

}
```

The first thing you need to do is to have this class extend Service:

```
package com.proandroidgames;

import android.app.Service;

public class SFMusic extends Service{

}
```

At this point, Eclipse may be throwing an error at you, because you have not implemented all of the methods that are required to extend Service. Just ignore that error for now. Add the following methods to your service:

```
package com.proandroidgames;

import android.app.Service;
import android.content.Intent;
import android.os.IBinder;

public class SFMusic extends Service{

        @Override
        public IBinder onBind(Intent arg0) {
                return null;
                }

        @Override
        public void onCreate() {
                super.onCreate();
            }

        public int onStartCommand(Intent intent, int flags, int startId) {
                return 1;
        }
        public void onStart(Intent intent, int startId) {

            }
        public void onStop() {

                }
```

```
           public IBinder onUnBind(Intent arg0) {
                        // TODO Auto-generated method stub
                        return null;
           }
           public void onPause() {

           }

           @Override
           public void onDestroy() {

           }

           @Override
           public void onLowMemory() {

           }

}
```

With the service code stubbed out, let's create two variables. The first is a Boolean
called isRunning. This will be used to query the service to find out if it is running. At
times, you will need to know if the service is running so you can either kill the music, if it
is still running, or restart it, if it has stopped.

> **NOTE:** Initially the isRunning Boolean will be set to false. When the service actually starts,
> you will set it to true.

The second variable that you need to create is the MediaPlayer, which will actually play
your music.

```
package com.proandroidgames;

import android.app.Service;
import android.media.MediaPlayer;
import android.content.Intent;
import android.os.IBinder;

public class SFMusic extends Service{
       public static boolean isRunning = false;
       MediaPlayer player;
       @Override
           public IBinder onBind(Intent arg0) {
                        return null;
                        }

       @Override
           public void onCreate() {
                        super.onCreate();
                   }

           public int onStartCommand(Intent intent, int flags, int startId) {
```

```
                    return 1;
            }
            public void onStart(Intent intent, int startId) {

            }
            public void onStop() {

            }

            public IBinder onUnBind(Intent argo) {
                        // TODO Auto-generated method stub
                        return null;
            }
            public void onPause() {

            }

            @Override
            public void onDestroy() {

            }

            @Override
            public void onLowMemory() {

        }

}
```

Next, you need to create a method in the service that will set the options for
MediaPlayer. These are the options that we create constants for in the engine: volume,
looping, and media file. This method will take in the constants that you created and pass
them directly to the MediaPlayer. You will call this method from the onCreate() method
so that, as soon as the service is created, the MediaPlayer options are set.

```
package com.proandroidgames;

import android.app.Service;
import android.media.MediaPlayer;
import android.content.Intent;
import android.os.IBinder;
import android.content.Context;

public class SFMusic extends Service{
            public static boolean isRunning = false;
            MediaPlayer player;
            @Override
            public IBinder onBind(Intent argo) {
                    return null;
                    }

            @Override
            public void onCreate() {
                    super.onCreate();
```

```
setMusicOptions(this,SFEngine.LOOP_BACKGROUND_MUSIC,SFEngine.R_VOLUME,SFEngine.L_VOLUME,
SFEngine.SPLASH_SCREEN_MUSIC);
            }
        public void setMusicOptions(Context context, boolean isLooped, int rVolume,
int lVolume, int soundFile){
                player = MediaPlayer.create(context, soundFile);
                player.setLooping(isLooped);
                player.setVolume(rVolume,lVolume);
        }
        public int onStartCommand(Intent intent, int flags, int startId) {
            return 1;
        }
        public void onStart(Intent intent, int startId) {

    }
        public void onStop() {

            }

        public IBinder onUnBind(Intent arg0) {
                    // TODO Auto-generated method stub
                    return null;
        }
        public void onPause() {

        }

        @Override
        public void onDestroy() {

        }

        @Override
        public void onLowMemory() {

        }

}
```

The last code that you need to add to the service indicates all of the places where the
media play is started and stopped. This code should be very easy to follow, but it is a
little scattered. Think about it logically; you are going to start the music in any of the
methods that deal with starting or creating and stop the music in any of the methods
that deal with stopping. Be sure to set the isRunning Boolean accordingly so that you
can correctly query if the service is running.

```
package com.proandroidgames;

import android.app.Service;
import android.content.Context;
import android.content.Intent;
import android.media.MediaPlayer;
import android.os.IBinder;
```

```
public class SFMusic extends Service{
        public static boolean isRunning = false;
        MediaPlayer player;

        @Override
        public IBinder onBind(Intent arg0) {
            return null;
            }

        @Override
        public void onCreate() {
            super.onCreate();

setMusicOptions(this,SFEngine.LOOP_BACKGROUND_MUSIC,SFEngine.R_VOLUME,SFEngine.L_VOLUME,
SFEngine.SPLASH_SCREEN_MUSIC);
            }
        public void setMusicOptions(Context context, boolean isLooped, int rVolume,
int lVolume, int soundFile){
                player = MediaPlayer.create(context, soundFile);
                player.setLooping(isLooped);
                player.setVolume(rVolume,lVolume);
        }
        public int onStartCommand(Intent intent, int flags, int startId) {
            try
            {
                player.start();
                isRunning = true;
                        }catch(Exception e){
                isRunning = false;
                player.stop();
                        }

                        return 1;
            }
            public void onStart(Intent intent, int startId) {

                    }
            public IBinder onUnBind(Intent arg0) {
                                    // TODO Auto-generated method stub
                                        return null;
                }
                public void onStop() {
                                        isRunning = false;
                }
                public void onPause() {       }
                @Override
                public void onDestroy() {
                                        player.stop();
                                        player.release();
                }
                @Override
                public void onLowMemory() {
                                        player.stop();
                }
```

```
}
```

The code for the service is now written. However, before you can use it, you need to associate the service with your Android project. Previously you used the AndroidManifest to associate a new Activity with the project. You follow the same procedure to associate your new SFMusic service with the project.

Open AndroidManifest.xml, and click the Application tab near the bottom of the editor window. Once you have the Application tab open, scroll to the bottom of the window to the Application Nodes section. Click the Add button to add a new node, and select Service from the list.

Click the new Service node in the Application Nodes windows, and navigate to Attributes for Service on the right-hand side of the editor window. You should now be able to click the Browse button to the right of the Name attribute. Locate your SFMusic service in the browser, and finish the operation.

Now, you are ready to use your music service in your game.

Playing Your Music

Open the SFEngine.java, and add a new public Thread() named musicThread. You will initialize this thread in the SFMainMenu.

```java
package com.proandroidgames;

import android.content.Context;
import android.content.Intent;
import android.view.View;

public class SFEngine {
                /*Constants that will be used in the game*/
                public static final int GAME_THREAD_DELAY = 4000;
                public static final int MENU_BUTTON_ALPHA = 0;
                public static final boolean HAPTIC_BUTTON_FEEDBACK = true;
                public static final int SPLASH_SCREEN_MUSIC = R.raw.warfieldedit;
                public static final int R_VOLUME = 100;
                public static final int L_VOLUME = 100;
                public static final boolean LOOP_BACKGROUND_MUSIC = true;
                public static Context context;
                public static Thread musicThread;

                /*Kill game and exit*/
                public boolean onExit(View v) {
        try
        {
                        return true;
        }catch(Exception e){
                        return false;
        }

                }

}
```

Now, open SFMainMenu.java, and create a new Thread() assigned to musicthread to run your music service.

```java
package com.proandroidgames;

import android.app.Activity;
import android.content.Intent;
import android.os.Bundle;
import android.view.View;
import android.view.View.OnClickListener;
import android.widget.ImageButton;


public class SFMainMenu extends Activity {
    /** Called when the activity is first created. */
    @Override
    public void onCreate(Bundle savedInstanceState) {
        super.onCreate(savedInstanceState);
        setContentView(R.layout.main);

        /** Fire up background music */
        SFEngine.musicThread = new Thread(){
                        public void run(){
                                        Intent bgmusic = new
Intent(getApplicationContext(), SFMusic.class);
                                        startService(bgmusic);
                                        SFEngine.context = getApplicationContext();
                        }
        };
        SFEngine.musicThread.start();

        final SFEngine engine = new SFEngine();

        /** Set menu button options */
        ImageButton start = (ImageButton)findViewById(R.id.btnStart);
        ImageButton exit = (ImageButton)findViewById(R.id.btnExit);

        start.getBackground().setAlpha(SFEngine.MENU_BUTTON_ALPHA);
        start.setHapticFeedbackEnabled(SFEngine.HAPTIC_BUTTON_FEEDBACK);

        exit.getBackground().setAlpha(SFEngine.MENU_BUTTON_ALPHA);
        exit.setHapticFeedbackEnabled(SFEngine.HAPTIC_BUTTON_FEEDBACK);

        start.setOnClickListener(new OnClickListener(){
                                                @Override
                                                public void onClick(View v) {
                                                                /** Start
Game!!!! */
                                                }
        });

        exit.setOnClickListener(new OnClickListener(){
                                                @Override
                                                public void onClick(View v) {
                                                                boolean clean =
false;
```

```
                                                                    clean =
engine.onExit(v);
                                                                    if (clean)
                                                                    {


int pid= android.os.Process.myPid();

android.os.Process.killProcess(pid);
                                                                    }
                                              }
                          );
     }

}
```

Finally, you need to kill the background music service during housekeeping. Go back to SFEngine, and add the following code to kill the service and thread:

```java
package com.proandroidgames;

import android.content.Context;
import android.content.Intent;
import android.view.View;

public class SFEngine {
                /*Constants that will be used in the game*/
                public static final int GAME_THREAD_DELAY = 4000;
                public static final int MENU_BUTTON_ALPHA = 0;
                public static final boolean HAPTIC_BUTTON_FEEDBACK = true;
                public static final int SPLASH_SCREEN_MUSIC = R.raw.warfieldedit;
                public static final int R_VOLUME = 100;
                public static final int L_VOLUME = 100;
                public static final boolean LOOP_BACKGROUND_MUSIC = true;
                public static Context context;
                public static Thread musicThread;

                /*Kill game and exit*/
                public boolean onExit(View v) {
        try
        {
                        Intent bgmusic = new Intent(context, SFMusic.class);
                        context.stopService(bgmusic);
                        musicThread.stop();
                        return true;
        }catch(Exception e){
                        return false;
        }

                }

}
```

Compile and run your game. You should now have a working splash screen with background music that exits cleanly. In the next chapter, you will begin to build the first level of the game, starting with its background.

Summary

In this chapter, you set forth the first code for your game. You created a splash screen that faded in and then faded out to the game's main menu. You also created the game's main menu with options to start and exit. Last, you used the media player and a raw music file to add some background music to your game.

In the next chapter, you will create a two-layer, scrolling background for your game.

Chapter 4

Drawing The Environment

In this chapter you are going to learn how to render a background to your game. The background sets the tone and the environment for the game. For Star Fighter, the environment is going to be a background of stars, planets, space ships, and debris. You are going to use OpenGL to set the background into the game and render it to the screen.

Given that a single background is pretty impressive, two backgrounds must be twice as impressive. Well, not quite – but two backgrounds that run at different speeds give your game a visual depth that can be very interesting. You will be adding a second layer of background to your game that will scroll at a faster speed than the first.

Later in the chapter, you will take a break from the game setting and work on making your game run at 60 frames per second. While many devices may not be able to run a fully completed game at a full 60 frames per second, it is the goal of most game developers.

No matter how good your game is, it will serve no purpose if the player cannot access it. Therefore, in this chapter you will also modify your main menu to be able to launch the game when the player selects the start option.

By this point in the book you should have a working splash screen that fades into the main menu of the game and some looping background music. This is a big accomplishment; however the code will more complicated in this chapter. Again, feel free to skip around the chapter, but realize that most of the examples will be cumulative in that they will all build in previous examples.

Finally, in this chapter, you be introduced to a good deal of OpenGL. I do realize that most casual Android developers may not have had too extensive of an exposure to OpenGL. I will try to give as much background and instructions in OpenGL as you proceed through the chapter.

With that said, let's jump right into drawing the background of the game.

Rendering the Background

In the previous chapter, you used Android's ImageView to display a bitmap as the splash screen of your game. This is an acceptable solution for a splash screen and a main menu. But there is too much overhead and not enough flexibility in this process to use it for the graphics of the game. If you were to somehow find a way to use this process to display your game graphics ,the game would run very slow, if it could load at all.

To quickly draw the background of this game to the screen, you need a tool that is both lightweight and flexible. Luckily, Android has an implementation of just such a tool: OpenGL ES. OpenGL ES is the OpenGL standard for Embedded Systems (I will just refer to it as OpenGL in this book for the ease of the discussion). It has been on Android, in various forms, from the first SDK releases. OpenGL offers a useful, flexible, and fairly established way to work with game graphics.

In the beginning, the implementation of OpenGL on Android was very buggy and not as feature rich as some other systems. However, as more Android versions have come out, the implementations of OpenGL have gotten more solid. This is not to say that there are not still —you will learn about at least one important OpenGL bug in this chapter.

You will be creating a fairly complicated two-layer, repeating, scrolling background for *Star Fighter*. Specifically, you will have a larger background image that is scrolling (and repeating) that is partially overlaid with a second scrolling image moving at a faster rate. This will give the background a complex look that has a 3-D effect. Figure 4–1 shows what the finished backgrounds will look like.

Figure 4–1. *The finished backgrounds*

To begin, you need a new activity to run your game. This activity will be launched when the player clicks on the Start button that you created in your main menu in the previous chapter.

Creating the Creating the Creating the

The game activity is the Android activity that will be launched when you start your actual game, at least the part of the game that the player will actually be playing (as opposed to the splash screen or main menu). While the splash screen and menu may seem like parts of the game, for this chapter's purposes, you are separating them out based on function.

You have created several key features of the game to this point, but you have yet to write any of the code that will power the game play. That is going to change now. You are going to create the activity that will run the game play of *Star Fighter*.

Create a new class in your main package named SFGame.java. After the class is created, open it in Eclipse. It should look like this:

```
package com.proandroidgames;

public class SFGame {

}
```

> **NOTE:** Keep in mind that if you have not followed this book in order, the code that you see here may differ from yours because you may have created your base with a different package or class name.

Modify your SFGame class to extend Activity, and include any unimplemented methods.

```
package com.proandroidgames;

import android.app.Activity;
import android.os.Bundle;

public class SFGame extends Activity {

    @Override
    public void onCreate(Bundle savedInstanceState) {
        super.onCreate(savedInstanceState);
        setContentView();
    }

}
```

> **TIP:** At this point, you should follow the directions in the previous chapter to associate the SFGame Activity with the StarFighter project using the AndroidManifest.

Save this file as it is. It cannot do much now. In fact, it is barely a shell of an activity, and if you were to run it now, you would be lucky to get a blank screen, but you would most likely receive a nice syntax error.

You need to build a view that the SFGame activity can display. The view will make the calls that display the game to the screen. The SFGame activity is the view's conduit to get to the screen.

Let's talk a little about what is going to happen next.

Creating a Game View

In Chapter 3, you used a premade Android view called an ImageView to display the splash screen and the main menu for your game. This is an acceptable method for displaying static graphics. However, you are created a limit pushing game here. A view with as much overhead and as limited of a function set as the ImageView simply will not give you the flexibility that you need to create a game. Therefore, you need to look elsewhere for you graphic rendering tools.

Android comes with just the right tool for the job, OpenGL. You will use OpenGL to display and manipulate the game graphics. It gives you the power and the flexibility that you need to quickly display 2D and 3D graphics and is perfect for the kind of game you are writing now.

If you have done any Android development in the past, you may have used the canvas to draw to the screen. OpenGL has its own type of canvas that you need to use to display OpenGL graphics to the screen. The GLSurfaceView will allow you the ability to display your games graphics to the screen.

To this point, you have created the SFGame activity, but you now need something for it to display. Let's create a new class named SFGameView:

```
package com.proandroidgames;

public class SFGameView{

}
```

Now, modify this class to extend GLSurfaceView.

```
package com.proandroidgames;

import android.opengl.GLSurfaceView;

public class SFGameView extends GLSurfaceView {

}
```

With the class that extends the GLSurfaceView created, you can add a reference to it in your SFGame activity. In the previous chapter, you set the value for setContentView() in your StarFighter activity to a layout. As of right now, the setContentView() value for the SFGame activity is not set, or it is set to a default main layout. However, you can set this value to a GLSurfaceView. Setting the SFGame setContentView() to the SFGameView that you just created will let you begin to work with and display OpenGL.

Open the SFGame activity, and create an instance of the SFGameView GLSurfaceView that you just created.

```
package com.proandroidgames;

import android.app.Activity;
import android.os.Bundle;

public class SFGame extends Activity {

        private SFGameView gameView;

            @Override
            public void onCreate(Bundle savedInstanceState) {
            super.onCreate(savedInstanceState);
            setContentView();
    }
}
```

Now, instantiate the SFGameView, and set the setContentView() to the new instance.

```
package com.proandroidgames;

import android.app.Activity;
import android.os.Bundle;

public class SFGame extends Activity {
    private SFGameView gameView;

    @Override
    public void onCreate(Bundle savedInstanceState) {
        super.onCreate(savedInstanceState);
        gameView = new SFGameView(this);
        setContentView(gameView);
    }
}
```

This is enough code to display the game using the SFGameView. However, you do want to think ahead here and consider things that can happen to your game as the player is using it. If you put in some extra time now, you can avoid some very painful headaches very simply.

Using onResume() and onPause()

One of the most common things that can happen is that the player can interrupt the game by giving another Activity focus. This can happen either intentionally—if the player starts another activity and gives it focus—or unintentionally—if the player receives a phone call during the game. Either situation can wreak havoc on your game if not handled properly. Surprisingly enough, these two situations are fairly easy to code for.

Android provides a couple of handlers just for situations where your activity could be interrupted. If your activity loses focus to another, whether intentionally or not, Android will send a pause event to your activity. When your activity becomes the active one again, Android will send it a resume event.

The Activity class can implement onPause() and onResume() to deal with these situations. Simply override these in your SFGame activity as follows:

```
package com.proandroidgames;

import android.app.Activity;
import android.os.Bundle;

public class SFGame extends Activity {

    private SFGameView gameView;

    @Override
    public void onCreate(Bundle savedInstanceState) {
        super.onCreate(savedInstanceState);
        gameView = new SFGameView(this);
        setContentView(gameView);
    }
  @Override
    protected void onResume() {

    }

    @Override
    protected void onPause() {

    }

}
```

Now, you can add some code that will pause and resume your game activity as necessary.

```
package com.proandroidgames;

import android.app.Activity;
import android.os.Bundle;

public class SFGame extends Activity {
    private SFGameView gameView;

    @Override
    public void onCreate(Bundle savedInstanceState) {
        super.onCreate(savedInstanceState);
        gameView = new SFGameView(this);
        setContentView(gameView);
    }
    @Override
    protected void onResume() {
        super.onResume();
        gameView.onResume();
```

```
    }

    @Override
    protected void onPause() {
        super.onPause();
        gameView.onPause();
    }

}
```

> **NOTE:** The onResume() and onPause() functions refer to the pausing of the activity execution itself, not the pausing of the game. Pausing the game is handled separately.

Save your SFGame class once again. You now have an activity that displays a GLSurfaceView. You need to create something for the SFGameView to display through the SFGame activity. What you need to create is a GLSurfaceView renderer.

Creating a Renderer

The GLSurfaceView that you created, SFGameView, is only a view for displaying OpenGL through. The GLSurfaceView needs the assistance of a renderer to do the heavy lifting. Theoretically, you could incorporate the renderer into the GLSurfaceView. However, I prefer having a clean separation of the code to give some distinction between the functions; it makes troubleshooting a little easier.

Create a new class in your StarFighter package called SFGameRenderer.

```
package com.proandroidgames;

public class SFGameRenderer{

}
```

Now you need to implement the GLSurfaceView's renderer.

```
package com.proandroidgames;

import android.opengl.GLSurfaceView.Renderer;

public class SFGameRenderer implements Renderer{

}
```
Be sure to add in the unimplemented methods:
```
package com.proandroidgames;

import javax.microedition.khronos.egl.EGLConfig;
import javax.microedition.khronos.opengles.GL10;

import android.opengl.GLSurfaceView.Renderer;

public class SFGameRenderer implements Renderer{
```

```
       @Override
       public void onDrawFrame(GL10 gl) {
              // TODO Auto-generated method stub

       }

       @Override
       public void onSurfaceChanged(GL10 gl, int width, int height) {

       }

       @Override
       public void onSurfaceCreated(GL10 gl, EGLConfig config) {

       }
}
```

The function of these methods should be fairly self-explanatory. The onDrawFrame()
method is called when the renderer is draws a frame to the screen. The
onSurfaceChanged() method is called when the size of the view has changed, even at
the time of the initial change. Finally, the onSurfaceCreated() method is called when the
GLSurface is created.

Let's start coding them in the order that they are called. First up is onSurfaceCreated().

Creating your OpenGL Surface

In onSurfaceCreated(), you are going to initialize your OpenGL and load your textures.

> **TIP:** In OpenGL parlance, a texture can also be an image, like your background. You will get to
> this later in the chapter, but technically, you will be using the background image for this game as
> a texture that is applied to two flat triangles and displayed.

The first step is to enable the 2-D texture mapping capabilities of OpenGL

```
package com.proandroidgames;

import javax.microedition.khronos.egl.EGLConfig;
import javax.microedition.khronos.opengles.GL10;
import android.opengl.GLSurfaceView.Renderer;

public class SFGameRenderer implements Renderer{
       @Override
       public void onDrawFrame(GL10 gl) {
       }
       @Override
       public void onSurfaceChanged(GL10 gl, int width, int height) {
       }

       @Override
```

```
        public void onSurfaceCreated(GL10 gl, EGLConfig config) {
              gl.glEnable(GL10.GL_TEXTURE_2D);
        }
}
```

Notice that the onSurfaceCreated() takes an instance of OpenGL (GL10 gl) as a parameter. This instance will be passed in to the method by the GLSurfaceView when the renderer is called. You do not have to worry about creating an instance of GL10 for this process; it will be done for you automatically.

Next, you want to tell OpenGL to test the depth of all of the objects in your surface. This will need some explaining. Even though you are creating a 2-D game, you will need to think in 3-D terms.

Imagine that the OpenGL environment is a stage. Everything that you want to draw in your game is an actor on this stage. Now, imagine that you are filming the actors as they move around on the stage. The resulting movie is a 2-D representation of what is happening. If one actor moves in front of another actor, that actor will not be visible on the film. However, if you are watching these actors live in a theater, depending on where you are sitting you may still be able to see the actor in the back.

This is the same idea that OpenGL is working under. Even though you are making a 2-D game, OpenGL is going to treat everything as if it were a 3-D object in 3-D space. In fact, one of the only differences to developing in 2-D and 3-D in OpenGL is how you tell OpenGL to render the final scene. Therefore, you need to be mindful of where your objects are placed in the 3-D space to make sure they render properly as a 2-D game. By enabling OpenGL depth testing next, you give OpenGL a means by which to text your textures and determine how they should be rendered.

```
package com.proandroidgames;

import javax.microedition.khronos.egl.EGLConfig;
import javax.microedition.khronos.opengles.GL10;
import android.opengl.GLSurfaceView.Renderer;

public class SFGameRenderer implements Renderer{
        @Override
        public void onDrawFrame(GL10 gl) {
        }
        @Override
        public void onSurfaceChanged(GL10 gl, int width, int height) {
        }

        @Override
        public void onSurfaceCreated(GL10 gl, EGLConfig config) {
              gl.glEnable(GL10.GL_TEXTURE_2D);
               gl.glClearDepthf(1.0f);
               gl.glEnable(GL10.GL_DEPTH_TEST);
               gl.glDepthFunc(GL10.GL_LEQUAL);

        }
}
```

The two last lines of code that you will add to this method concern blending. You don't have to be too concerned about this right now, because you really won't notice the effects of this code until much later in this chapter. All of the images that you are going to draw in your game are going to have areas that should be transparent. These two lines of code will set OpenGL's blending feature to create transparency.

```
package com.proandroidgames;

import javax.microedition.khronos.egl.EGLConfig;
import javax.microedition.khronos.opengles.GL10;
import android.opengl.GLSurfaceView.Renderer;

public class SFGameRenderer implements Renderer{
        @Override
        public void onDrawFrame(GL10 gl) {
        }
        @Override
        public void onSurfaceChanged(GL10 gl, int width, int height) {
        }

        @Override
        public void onSurfaceCreated(GL10 gl, EGLConfig config) {
            gl.glEnable(GL10.GL_TEXTURE_2D);
             gl.glClearDepthf(1.0f);
             gl.glEnable(GL10.GL_DEPTH_TEST);
             gl.glDepthFunc(GL10.GL_LEQUAL);

             gl.glEnable(GL10.GL_BLEND);
        gl.glBlendFunc(GL10.GL_ONE, GL10.GL_ONE);
            }
}
```

Loading Game Textures

The next thing you should do in the onSurfaceCreated() method is load your textures. However, that is going to be a somewhat involved process, and you will tackle it in the next section. For now, put a comment in the code to indicate that you are coming back to it, and let's move on to onSurfaceChanged().

> **NOTE:** All of the textures you add throughout the game will be added in the onSurfaceCreated() method.

```
public class SFGameRenderer implements Renderer{
        @Override
        public void onDrawFrame(GL10 gl) {
        }
        @Override
        public void onSurfaceChanged(GL10 gl, int width, int height) {
        }

        @Override
        public void onSurfaceCreated(GL10 gl, EGLConfig config) {
```

```
            gl.glEnable(GL10.GL_TEXTURE_2D);
             gl.glClearDepthf(1.0f);
            gl.glEnable(GL10.GL_DEPTH_TEST);
            gl.glDepthFunc(GL10.GL_LEQUAL);

            gl.glEnable(GL10.GL_BLEND);
             gl.glBlendFunc(GL10.GL_ONE, GL10.GL_ONE);

            //TODO Add texture loading for background image
        }
}
```

The onSurfacedChanged() method is going to handle all of the setup needed to display your images. Every time the screen is resized, the orientation is changed, and on the initial startup, this method is called.

You need to set up glViewport() and call the rendering routine to complete onSurfacedChanged().

The glViewport() method takes four parameters. The first two parameters are the x and y coordinates of the lower left-hand corner of the screen. Typically, these values will be (0,0) because the lower left corner of the screen will be where the x and y axes meet— the 0 coordinate of each. The next two parameters of the glViewport() method are the width and the height of your viewport. Unless you want your game to be smaller than the device's screen, these should be set to the width and the height of the device.

```
public class SFGameRenderer implements Renderer{
        @Override
        public void onDrawFrame(GL10 gl) {
        }
        @Override
        public void onSurfaceChanged(GL10 gl, int width, int height) {

            gl.glViewport(0, 0, width,height);
        }

...

}
```

Notice that the calling surface, in this case SFGameView, sends in width and height parameters to the onSurfacedChanged() method. You can just set the width and the height of the glViewport() to the corresponding width and height sent in by SFGameView.

> **NOTE:** The width and height sent in by SFGameView will represent the width and height of the device minus the notification bar at the top of the screen.

If the glViewport() represents the lens through which your scene is filmed, the glOrthof() is the image processor. With the view port set, all you have to do now is use glOrthof() to render the surface.

Rendering the Surface

To access glOrthof() you need to put OpenGL into projection matrix mode. OpenGL has different matrix modes that let you access different parts of the engine. Throughout this book, you will access most if not all of them. This is the first one you will work with. Projection matrix mode gives you access to the way in which your scene is rendered.

To access projection matrix mode you need to set glMatrixMode() to GL_PROJECTION.

```
public class SFGameRenderer implements Renderer{
        @Override
        public void onDrawFrame(GL10 gl) {
        }

...

        @Override
        public void onSurfaceCreated(GL10 gl, EGLConfig config) {
            gl.glEnable(GL10.GL_TEXTURE_2D);
            gl.glClearDepthf(1.0f);
            gl.glEnable(GL10.GL_DEPTH_TEST);
            gl.glDepthFunc(GL10.GL_LEQUAL);

            gl.glEnable(GL10.GL_BLEND);
             gl.glBlendFunc(GL10.GL_ONE, GL10.GL_ONE);

            //TODO Add texture loading for background image
        }
}
```

Now that OpenGL is in projection matrix mode, you need to load the current identity. Think of the identity as the default state of OpenGL.

```
public class SFGameRenderer implements Renderer{
        @Override
        public void onDrawFrame(GL10 gl) {
        }

...

        @Override
        public void onSurfaceCreated(GL10 gl, EGLConfig config) {
            gl.glEnable(GL10.GL_TEXTURE_2D);
            gl.glClearDepthf(1.0f);
            gl.glEnable(GL10.GL_DEPTH_TEST);
            gl.glDepthFunc(GL10.GL_LEQUAL);
             gl.glEnable(GL10.GL_BLEND);
              gl.glBlendFunc(GL10.GL_ONE, GL10.GL_ONE);

            //TODO Add texture loading for background image
        }
}
```

With the identity is loaded, you can set up glOrthof(), which will set up an orthogonal, two-dimensional rendering of your scene. This call takes six parameters, each of which defines a clipping plane.

The clipping planes indicate to the renderer where to stop rendering. In other words, any images that fall outside of the clipping planes will not be picked up by glOrthof(). The six clipping planes are the left, right, bottom, top, near, and far. These represent points on the x, y, and z axes.

```java
public class SFGameRenderer implements Renderer{
        @Override
        public void onDrawFrame(GL10 gl) {
        }
        @Override
        public void onSurfaceChanged(GL10 gl, int width, int height) {

                gl.glViewport(0, 0, width,height);

                gl.glMatrixMode(GL10.GL_PROJECTION);
                gl.glLoadIdentity();
                gl.glOrthof(0f, 1f, 0f, 1f, -1f, 1f);

        }

        @Override
        public void onSurfaceCreated(GL10 gl, EGLConfig config) {
                gl.glEnable(GL10.GL_TEXTURE_2D);
                gl.glClearDepthf(1.0f);
                gl.glEnable(GL10.GL_DEPTH_TEST);
                gl.glDepthFunc(GL10.GL_LEQUAL);

                gl.glEnable(GL10.GL_BLEND);
                 gl.glBlendFunc(GL10.GL_ONE, GL10.GL_ONE);

                //TODO Add texture loading for background image
        }
}
```

That is all you have to do to set up the rendering and projection of your game. Go ahead and save SFGameRenderer; you will come back to onDrawFrame() later in this chapter.

With the onSurfaceCreated() and onSurfaceChanged() methods set up, you can go back to that comment that you added to onSurfaceCreated(). In the next section of this chapter, you are going to load your background image as a texture and call it from onSurfaceCreated().

Loading an Image Using OpenGL

Images in OpenGL are loaded as textures. This is to say that an image, any image that you want to display using OpenGL, is really treated as a texture that is being applied to a 3-D object.

For this game, you are creating 2-D graphics, but OpenGL is going to treat them as 3-D objects. Therefore, you will be building squares and triangles to map your images onto. Once your images are mapped as textures onto these flat shapes, you can send them into the renderer. It really sounds more complicated than it is.

Let's start by copying a file into Eclipse to use as the background. The image that I used is called backgroundstars.png and is shown in Figure 4–2.

Figure 4–2. *The background image*

If you are using a Motorola Droid model phone, there's is a bug in OpenGL that extends back to at least the Froyo version of Android. Luckily though, there is a workaround.

I personally have a Droid X and have seen this bug for myself. If you load an image as a texture using OpenGL on a Droid, you may end up seeing nothing but a white box where the image should be. The bug has to do with the size and placement of the image in your Android package.

For most normal installations of Android, the images can be placed in any of the res/drawable-[density] folders and be any dimension. In the last chapter, you placed a few images of differing size dimensions into the res/drawable-hdpi folder, and hopefully, you had no problems displaying them.

To avoid this dreaded Droid white box bug follow these two steps. First, create a new drawable folder under your res called drawable-nopi. Older versions of Android came with this folder installed; I can only assume that something on the Droid phones is still referencing it. All of the images that you want to display using OpenGL should now be placed in this new res/drawable-nopi folder.

Second, you must ensure that your images are a derivative of 256 · 256 (a power of 2). The image for the background (see Figure 4–1) is 256 · 256 pixels. However, I have found that 128 · 128 and 64 · 64 work as well. Hopefully, this bug will be fixed in future versions of the Droid phones or the Android software.

That being said, take the image that you are using for your background, and copy it into your respective res/drawable folder. You can now reference it using the R.java file.

Now, create a new class, SFBackground. This new class file will be called to load the image as a texture and return it back to the renderer.

```
package com.proandroidgames;

public class SFBackground {

}
```

You are going to call the SFBackground.loadTexture() method from the SFGameRenderer to load up the background to OpenGL. But first you need to build the constructor. The constructor for the SFBackground class is going to set up all of the variables that you will need to interact with OpenGL.

You will need an array to hold the mapping coordinates of your texture, an array to hold the coordinates of your vertices, and an array to hold the indices of the vertices. You will also be creating an array of pointers to your textures.

> **NOTE:** In this class, you will only be loading one texture into the class, but in future chapters, you will be loading multiple textures into one class. Therefore, in an effort to make the code as generic as possible, you will use the same structure for most of the texture loading classes.

```
package com.proandroidgames;

public class SFBackground {
        private int[] textures = new int[1];

        private float vertices[] = {
                        0.0f, 0.0f, 0.0f,
                        1.0f, 0.0f, 0.0f,
                        1.0f, 1.0f, 0.0f,
                        0.0f, 1.0f, 0.0f,
                };
        private float texture[] = {
                        0.0f, 0.0f,
                        1.0f, 0f,
                        1, 1.0f,
                        0f, 1f,
                };
        private byte indices[] = {
                        0,1,2,
                         0,2,3,
                };
        public SFBackground() {

        }
}
```

In the next section you will add the arrays that will build polygons to hold your texture.

Vertices, Textures, and Indices . . . Oh My!

Let's briefly discuss what the vertex, texture, and index values represent. The vertices[] array lists a series of points. Each row here represents the x, y, and z value of a corner of a square. In this case, you are making a square that is the full size of the screen. This will ensure that the image covers the entire background area.

The texture[] array represents where the corners of the image (i.e., texture) will line up with the corners of the square you created. Again, in this case, you want the texture to cover the entire square, which in turn is covering the entire background. The textures[] array hold a pointer to each texture that you are loading onto your shape. You are hard coding this to 1, because you will be loading only one background image onto this shape.

Finally, the indices[] array holds the definition for the face of the square. The face of the square is broken into two triangles. The values in this array are the corners of those triangles in counter-clockwise order. Notice that one line (two points) overlap (0 and 2). Figure 4–3 illustrates this concept.

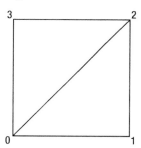

Figure 4–3. *Labeled index points*

Now, create some buffers that we can hold these arrays in. The buffers can then be loaded into OpenGL.

```java
package com.proandroidgames;

import java.nio.ByteBuffer;
import java.nio.FloatBuffer;

public class SFBackground {

        private FloatBuffer vertexBuffer;
        private FloatBuffer textureBuffer;
        private ByteBuffer indexBuffer;

        private int[] textures = new int[1];

        private float vertices[] = {
                        0.0f, 0.0f, 0.0f,
                        1.0f, 0.0f, 0.0f,
                        1.0f, 1.0f, 0.0f,
                        0.0f, 1.0f, 0.0f,
```

```
                   };
        private float texture[] = {
                        0.0f, 0.0f,
                        1.0f, 0.0f,
                        1.0, 1.0f,
                        0.0f, 1.0f,
                   };
        private byte indices[] = {
                        0,1,2,
                        0,2,3,
                   };
        public SFBackground() {

        }

}
```

In the constructor for the SFBackground class, you are going to populate the appropriate buffers with the appropriate arrays.

```
package com.proandroidgames;

import java.nio.ByteOrder;
import java.nio.ByteBuffer;
import java.nio.FloatBuffer;

public class SFBackground {

        private FloatBuffer vertexBuffer;
        private FloatBuffer textureBuffer;
        private ByteBuffer indexBuffer;

        private int[] textures = new int[1];

        private float vertices[] = {
                        0.0f, 0.0f, 0.0f,
                        1.0f, 0.0f, 0.0f,
                        1.0f, 1.0f, 0.0f,
                        0.0f, 1.0f, 0.0f,
                   };
        private float texture[] = {
                        0.0f, 0.0f,
                        1.0f, 0.0f,
                        1.0, 1.0f,
                        0.0f, 1.0f,
                   };
        private byte indices[] = {
                        0,1,2,
                        0,2,3,
                   };

        public SFBackground() {

                ByteBuffer byteBuf = ByteBuffer.allocateDirect(vertices.length * 4);
                byteBuf.order(ByteOrder.nativeOrder());
                vertexBuffer = byteBuf.asFloatBuffer();
                vertexBuffer.put(vertices);
```

```
                    vertexBuffer.position(0);

                    byteBuf = ByteBuffer.allocateDirect(texture.length * 4);
                    byteBuf.order(ByteOrder.nativeOrder());
                    textureBuffer = byteBuf.asFloatBuffer();
                    textureBuffer.put(texture);
                    textureBuffer.position(0);

                    indexBuffer = ByteBuffer.allocateDirect(indices.length);
                    indexBuffer.put(indices);
                    indexBuffer.position(0);

              }

        }
```

The code here should be self-explanatory. You are creating a ByteBuffer with the values of the vertex and texture arrays. Notice that the number of values in each of these arrays is multiplied by 4 to allocate space in the ByteBuffer. This is because the values in the arrays are floats, and floats are four times the size of bytes. The index array is integers and it can be loaded directly into the indexBuffer.

Creating the loadTexture() Method

Next, you need to create the loadTexture() method. The loadTexture() method will take in an image pointer and then load the image into a stream. The stream will then be loaded as a texture into OpenGL. During the drawing process you will map this texture onto the vertices.

```
package com.proandroidgames;

import javax.microedition.khronos.opengles.GL10;

import java.nio.ByteBuffer;
import java.nio.ByteOrder;
import java.nio.FloatBuffer;
import android.content.Context;
import android.graphics.Bitmap;
import android.graphics.BitmapFactory;
import android.opengl.GLUtils;
import java.io.IOException;
import java.io.InputStream;

public class SFBackground {


...


        public SFBackground() {

...


        }
        public void loadTexture(GL10 gl,int texture, Context context) {
```

```
InputStream imagestream = context.getResources().openRawResource(texture);
Bitmap bitmap = null;
try {

        bitmap = BitmapFactory.decodeStream(imagestream);

}catch(Exception e){

}finally {
   //Always clear and close
   try {
           imagestream.close();
           imagestream = null;
     } catch (IOException e) {
     }
}

gl.glGenTextures(1, textures, 0);
gl.glBindTexture(GL10.GL_TEXTURE_2D, textures[0]);

  gl.glTexParameterf(GL10.GL_TEXTURE_2D, GL10.GL_TEXTURE_MIN_FILTER,
GL10.GL_NEAREST);
        gl.glTexParameterf(GL10.GL_TEXTURE_2D, GL10.GL_TEXTURE_MAG_FILTER,
GL10.GL_LINEAR);

        gl.glTexParameterf(GL10.GL_TEXTURE_2D, GL10.GL_TEXTURE_WRAP_S,
GL10.GL_REPEAT);
        gl.glTexParameterf(GL10.GL_TEXTURE_2D, GL10.GL_TEXTURE_WRAP_T,
GL10.GL_REPEAT);

        GLUtils.texImage2D(GL10.GL_TEXTURE_2D, 0, bitmap, 0);

        bitmap.recycle();
   }

}
```

The first part of loadTexture() is pretty easy. It takes in the pointer and loads the resulting image into a bitmap stream. The stream is then closed.

The second part of loadTexture(), however, is fairly heavy in OpenGL. The first line generates a texture pointer, which is structured like a dictionary.

```
gl.glGenTextures(1, textures, 0);
```

The first parameter is the number of texture names that you need generated. When it comes time to bind the textures to a set of vertices, you will call them out of OpenGL by name. Here, you are only loading one texture, so you only need one texture name generated. The second parameter is the array of ints that you created to hold the number for each texture. Again, there is only one value in this array right now. Finally, the last parameter holds the offset for the pointer into the array. Since your array is zero-based, the offset is 0.

The second line binds the texture into OpenGL.

```
gl.glBindTexture(GL10.GL_TEXTURE_2D, textures[0]);
```

If you were loading two textures together, you would have two each of these first two lines: one to load the first image and one to load the second.

The next two lines deal with how OpenGL is to map the texture onto the vertices. You want the mapping to take place quickly but produce sharpened pixels.

```
gl.glTexParameterf(GL10.GL_TEXTURE_2D, GL10.GL_TEXTURE_MIN_FILTER, GL10.GL_NEAREST);
gl.glTexParameterf(GL10.GL_TEXTURE_2D, GL10.GL_TEXTURE_MAG_FILTER, GL10.GL_LINEAR);
```

The following two lines are important. Star Fighter is a scrolling shooter game, so the background should continuously scroll to give the illusion that the playable character is flying through space. Obviously, the image you are using for the background is finite. Therefore, to create the illusion that your player is flying through the endless vastness of space, the image must repeat ad infinitum. Luckily, OpenGL can handle this for you.

```
gl.glTexParameterf(GL10.GL_TEXTURE_2D, GL10.GL_TEXTURE_WRAP_S, GL10.GL_REPEAT);
gl.glTexParameterf(GL10.GL_TEXTURE_2D, GL10.GL_TEXTURE_WRAP_T, GL10.GL_REPEAT);
```

In these two lines, you are telling OpenGL to continuously repeat your background texture in the S and T directions. Right now, your vertices are the size of the screen, and the initial background texture will be mapped directly on top of it. When it comes time to scroll the background (in the next section of this chapter), you will actually be moving the texture on the vertices rather than moving the vertices. By moving the textures, you allow OpenGL to repeat the texture for you, to cover vertex that is exposed when you move the texture. It is a very handy feature of OpenGL, especially in game development.

Finally, in the last two line of the loadTexture() method, you associate the bitmap input stream that you created with the first texture. The bitmap stream is then recycled.

```
GLUtils.texImage2D(GL10.GL_TEXTURE_2D, 0, bitmap, 0);
bitmap.recycle();
```

Mapping Your Texture

The last piece of code you need to write to complete your SFBackground class is the method that will draw the texture onto the vertices.

```
package com.proandroidgames;

import javax.microedition.khronos.opengles.GL10;

import java.nio.ByteBuffer;
import java.nio.ByteOrder;
import java.nio.FloatBuffer;
import android.content.Context;
import android.graphics.Bitmap;
import android.graphics.BitmapFactory;
import android.opengl.GLUtils;
import java.io.IOException;
import java.io.InputStream;

public class SFBackground {
```

...

```java
        public void draw(GL10 gl) {

                gl.glBindTexture(GL10.GL_TEXTURE_2D, textures[0]);

                gl.glFrontFace(GL10.GL_CCW);
                gl.glEnable(GL10.GL_CULL_FACE);
                gl.glCullFace(GL10.GL_BACK);

                gl.glEnableClientState(GL10.GL_VERTEX_ARRAY);
                gl.glEnableClientState(GL10.GL_TEXTURE_COORD_ARRAY);

                gl.glVertexPointer(3, GL10.GL_FLOAT, 0, vertexBuffer);
                gl.glTexCoordPointer(2, GL10.GL_FLOAT, 0, textureBuffer);

                 gl.glDrawElements(GL10.GL_TRIANGLES, indices.length,
GL10.GL_UNSIGNED_BYTE, indexBuffer);

                gl.glDisableClientState(GL10.GL_VERTEX_ARRAY);
                gl.glDisableClientState(GL10.GL_TEXTURE_COORD_ARRAY);
                gl.glDisable(GL10.GL_CULL_FACE);

        }

        public SFBackground() {

...

}

        public void loadTexture(GL10 gl,int texture, Context context) {
                InputStream imagestream = context.getResources().openRawResource(texture);
                Bitmap bitmap = null;
                try {

                    bitmap = BitmapFactory.decodeStream(imagestream);

                }catch(Exception e){

                }finally {

                    try {
                            imagestream.close();
                            imagestream = null;
                    } catch (IOException e) {
                    }
                }

                gl.glGenTextures(1, textures, 0);
                gl.glBindTexture(GL10.GL_TEXTURE_2D, textures[0]);

                 gl.glTexParameterf(GL10.GL_TEXTURE_2D, GL10.GL_TEXTURE_MIN_FILTER,
GL10.GL_NEAREST);
```

```
            gl.glTexParameterf(GL10.GL_TEXTURE_2D, GL10.GL_TEXTURE_MAG_FILTER,
GL10.GL_LINEAR);

            gl.glTexParameterf(GL10.GL_TEXTURE_2D, GL10.GL_TEXTURE_WRAP_S,
GL10.GL_REPEAT);
            gl.glTexParameterf(GL10.GL_TEXTURE_2D, GL10.GL_TEXTURE_WRAP_T,
GL10.GL_REPEAT);

        GLUtils.texImage2D(GL10.GL_TEXTURE_2D, 0, bitmap, 0);

        bitmap.recycle();
    }

}
```

The draw() method is going to be called every time you want to draw the background, as opposed to the loadTexture() method, which will be called only when you initialize the game.

This first line of this method binds the texture to your target. Think of it as putting a bullet in the chamber of a gun; the texture is loaded up and ready to be used.

```
gl.glBindTexture(GL10.GL_TEXTURE_2D, textures[0]);
```

The next three lines in the draw() method tell OpenGL to enable culling and basically ignore any vertices that are not on the front face. Since you are rendering the game in a 2-D orthogonal view, you don't want OpenGL to spend precious processor time dealing with vertices that the player will never see. Right now, all of your vertices are front facing, but this is good code to have in there anyway.

```
gl.glFrontFace(GL10.GL_CCW);
gl.glEnable(GL10.GL_CULL_FACE);
gl.glCullFace(GL10.GL_BACK);
```

The next four lines enable the vertex and texture states and loads the vertices and texture buffers into OpenGL.

```
gl.glEnableClientState(GL10.GL_VERTEX_ARRAY);
gl.glEnableClientState(GL10.GL_TEXTURE_COORD_ARRAY);
gl.glVertexPointer(3, GL10.GL_FLOAT, 0, vertexBuffer);
gl.glTexCoordPointer(2, GL10.GL_FLOAT, 0, textureBuffer);
```

Finally, the texture is drawn onto the vertices, and all of the states that were enabled are disabled.

```
gl.glDrawElements(GL10.GL_TRIANGLES, indices.length, GL10.GL_UNSIGNED_BYTE,
indexBuffer);
gl.glDisableClientState(GL10.GL_VERTEX_ARRAY);
gl.glDisableClientState(GL10.GL_TEXTURE_COORD_ARRAY);
gl.glDisable(GL10.GL_CULL_FACE);
```

Your SFBackground class is now complete and ready to be called by the SFGameRenderer. Save the SFBackground.java file and reopen SFGameRenderer.

Calling loadTexture() and draw()

You need to add in the appropriate calls to both the loadTexture() and the draw()
methods of SFBackground. The loadTexture() method will be called from the
onSurfaceCreated() method of SFGameRenderer.

Because the loadTexture() method of SFBackground takes an image pointer as a
parameter, you need to add a new constant to the SFEngine. Open SFEngine and add the
following constant to point to the backgroundstars.png file that you added to the
drawable folder.

```
package com.proandroidgames;

import android.app.Activity;
import android.content.Intent;
import android.os.Bundle;
import android.view.View;
import android.view.View.OnClickListener;
import android.widget.ImageButton;
package com.proandroidgames;

import android.content.Context;
import android.content.Intent;
import android.view.View;

public class SFEngine {
        /*Constants that will be used in the game*/
        public static final int GAME_THREAD_DELAY = 4000;
        public static final int MENU_BUTTON_ALPHA = 0;
        public static final boolean HAPTIC_BUTTON_FEEDBACK = true;
        public static final int SPLASH_SCREEN_MUSIC = R.raw.warfieldedit;
        public static final int R_VOLUME = 100;
        public static final int L_VOLUME = 100;
        public static final boolean LOOP_BACKGROUND_MUSIC = true;
        public static Context context;
        public static Thread musicThread;
        public static final int BACKGROUND_LAYER_ONE = R.drawable.backgroundstars;

        /*Kill game and exit*/
        public boolean onExit(View v) {
        try
        {
                Intent bgmusic = new Intent(context, sfmusic.class);
                context.stopService(bgmusic);
                musicThread.stop();
                return true;
        }catch(Exception e){
                return false;
        }

        }

}
```

You will now call the loadTexture() method of the SFBackground class and pass it this constant. This will load the background stars image as a texture into OpenGL.

Save SFEngine, and go back to SFGameRenderer. You will now instantiate a new SFBackground and call its loadTexture() method from onSurfaceCreated(). It is best to instantiate the new SFBackground where it can be accessed throughout the class. You will be making several calls to SFBackground in this class.

```
package com.proandroidgames;

import javax.microedition.khronos.egl.EGLConfig;
import javax.microedition.khronos.opengles.GL10;

import android.opengl.GLSurfaceView.Renderer;

public class SFGameRenderer implements Renderer{

        private SFBackground background = new SFBackground();

        @Override
        public void onDrawFrame(GL10 gl) {

        }

        @Override
        public void onSurfaceChanged(GL10 gl, int width, int height) {
                gl.glViewport(0, 0, width,height);

                gl.glMatrixMode(GL10.GL_PROJECTION);
                gl.glLoadIdentity();

                gl.glOrthof(0f, 1f, 0f, 1f, -1f, 1f);

        }

        @Override
        public void onSurfaceCreated(GL10 gl, EGLConfig config) {

                gl.glEnable(GL10.GL_TEXTURE_2D);
                gl.glClearDepthf(1.0f);
                gl.glEnable(GL10.GL_DEPTH_TEST);
                gl.glDepthFunc(GL10.GL_LEQUAL);

                gl.glEnable(GL10.GL_BLEND);
                gl.glBlendFunc(GL10.GL_ONE, GL10.GL_ONE);

                background.loadTexture(gl,SFEngine.BACKGROUND_LAYER_ONE,
SFEngine.context);

        }

}
```

At this point, if you called the draw() method of SFBackground you would have a static image of the star field. However, a static background is not what you are going for in this game. *Star Fighter* has the main playable character racing through space to fight the enemy, and to simulate that race through space, the background needs to scroll. In the next section, you are going create a method that will scroll the background as though you are flying through the star field.

Scrolling the Background

Compared to what you have accomplished thus far in this chapter, writing the method to scroll the background is going to be very easy. In **SFGameRenderer**, create a new method named scrollBackground1().

You also need a new float named bgScroll1. This float will keep track of how much the background has scrolled when you are not in the method. Since you need the value to persist outside of the scrollBackground1() method, create it where the class has access to it.

> **NOTE:** You are naming this method scrollBackground1() because, later in this chapter, you will be creating a scrollBackground2() that will scroll a second layer of the background.

```
package com.proandroidgames;

import javax.microedition.khronos.egl.EGLConfig;
import javax.microedition.khronos.opengles.GL10;

import android.opengl.GLSurfaceView.Renderer;

public class SFGameRenderer implements Renderer{
        private SFBackground background = new SFBackground();

        private float bgScroll1;

        @Override
        public void onDrawFrame(GL10 gl) {
                // TODO Auto-generated method stub
                }

        private void scrollBackground1(GL10 gl){

        }

        @Override
        public void onSurfaceChanged(GL10 gl, int width, int height) {
                // TODO Auto-generated method stub

                gl.glViewport(0, 0, width,height);

                gl.glMatrixMode(GL10.GL_PROJECTION);
                gl.glLoadIdentity();

                gl.glOrthof(0f, 1f, 0f, 1f, -1f, 1f);

        }
```

```
        @Override
        public void onSurfaceCreated(GL10 gl, EGLConfig config) {
                // TODO Auto-generated method stub

                gl.glEnable(GL10.GL_TEXTURE_2D);
                gl.glClearDepthf(1.0f);
                gl.glEnable(GL10.GL_DEPTH_TEST);
                gl.glDepthFunc(GL10.GL_LEQUAL);

                gl.glEnable(GL10.GL_BLEND);
                gl.glBlendFunc(GL10.GL_ONE, GL10.GL_ONE);

                    background.loadTexture(gl,SFEngine.BACKGROUND_LAYER_ONE,
SFEngine.context);

        }

}
```

The first thing you are going to do in this method is test to ensure that the value of bgScroll1 will not exceed the largest possible value for a float and throw an exception. The chances of bgScroll1 going that high are very slim, especially when you see what we will be incrementing it by. However, it is always better to play things safe.

Test that bgScroll1 is not equal to the largest size for a float. If bgScroll1 is the maximum size for a float, set it to zero.

```
package com.proandroidgames;

import javax.microedition.khronos.egl.EGLConfig;
import javax.microedition.khronos.opengles.GL10;

import android.opengl.GLSurfaceView.Renderer;

public class SFGameRenderer implements Renderer{
        private SFBackground background = new SFBackground();

        private float bgScroll1;

        @Override
        public void onDrawFrame(GL10 gl) {
                // TODO Auto-generated method stub
                }

        private void scrollBackground1(GL10 gl){
                if (bgScroll1 == Float.MAX_VALUE){
                        bgScroll1 = 0f;
                }

        }


        ...

}
```

Earlier in this chapter, we discussed two of the matrix modes of OpenGL: texture and projection. You have to put OpenGL in texture matrix mode to scroll the texture on the vertices.

> **NOTE:** Remember you are actually moving the texture on the vertices here. You are not moving the vertices.

Because you are not moving the vertices, you need to ensure that they are in the correct place and that nothing moved unintentionally. Why? This is one of the tricky parts of learning OpenGL.

OpenGL Matrices

Setting OpenGL to texture matrix mode, or even model view matrix mode (used to move and scale the vertices) will give you access to *all* of the textures and *all* of the vertices respectively in OpenGL at that time. This means that when you put OpenGL into texture matrix mode and move a texture 1 unit on the x axis, you are actually moving all of the textures you have within OpenGL at that moment 1 unit on the x axis.

This situation could be problematic in a game where you could have any number of items all moving and scaling at different rates and directions at any given time. However, if OpenGL works with all of the textures at once and all of the vertices at once, how do you move individual items separately?

This may sound confusing right now, but there is a logical way to work around the situation.

All of the matrix modes are kept on a stack. The process is to push the mode off of the stack (in this case, texture matrix mode). Once the mode is off of the stack, you move all of the textures and redraw only the textures that you want effected by that particular movement. You then pop the texture back on the stack and repeat the process for the next texture that you want to move.

You have to be careful to reset the matrix mode back to its default state before you begin working with it, or it will have the last value you set it to. For example, let's say you have texture A and texture B. You want to move texture A 1 unit on the x axis and 1 unit on the y axis. You want to move texture B just 1 unit on the x axis. You push the texture matrix off of the stack and move it 1 unit each on the x and y axes. You then draw texture A and pop the matrix back on the stack. That was easy.

Now, you move on to texture B. You push the matrix off the stack and move the matrix 1 unit on the x axis. However, the matrix is already set to (1,1) because the last operation that you did on texture A was to move the texture matrix 1 unit on each axis. So you inadvertently end up moving texture B 2 units on the x axis and 1 unit on the y axis. Therefore, you need to reset the matrix to its default state after you push it off the stack to make sure that you start with the default units. Resetting the matrix is accomplished using the glLoadIdentity() call.

The OpenGL operation that you will be performing to scroll your background is glTranslatef(). The glTranslatef() method takes three parameters, the values x, y, and z. It will adjust the current matrix according to the values provided. You are going to store the value that you are scrolling your background by in a constant. Add the following constant to SFEngine.

```
public static float SCROLL_BACKGROUND_1 = .002f;
```

Save SFEngine and move back to SFGameRenderer. Your first step in scrolling the background texture is to push the model matrix mode off the stack and reset it, just in case any moving there done in the future affects the model mode. Then you are going to push the texture matrix off the stack and do your scrolling.

Add the following lines to the scrollBackground1() method:

```
                gl.glMatrixMode(GL10.GL_MODELVIEW);
                 gl.glLoadIdentity();
                 gl.glPushMatrix();
                 gl.glScalef(1f, 1f, 1f);
                 gl.glTranslatef(0f, 0f, 0f);
package com.proandroidgames;

import javax.microedition.khronos.egl.EGLConfig;
import javax.microedition.khronos.opengles.GL10;

import android.opengl.GLSurfaceView.Renderer;

public class SFGameRenderer implements Renderer{
        private SFBackground background = new SFBackground();

        private float bgScroll1;

        @Override
        public void onDrawFrame(GL10 gl) {
                // TODO Auto-generated method stub
                }

        private void scrollBackground1(GL10 gl){
                if (bgScroll1 == Float.MAX_VALUE){
                        bgScroll1 = 0f;
                }
                /*This code just resets the scale and translate of the
                  Model matrix mode, we are not moving it*/
                gl.glMatrixMode(GL10.GL_MODELVIEW);
                 gl.glLoadIdentity();
                 gl.glPushMatrix();
                 gl.glScalef(1f, 1f, 1f);
                 gl.glTranslatef(0f, 0f, 0f);
        }

        @Override
        public void onSurfaceChanged(GL10 gl, int width, int height) {
                // TODO Auto-generated method stub

                gl.glViewport(0, 0, width,height);
```

```
        gl.glMatrixMode(GL10.GL_PROJECTION);
        gl.glLoadIdentity();

        gl.glOrthof(0f, 1f, 0f, 1f, -1f, 1f);

    }

    @Override
    public void onSurfaceCreated(GL10 gl, EGLConfig config) {
            // TODO Auto-generated method stub

        gl.glEnable(GL10.GL_TEXTURE_2D);
        gl.glClearDepthf(1.0f);
        gl.glEnable(GL10.GL_DEPTH_TEST);
        gl.glDepthFunc(GL10.GL_LEQUAL);

        gl.glEnable(GL10.GL_BLEND);
        gl.glBlendFunc(GL10.GL_ONE, GL10.GL_ONE);

        background.loadTexture(gl,SFEngine.BACKGROUND_LAYER_ONE,
SFEngine.context);

    }

}
```

Again, this code is more housekeeping than anything at this point.

Transforming the Texture

Now, you are going to load up the texture matrix mode and perform your scrolling. You are going to adjust the y axis by the value in bgScroll1. The result of this is that the background will move along the y axis by the amount in bgScroll1.

```
package com.proandroidgames;

import javax.microedition.khronos.egl.EGLConfig;
import javax.microedition.khronos.opengles.GL10;

import android.opengl.GLSurfaceView.Renderer;

public class SFGameRenderer implements Renderer{
        private SFBackground background = new SFBackground();
        private float bgScroll1;

        @Override
        public void onDrawFrame(GL10 gl) {
                // TODO Auto-generated method stub

        }
        private void scrollBackground1(GL10 gl){
                if (bgScroll1 == Float.MAX_VALUE){
                        bgScroll1 = 0f;
                }
                    gl.glMatrixMode(GL10.GL_MODELVIEW);
              gl.glLoadIdentity();
```

```
            gl.glPushMatrix();
            gl.glScalef(1f, 1f, 1f);
            gl.glTranslatef(0f, 0f, 0f);

            gl.glMatrixMode(GL10.GL_TEXTURE);
            gl.glLoadIdentity();
            gl.glTranslatef(0.0f, bgScroll1, 0.0f);  //scrolling the texture

    }

    @Override
    public void onSurfaceChanged(GL10 gl, int width, int height) {
            // TODO Auto-generated method stub

            gl.glViewport(0, 0, width,height);

            gl.glMatrixMode(GL10.GL_PROJECTION);
            gl.glLoadIdentity();

            gl.glOrthof(0f, 1f, 0f, 1f, -1f, 1f);

    }

    @Override
    public void onSurfaceCreated(GL10 gl, EGLConfig config) {
            // TODO Auto-generated method stub

                gl.glEnable(GL10.GL_TEXTURE_2D);
            gl.glClearDepthf(1.0f);
            gl.glEnable(GL10.GL_DEPTH_TEST);
            gl.glDepthFunc(GL10.GL_LEQUAL);

            gl.glEnable(GL10.GL_BLEND);
            gl.glBlendFunc(GL10.GL_ONE, GL10.GL_ONE);

                background.loadTexture(gl,SFEngine.BACKGROUND_LAYER_ONE,
    SFEngine.context);

    }

}
```

The final things that you need to do in scrollBackground1() is to draw the background by calling the draw() method of the SFBackground, pop the matrix back on the stack, and increment bgScroll1.

```
package com.proandroidgames;

import javax.microedition.khronos.egl.EGLConfig;
import javax.microedition.khronos.opengles.GL10;

import android.opengl.GLSurfaceView.Renderer;

public class SFGameRenderer implements Renderer{
        private SFBackground background = new SFBackground();
        private float bgScroll1;
```

```java
    @Override
    public void onDrawFrame(GL10 gl) {
        // TODO Auto-generated method stub

    }
    private void scrollBackground1(GL10 gl){
        if (bgScroll1 == Float.MAX_VALUE){
            bgScroll1 = 0f;
        }

        gl.glMatrixMode(GL10.GL_MODELVIEW);
        gl.glLoadIdentity();
        gl.glPushMatrix();
        gl.glScalef(1f, 1f, 1f);
        gl.glTranslatef(0f, 0f, 0f);

        gl.glMatrixMode(GL10.GL_TEXTURE);
        gl.glLoadIdentity();
        gl.glTranslatef(0.0f, bgScroll1, 0.0f);

        background.draw(gl);
        gl.glPopMatrix();
        bgScroll1 +=  SFEngine.SCROLL_BACKGROUND_1;
        gl.glLoadIdentity();

    }

    @Override
    public void onSurfaceChanged(GL10 gl, int width, int height) {
        // TODO Auto-generated method stub

        gl.glViewport(0, 0, width,height);

        gl.glMatrixMode(GL10.GL_PROJECTION);
        gl.glLoadIdentity();

        gl.glOrthof(0f, 1f, 0f, 1f, -1f, 1f);

    }

    @Override
    public void onSurfaceCreated(GL10 gl, EGLConfig config) {
        // TODO Auto-generated method stub

        gl.glEnable(GL10.GL_TEXTURE_2D);
        gl.glClearDepthf(1.0f);
        gl.glEnable(GL10.GL_DEPTH_TEST);
        gl.glDepthFunc(GL10.GL_LEQUAL);

        gl.glEnable(GL10.GL_BLEND);
        gl.glBlendFunc(GL10.GL_ONE, GL10.GL_ONE);

        background.loadTexture(gl,SFEngine.BACKGROUND_LAYER_ONE,
SFEngine.context);

    }
```

```
}
```

That small method is all you need to be able to scroll the background of your game. Just to recap what the method does:

- It resets the model matrix to make sure it has not been inadvertently moved.

- It loads the texture matrix and moves it along the y axis by the value in SCROLL_BACKGROUND_1.

- It draws the background and pops the matrix back on the stack.

This scrolling will give you a nice moving star field that your player's ship can fly through. Try running your game now, and take a look at how the background scrolls. It is also a good time to do some debugging if there are any problems, before you move on to more complicated code. However, especially by today's gaming standards, the current background is fairly plain. You need to do something to give it a little oomph.

In the next section, you are going to add a second layer to the background. This will give the background of your game some depth, even for a 2-D game. If you have seen any two-layer side-scrolling game, like *Super Mario Brothers*, you should have noticed that the two layers scroll at different rates. You will give your game this two-layer, two-speed scrolling effect in the following section.

Adding a Second Layer

At this point, you have initialized OpenGL, loaded your background image as a texture, and created a method to scroll that texture down the background of the game. Now, it is time to create a second layer of the background. This second layer is going to be very easy to create, especially in comparison to the benefits that you will get back from it in the look of your game.

Much of the implementation of the second layer is actually already done; you just need to create a new scrolling function, add a couple of new constants, and instantiate a new copy of your SFBackground.

First, add a new image to your res/drawable folder. The image that I have used is called debris.png.

> **NOTE:** Because you have just done most of this work for the first layer of the background, I will not be going into as much detail as in the previous section of this chapter.

With the image having been placed in your res/drawable folder, you can add two more constants to the SFEngine. The first is a pointer to the new image file that can be passed to the loadTexture() method of SFBackground, and the second a float that will hold the scroll value for the second layer of the background. This float constant is the key part in the second layer of the background because it will make the second layer scroll faster than the first – giving your game some added depth.

Add the following constants to your SFEngine.

```
public static float SCROLL_BACKGROUND_2  = .007f;
public static final int BACKGROUND_LAYER_TWO = R.drawable.debris;
```

Notice that the SCROLL_BACKGROUND_2 is set to a higher (decimal) value than SCROLL_BACKGROUND_1. Having a larger value will mean that the y axis is incremented greater and thus the second layer of the background will seem to move faster than the first. If the second layer scrolls faster than the first, the illusion will be that the background has depth.

Next, go back to your SFGameRenderer and instantiate a new copy of SFBackground called background2. Notice that you are reusing the SFBackground class. This reuse is part of the difference between game engine code and game-specific code. Because the SFBackground was built to be general, to load and draw whatever image was passed to it as a texture, it is part of the engine and can be reused for any of our background layers.

Because you are instantiating a new copy of SFBackground, you should also create a new float called bgScroll2. This float will keep track of the cumulative scrolling factor of the second layer of the background as opposed to the scrolling of the first layer of the background, which is held in the bgScroll1 float.

```
package com.proandroidgames;

import javax.microedition.khronos.egl.EGLConfig;
import javax.microedition.khronos.opengles.GL10;

import android.opengl.GLSurfaceView.Renderer;

public class SFGameRenderer implements Renderer{
        private SFBackground background = new SFBackground();
        private SFBackground background2 = new SFBackground();
        private float bgScroll1;
        private float bgScroll2;
        @Override
        public void onDrawFrame(GL10 gl) {
                // TODO Auto-generated method stub

        }
        private void scrollBackground1(GL10 gl){
                if (bgScroll1 == Float.MAX_VALUE){
                        bgScroll1 = 0f;
                }

            gl.glMatrixMode(GL10.GL_MODELVIEW);
            gl.glLoadIdentity();
            gl.glPushMatrix();
            gl.glScalef(1f, 1f, 1f);
            gl.glTranslatef(0f, 0f, 0f);

            gl.glMatrixMode(GL10.GL_TEXTURE);
            gl.glLoadIdentity();
            gl.glTranslatef(0.0f, bgScroll1, 0.0f);
```

```
        background.draw(gl);
        gl.glPopMatrix();
        bgScroll1 +=  SFEngine.SCROLL_BACKGROUND_1;
        gl.glLoadIdentity();


    }

    @Override
    public void onSurfaceChanged(GL10 gl, int width, int height) {
            // TODO Auto-generated method stub

            gl.glViewport(0, 0, width,height);

            gl.glMatrixMode(GL10.GL_PROJECTION);
            gl.glLoadIdentity();

            gl.glOrthof(0f, 1f, 0f, 1f, -1f, 1f);

    }

    @Override
    public void onSurfaceCreated(GL10 gl, EGLConfig config) {
            // TODO Auto-generated method stub

            gl.glEnable(GL10.GL_TEXTURE_2D);
            gl.glClearDepthf(1.0f);
            gl.glEnable(GL10.GL_DEPTH_TEST);
            gl.glDepthFunc(GL10.GL_LEQUAL);

            gl.glEnable(GL10.GL_BLEND);
            gl.glBlendFunc(GL10.GL_ONE, GL10.GL_ONE);

              background.loadTexture(gl,SFEngine.BACKGROUND_LAYER_ONE,
    SFEngine.context);

    }

}
```

Loading a Second Texture

Now that you have the copy of SFBackground instantiated for the second layer, you can load the texture for it. You are going to call the same loadTexture() method that you called for the first layer of the background. You will make the call the loadTexture() for the second layer of the background right after you make the call for the first in the onSurfaceCreated() method of the SFGameRenderer.

```
package com.proandroidgames;

import javax.microedition.khronos.egl.EGLConfig;
import javax.microedition.khronos.opengles.GL10;

import android.opengl.GLSurfaceView.Renderer;
```

```
public class SFGameRenderer implements Renderer{
        private SFBackground background = new SFBackground();
        private SFBackground background2 = new SFBackground();
        private float bgScroll1;
        private float bgScroll2;

...


        @Override
        public void onSurfaceCreated(GL10 gl, EGLConfig config) {
                // TODO Auto-generated method stub

            gl.glEnable(GL10.GL_TEXTURE_2D);
            gl.glClearDepthf(1.0f);
            gl.glEnable(GL10.GL_DEPTH_TEST);
            gl.glDepthFunc(GL10.GL_LEQUAL);

            gl.glEnable(GL10.GL_BLEND);
            gl.glBlendFunc(GL10.GL_ONE, GL10.GL_ONE);

             background.loadTexture(gl,SFEngine.BACKGROUND_LAYER_ONE,
SFEngine.context);
                background2.loadTexture(gl,SFEngine.BACKGROUND_LAYER_TWO,
SFEngine.context);

        }

}
```

Be sure that when you call the loadTexture() method for the second layer of the background that you pass it the correct image pointer. Earlier, you created a new constant in the SFEngine called BACKGROUND_LAYER_TWO with a pointer to a new image; this is the pointer that you should be passing to the loadTexture() method of background2.

You now have a new layer of the background instantiated, and you are loading a texture into it. Next, you need to write a new method to control the scrolling.

Scrolling Layer Two

You are going to do something a little different in this scrolling method than in the scrolling method for the first layer of the background. Because the second layer of the background is just smaller images that should not dominate the overall look of the background, you are going to resize the vertices in the model matrix view so that the second-layer texture's vertices are half the width of the screen. Then, you will move the vertices along the x axis, so the image appears to be half off the screen to the right-hand side.

Create a new method in your SFGameRenderer called scrollBackground2(). You should also insert the same test that you had in scrollBackground1() to make sure that bgScroll2 has not exceeded the maximum size of a float.

```java
package com.proandroidgames;

import javax.microedition.khronos.egl.EGLConfig;
import javax.microedition.khronos.opengles.GL10;

import android.opengl.GLSurfaceView.Renderer;

public class SFGameRenderer implements Renderer{
        private SFBackground background = new SFBackground();
        private SFBackground background2 = new SFBackground();
        private float bgScroll1;
        private float bgScroll2;


        @Override
        public void onDrawFrame(GL10 gl) {
                // TODO Auto-generated method stub

        }
        private void scrollBackground1(GL10 gl){
                if (bgScroll1 == Float.MAX_VALUE){
                        bgScroll1 = 0f;
                }

            gl.glMatrixMode(GL10.GL_MODELVIEW);
            gl.glLoadIdentity();
            gl.glPushMatrix();
            gl.glScalef(1f, 1f, 1f);
            gl.glTranslatef(0f, 0f, 0f);

            gl.glMatrixMode(GL10.GL_TEXTURE);
            gl.glLoadIdentity();
            gl.glTranslatef(0.0f,bgScroll1, 0.0f);

            background.draw(gl);
            gl.glPopMatrix();
            bgScroll1 +=  SFEngine.SCROLL_BACKGROUND_1;
            gl.glLoadIdentity();


        }

        private void scrollBackground2(GL10 gl){
                if (bgScroll2 == Float.MAX_VALUE){
                        bgScroll2 = 0f;
                }

        }

        ...

}
```

Working with the Matrices

Here is where the code for scrollBackground2() is going to change a little. In scrollBackground1(), you added some housekeeping code to make sure that the model matrix had not changed and reset it to a default value. In scrollBackground2(), you are going to perform two transformations on the model matrix. First, you are going to scale the model matrix on the x axis so that it is half the size of the screen. Then you are going to move the model matrix on the x axis so that it is half off the right hand side of the screen.

Because you are performing these actions on the model matrix and not the texture matrix, you will be transforming the vertices and not the texture applied to it. That is, while visually you will see the texture shrink and move to the side of the screen, you are actually shrinking and moving the vertices, not the texture.

You will set the x value of the glScale() method to .5 to shrink the vertices by half on the x axis. Be careful to understand that setting the axis to .5 does not mean you want to add .5 units to it. All of the values are multiplied. Therefore, by setting the x of glScale() to .5, you are telling OpenGL to multiple the current value of x by .5, thus (in your case) shrinking the x axis by half.

```
package com.proandroidgames;

import javax.microedition.khronos.egl.EGLConfig;
import javax.microedition.khronos.opengles.GL10;

import android.opengl.GLSurfaceView.Renderer;

public class SFGameRenderer implements Renderer{
        private SFBackground background = new SFBackground();
        private SFBackground background2 = new SFBackground();
        private float bgScroll1;
        private float bgScroll2;

        @Override
        public void onDrawFrame(GL10 gl) {
                // TODO Auto-generated method stub

        }
        private void scrollBackground1(GL10 gl){
                if (bgScroll1 == Float.MAX_VALUE){
                        bgScroll1 = 0f;
                }

            gl.glMatrixMode(GL10.GL_MODELVIEW);
            gl.glLoadIdentity();
            gl.glPushMatrix();
            gl.glScalef(1f, 1f, 1f);
            gl.glTranslatef(0f, 0f, 0f);

            gl.glMatrixMode(GL10.GL_TEXTURE);
            gl.glLoadIdentity();
            gl.glTranslatef(0.0f,bgScroll1, 0.0f);
```

```java
            background.draw(gl);
            gl.glPopMatrix();
            bgScroll1 +=  SFEngine.SCROLL_BACKGROUND_1;
            gl.glLoadIdentity();


    }
    private void scrollBackground2(GL10 gl){
            if (bgScroll2 == Float.MAX_VALUE){
                    bgScroll2 = 0f;
            }

        gl.glMatrixMode(GL10.GL_MODELVIEW);
        gl.glLoadIdentity();
        gl.glPushMatrix();
        gl.glScalef(.5f, 1f, 1f);
        gl.glTranslatef(1.5f, 0f, 0f);

    }
    @Override
    public void onSurfaceChanged(GL10 gl, int width, int height) {
            // TODO Auto-generated method stub

            gl.glViewport(0, 0, width,height);

            gl.glMatrixMode(GL10.GL_PROJECTION);
            gl.glLoadIdentity();

            gl.glOrthof(0f, 1f, 0f, 1f, -1f, 1f);

    }

    @Override
    public void onSurfaceCreated(GL10 gl, EGLConfig config) {
            // TODO Auto-generated method stub

            gl.glEnable(GL10.GL_TEXTURE_2D);
            gl.glClearDepthf(1.0f);
            gl.glEnable(GL10.GL_DEPTH_TEST);
            gl.glDepthFunc(GL10.GL_LEQUAL);

            gl.glEnable(GL10.GL_BLEND);
            gl.glBlendFunc(GL10.GL_ONE, GL10.GL_ONE);

              background.loadTexture(gl,SFEngine.BACKGROUND_LAYER_ONE,
    SFEngine.context);
                background2.loadTexture(gl,SFEngine.BACKGROUND_LAYER_TWO,
    SFEngine.context);

        }

}
```

Notice the difference between scrollBackground1() and scrollBackground2(). Because scrollBackground2() works directly with the model matrix, you want to make sure that the you have the code in place in scrollBackground1() to reset this. Otherwise, your star field background will end up being transformed by half and pushed to the right-hand side of the screen.

Finishing the scrollBackground2() Method

The remainder of the scrollBackground2() method is the same as scrollBackground1().
You need to move the background texture along the y axis by the value in bgScroll2
and then increment that value by SCROLL_BACKGROUND_2.

```java
package com.proandroidgames;

import javax.microedition.khronos.egl.EGLConfig;
import javax.microedition.khronos.opengles.GL10;

import android.opengl.GLSurfaceView.Renderer;

public class SFGameRenderer implements Renderer{
        private SFBackground background = new SFBackground();
        private SFBackground background2 = new SFBackground();
        private float bgScroll1;
        private float bgScroll2;

        @Override
        public void onDrawFrame(GL10 gl) {
                // TODO Auto-generated method stub

        }
        private void scrollBackground1(GL10 gl){
                if (bgScroll1 == Float.MAX_VALUE){
                        bgScroll1 = 0f;
                }

            gl.glMatrixMode(GL10.GL_MODELVIEW);
            gl.glLoadIdentity();
            gl.glPushMatrix();
            gl.glScalef(1f, 1f, 1f);
            gl.glTranslatef(0f, 0f, 0f);

            gl.glMatrixMode(GL10.GL_TEXTURE);
            gl.glLoadIdentity();
            gl.glTranslatef(0.0f,bgScroll1, 0.0f);

            background.draw(gl);
            gl.glPopMatrix();
            bgScroll1 +=  SFEngine.SCROLL_BACKGROUND_1;
            gl.glLoadIdentity();


        }
        private void scrollBackground2(GL10 gl){
                if (bgScroll2 == Float.MAX_VALUE){
                        bgScroll2 = 0f;
                }

            gl.glMatrixMode(GL10.GL_MODELVIEW);
```

```
                gl.glLoadIdentity();
                gl.glPushMatrix();
                gl.glScalef(.5f, 1f, 1f);
                gl.glTranslatef(1.5f, 0f, 0f);

                gl.glMatrixMode(GL10.GL_TEXTURE);
                gl.glLoadIdentity();
                gl.glTranslatef( 0.0f,bgScroll2, 0.0f);

                background2.draw(gl);
                gl.glPopMatrix();
                bgScroll2 +=  SFEngine.SCROLL_BACKGROUND_2;
                gl.glLoadIdentity();
        }
        @Override
        public void onSurfaceChanged(GL10 gl, int width, int height) {
                // TODO Auto-generated method stub

                gl.glViewport(0, 0, width,height);

                gl.glMatrixMode(GL10.GL_PROJECTION);
                gl.glLoadIdentity();

                gl.glOrthof(0f, 1f, 0f, 1f, -1f, 1f);

        }

        @Override
        public void onSurfaceCreated(GL10 gl, EGLConfig config) {
                // TODO Auto-generated method stub

                gl.glEnable(GL10.GL_TEXTURE_2D);
                gl.glClearDepthf(1.0f);
                gl.glEnable(GL10.GL_DEPTH_TEST);
                gl.glDepthFunc(GL10.GL_LEQUAL);

                gl.glEnable(GL10.GL_BLEND);
                gl.glBlendFunc(GL10.GL_ONE,  GL10.GL_ONE);

                    background.loadTexture(gl,SFEngine.BACKGROUND_LAYER_ONE,
        SFEngine.context);
                    background2.loadTexture(gl,SFEngine.BACKGROUND_LAYER_TWO,
        SFEngine.context);

        }

}
```

You have done a lot of coding thus far in this chapter, and you have a fairly complete environment in which your player can experience the game. However, one very important part of SFGameRenderer is left to code; the onDrawFrame() method. This method will not only control the scrolling (and ultimately the drawing) of your backgrounds, it will also control the frame rate at which your game runs.

Running at 60 Frames per Second

The holy grail of game run speeds is 60 frames per second. Your game should run at, or as close as possible to, 60 frames per second to have a smooth game play experience. In this section of the chapter, you are going to write a quick thread pausing routine that will ensure your games runs around 60 frames per second.

The good thing about using a GLSurfaceView renderer as the main launching point of your game (SFGameRenderer) is that it is already threaded for you. Unless you explicitly set it otherwise, the onDrawFrame() method is called continuously. You do not need to worry about manually setting up any extra threads for the game execution or calling the game methods in a loop. When you set up the SFGameRenderer as the main view of the activity, a threading action is executed that will continuously call the onDrawFrame() method of SFGameRenderer.

Therefore, you need to marshal how this method runs in order to limit it to running just 60 times in one second.

You can put a quick pausing routine in the onDrawFrame() that will put the thread to sleep for a specific amount of time. The amount of time that you want to put the thread to sleep will be one second divided by 60. You will store this value in a constant in the SFEngine.

```
public class SFEngine {
        /*Constants that will be used in the game*/
        public static final int GAME_THREAD_DELAY = 4000;
        public static final int MENU_BUTTON_ALPHA = 0;
        public static final boolean HAPTIC_BUTTON_FEEDBACK = true;
        public static final int SPLASH_SCREEN_MUSIC = R.raw.warfieldedit;
        public static final int R_VOLUME = 100;
        public static final int L_VOLUME = 100;
        public static final boolean LOOP_BACKGROUND_MUSIC = true;
        public static final int GAME_THREAD_FPS_SLEEP = (1000/60);
        public static Context context;
        public static Thread musicThread;
        public static Display display;
        public static float SCROLL_BACKGROUND_1  = .002f;
        public static float SCROLL_BACKGROUND_2  = .007f;
        public static final int BACKGROUND_LAYER_ONE = R.drawable.backgroundstars;
        public static final int BACKGROUND_LAYER_TWO = R.drawable.debris;

        /*Kill game and exit*/
        public boolean onExit(View v) {
        try
        {
                Intent bgmusic = new Intent(context, sfmusic.class);
                context.stopService(bgmusic);
                musicThread.stop();

                return true;
        }catch(Exception e){
                return false;
        }
```

```
        }

}
```

> **TIP:** In Chapter 5, you will have the option of modifying this formula slightly. As you add more
> objects to it, you will want to take into account the amount of time OpenGL needs to render your
> game. For right now, this formula should be just fine.

Pausing the Game Loop

Now that the constant is created, you can set up the pausing routine in the
onDrawFrame() method. At the top of the method, insert Thread.sleep().

```java
package com.proandroidgames;

import javax.microedition.khronos.egl.EGLConfig;
import javax.microedition.khronos.opengles.GL10;

import android.opengl.GLSurfaceView.Renderer;

public class SFGameRenderer implements Renderer{
        private SFBackground background = new SFBackground();
        private SFBackground background2 = new SFBackground();
        private float bgScroll1;
        private float bgScroll2;

        @Override
        public void onDrawFrame(GL10 gl) {
                // TODO Auto-generated method stub
                try {
                        Thread.sleep(SFEngine.GAME_THREAD_FPS_SLEEP);
                } catch (InterruptedException e) {
                        // TODO Auto-generated catch block
                        e.printStackTrace();
                }

        }
        private void scrollBackground1(GL10 gl){
                if (bgScroll1 == Float.MAX_VALUE){
                        bgScroll1 = 0f;
                }

            gl.glMatrixMode(GL10.GL_MODELVIEW);
            gl.glLoadIdentity();
            gl.glPushMatrix();
            gl.glScalef(1f, 1f, 1f);
            gl.glTranslatef(0f, 0f, 0f);

            gl.glMatrixMode(GL10.GL_TEXTURE);
            gl.glLoadIdentity();
            gl.glTranslatef(0.0f,bgScroll1, 0.0f);
```

```java
            background.draw(gl);
            gl.glPopMatrix();
            bgScroll1 +=  SFEngine.SCROLL_BACKGROUND_1;
            gl.glLoadIdentity();


    }
    private void scrollBackground2(GL10 gl){
            if (bgScroll2 == Float.MAX_VALUE){
                    bgScroll2 = 0f;
            }

        gl.glMatrixMode(GL10.GL_MODELVIEW);
        gl.glLoadIdentity();
        gl.glPushMatrix();
        gl.glScalef(.5f, 1f, 1f);
        gl.glTranslatef(1.5f, 0f, 0f);

        gl.glMatrixMode(GL10.GL_TEXTURE);
        gl.glLoadIdentity();
        gl.glTranslatef( 0.0f,bgScroll2, 0.0f);

        background2.draw(gl);
        gl.glPopMatrix();
        bgScroll2 +=  SFEngine.SCROLL_BACKGROUND_2;
        gl.glLoadIdentity();
    }
    @Override
    public void onSurfaceChanged(GL10 gl, int width, int height) {
            // TODO Auto-generated method stub

            gl.glViewport(0, 0, width,height);

            gl.glMatrixMode(GL10.GL_PROJECTION);
            gl.glLoadIdentity();

            gl.glOrthof(0f, 1f, 0f, 1f, -1f, 1f);

    }


    @Override
    public void onSurfaceCreated(GL10 gl, EGLConfig config) {
    // TODO Auto-generated method stub

            gl.glEnable(GL10.GL_TEXTURE_2D);
            gl.glClearDepthf(1.0f);
            gl.glEnable(GL10.GL_DEPTH_TEST);
            gl.glDepthFunc(GL10.GL_LEQUAL);

            gl.glEnable(GL10.GL_BLEND);
            gl.glBlendFunc(GL10.GL_ONE, GL10.GL_ONE);

             background.loadTexture(gl,SFEngine.BACKGROUND_LAYER_ONE,
SFEngine.context);
             background2.loadTexture(gl,SFEngine.BACKGROUND_LAYER_TWO,
SFEngine.context);
```

```
        }
    }
```

Now, anything that you place *after* the try. . .catch containing the Thread.sleep() will only run 60 times per second. You are going to use this onDrawFrame() with the pausing routine as your game loop. Everything that you need to call to place into your game you will do from here.

Clearing the OpenGL Buffers

The first step in your game loop is to clear the OpenGL buffers. This will prepare OpenGL for all of the rendering and transforming that you are about to do.

```
@Override
    public void onDrawFrame(GL10 gl) {
            // TODO Auto-generated method stub
            try {
                    Thread.sleep(SFEngine.GAME_THREAD_FPS_SLEEP);
            } catch (InterruptedException e) {
                    // TODO Auto-generated catch block
                    e.printStackTrace();
            }
            gl.glClear(GL10.GL_COLOR_BUFFER_BIT | GL10.GL_DEPTH_BUFFER_BIT);

    }
```

Once the buffers have been cleared, you can call the two scrolling methods that you created in the last section of this chapter. These two methods will move and draw the two layers of the background appropriately.

```
@Override
    public void onDrawFrame(GL10 gl) {
            // TODO Auto-generated method stub
            try {
                    Thread.sleep(SFEngine.GAME_THREAD_FPS_SLEEP);
            } catch (InterruptedException e) {
                    // TODO Auto-generated catch block
                    e.printStackTrace();
            }
            gl.glClear(GL10.GL_COLOR_BUFFER_BIT | GL10.GL_DEPTH_BUFFER_BIT);

            scrollBackground1(gl);
            scrollBackground2(gl);

    }
```

Finally, you are going to call the transparency blending function of OpenGL. This OpenGL function will make sure everything that you are supposed to be able to see through is transparent. Without this function, you will not see through the vertices around your texture.

```
@Override
    public void onDrawFrame(GL10 gl) {
```

```
        // TODO Auto-generated method stub
        try {
                Thread.sleep(SFEngine.GAME_THREAD_FPS_SLEEP);
        } catch (InterruptedException e) {
                // TODO Auto-generated catch block
                e.printStackTrace();
        }
        gl.glClear(GL10.GL_COLOR_BUFFER_BIT | GL10.GL_DEPTH_BUFFER_BIT);

        scrollBackground1(gl);
        scrollBackground2(gl);

        //All other game drawing will be called here

        gl.glEnable(GL10.GL_BLEND);
        gl.glBlendFunc(GL10.GL_ONE, GL10.GL_ONE);
}
```

Congratulations! You just successfully used OpenGL to create a two-layer, dual-speed scrolling background. Your last step before you can run your game is to wire up the Start button from the main menu to call the SFGame activity.

Modify the Main Menu

Open the SFMainMenu file that you created in the last chapter. In Chapter 3, you created an onClickListener() for the start button. You are going to add a new intent to this method for the SFGame activity. Adding this activity to the onClickListener() will start your game activity when the player clicks (or touches) the Start button on the main menu.

```
start.setOnClickListener(new OnClickListener(){
        @Override
        public void onClick(View v) {
        /** Start Game!!!! */
        Intent game = new Intent(getApplicationContext(),SFGame.class);
        SFMainMenu.this.startActivity(game);

    }
});
```

You can compile and run your code. You should see the splash screen fade into the main menu. If you click the Start button on the main menu, you should be launched into your game where you will see the two layers of your background scroll by at different speeds to the sounds of your background music.

Click the back menu button on your device to return to the main menu, and click the exit button to exit the game and kill the threads.

> **CAUTION:** Keep in mind that you have not yet put in some important housekeeping code. For example, if you were to just leave the focus of the game, the threads would continue to run (so too the music). You will add in code to take care of this later in this book. For now, when you are testing your game, make sure you kill the threads by clicking the exit button.

Summary

In this chapter, you learned several key skills that a game developer needs to add backgrounds to your games. Specifically, you should now have a basic understanding of the following:

- Creating a `GLSurface` instance
- Creating a renderer
- Initializing OpenGL
- Loading a texture from an image
- Modifying the OpenGL matrices
- Pushing and popping a matrix
- Using `glScale()` and `glTranslatef()` to move textures and vertices
- Marshalling a renderer using `Thread.sleep()`

In the next chapter, you will add your first playable character to the game.

Chapter 5

Creating Your Character

To this point in the book, you have done quite a bit of developing, and you have learned a lot about OpenGL and Android—so much that you should be fairly comfortable now with the slight differences between OpenGL and any of the other API tools you may have used in the past.

You have not written an exorbitant amount of code thus far. But what you have written has made a great start to your game and a big visual impact. You have accomplished developing a two-layer dual-speed scrolling background, background music, splash screen, and main menu system. All of these items have one thing in common, as far as a playable game is concerned: they are pretty boring.

That is to say, a gamer is not going to buy your game to watch a fancy two-layer background scroll by. The gamer needs some action to control. This is what Chapter 5: Create Your Character is all about.

In this chapter, you will create your playable character. By the end of this chapter, you will have an animated character that the player can move on the screen. The first section of this chapter will introduce you to a staple of 2-D game development—sprite animation. Then, using OpenGL ES, you will load different sprites from a full sprite sheet to create the illusion of an animated character. You will learn how to load different sprites at key points in the action to make your character look like it is banking in flight.

Animating Sprites

One of the most time-honored tools in the 2-D game developer's belt is sprite animation. Think back to any of your favorite 2-D games, chances are the animation of any of the characters was achieved using sprite animation.

A sprite is technically any graphic element in a 2-D game. Your main playable character is, therefore, a sprite by definition. Sprites, by themselves, are just static images that sit on the screen and do not change. Sprite animation is the process that you are going to use to give your character some life, even if that character is just a spaceship.

> **CAUTION:** Do not confuse *animation* with *movement*. Moving a sprite (image, texture, vertex, or model) around the screen is not the same as animating a sprite; the two concepts and skills are mutually exclusive.

Sprite animation is accomplished using a flip-book style effect. Think of almost any 2-D game, for example, *Mario Brothers*. *Mario Brothers* is one of the best examples of 2-D platform gaming that incorporates sprite animation. In the game, you move Mario left or right through a side-scrolling environment. Mario walks, and sometimes runs, in the direction that you move him. His legs are clearly animated in a walking sequence.

This walking animation is actually made up of a series of still pictures. Each picture depicts a different point in the walking action. When the player moves the character to the left or to the right, the different images are swapped out, giving the illusion that Mario is walking.

In the game *Star Fighter*, you are going to employ the same method to create some animation for your main character. The main playable character in *Star Fighter* is a spaceship; therefore, it will not require walking animation. Spaceships do require some animating though. In this chapter, you will create animations for banking to the right and banking to the left as the player is flying. In future chapters, you will create animations for exploding in a collision.

The great part about sprite animation is that you learned all of the skills that are needed to implement it in the previous chapter. That is, you learned how to load a texture into OpenGL. More importantly, you learned to map a texture onto a set of vertices. The key to sprite animation is how the texture is mapped onto your vertices.

The textures used in implementing sprite animation are not technically separate images. The time and power that would be needed to load and map a new texture 60 times per second—if you could even do it—would far exceed the capabilities of an Android device. Rather, you will use something called a sprite sheet.

A sprite sheet is a single image that contains on it all of the separate images required to perform sprite animation. Figure 5–1 shows the sprite sheet for the main playable ship.

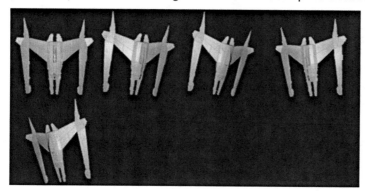

Figure 5–1. *Main character sprite sheet*

> **NOTE:** The sprite sheet in Figure 5–1 is only partially shown. The actual image as it is loaded into OpenGL is 512×512. The bottom half of the image, which is nothing but transparency, has been cropped for better display in the book.

How do you animate one image that is full of smaller ones? It is actually easier than you may think. You will load the image as one texture, but you will only be displaying the portion of the texture that has the image that you want to show the player. When you want to animate the image, you simply use `glTranslateF()` to move to the next part of the image that you want to display.

Don't worry if this concept doesn't quite make sense yet; you are going to put it into action in the next sections of this chapter. The first step, however, is to create a class that will handle drawing and loading your playable character.

> **NOTE:** You may be wondering why the ships in the sprite sheet are facing down rather than up; especially since the playable character will be at the bottom of the screen flying up toward the top. This is because OpenGL renders all bitmaps from the last line to the first. Therefore, when OpenGL renders this sprite sheet it will appear on the screen as in Figure 5–2.

Figure 5–2. *How the sprite sheet will look on screen*

Yes, you could use draw the sprite sheet the correct way and then use OpenGL to rotate the texture to the correct position. However, it is easy enough to invert the sprite sheet using any imaging software, and that way, you save OpenGL the cycles and trouble of inverting it for you.

Loading Your Character

In the previous chapter, you created a class that loaded a texture for a background image and then drew that image when called. The mechanics that you used to create that class will be the same as those that you will need to load up and draw your main character. You will make small adjustments to allow for the use of a sprite sheet, but otherwise, this code should look familiar.

Start by creating a new class in your project package named SFGoodGuy:

```
package com.proandroidgames;

public class SFGoodGuy {

}
```

In the SFGoodGuy() class, stub out a constructor, a draw() method, and a loadTexture() method.

> **TIP:** Remember, you can use the alt + shift + O shortcut in Eclipse to expose any missing imports that you may need.

```
package com.proandroidgames;

public class SFGoodGuy {

        public SFGoodGuy() {

        }
        public void draw(GL10 gl) {
```

```
        }
        public void loadTexture(GL10 gl,int texture, Context context) {

        }
}
```

Next, establish the buffers that you will use in the class. Again, this should look identical to what you did in the previous chapter when working with the background for the game.

You can also add the code to create the vertices[] array. The vertices will be the same as those used in for the background.

```
package com.proandroidgames;

public class SFGoodGuy {

        private FloatBuffer vertexBuffer;
        private FloatBuffer textureBuffer;
        private ByteBuffer indexBuffer;
        private int[] textures = new int[1];

        private float vertices[] = {
                0.0f, 0.0f, 0.0f,
                1.0f, 0.0f, 0.0f,
                1.0f, 1.0f, 0.0f,
                0.0f, 1.0f, 0.0f,
        };

        public SFGoodGuy() {

        }
        public void draw(GL10 gl) {

        }
        public void loadTexture(GL10 gl,int texture, Context context) {

        }
}
```

Now, create the array for the texture mapping.

Creating Texture Mapping Arrays

Texture mapping is where the SFGoodGuy() class will deviate from what you used when loading the background. The texture that you will load into this class is a large sprite sheet that contains five images of the main playable character. Your goal is to display only one of these images at a time.

The key to understanding how to tell OpenGL the location of the image that you want to display is how the images are configured on the sprite sheet. Take a look, again, at the sprite sheet in Figure 5–1. Notice that the images are laid out evenly with four images in the first row and one image in the second. With only four images in the first row of the texture, and the entire texture being 1 unit long, you can surmise that you will only need to display one-fourth of the entire texture to display one of the four images on the first row.

This means that rather than mapping the full texture—from (0,0) to (1,1)—like you did for the background, you only need to map a quarter of it—from (0,0) to (0,.25). You will only be mapping, and thus displaying, the first image of the ship by only using .25, or one-fourth, of the texture.

Create your texture array like this:

```
package com.proandroidgames;

public class SFGoodGuy {

        private FloatBuffer vertexBuffer;
        private FloatBuffer textureBuffer;
        private ByteBuffer indexBuffer;
        private int[] textures = new int[1];

        private float vertices[] = {
                0.0f, 0.0f, 0.0f,
                1.0f, 0.0f, 0.0f,
                1.0f, 1.0f, 0.0f,
                0.0f, 1.0f, 0.0f,
        };

        private float texture[] = {
                0.0f, 0.0f,
                0.25f, 0.0f,
                0.25f, 0.25f,
                0.0f, 0.25f,
        };

        public SFGoodGuy() {

        }
        public void draw(GL10 gl) {

        }
        public void loadTexture(GL10 gl,int texture, Context context) {

        }
}
```

The indices array, the draw() method, and the constructor are all the same as those used in the SFBackground class:

```
package com.proandroidgames;

import java.io.IOException;
import java.io.InputStream;
import java.nio.ByteBuffer;
import java.nio.ByteOrder;
import java.nio.FloatBuffer;
```

```java
import javax.microedition.khronos.opengles.GL10;

import android.content.Context;
import android.graphics.Bitmap;
import android.graphics.BitmapFactory;
import android.opengl.GLUtils;

public class SFGoodGuy {

        private FloatBuffer vertexBuffer;
        private FloatBuffer textureBuffer;
        private ByteBuffer indexBuffer;
        private int[] textures = new int[1];

        private float vertices[] = {
                0.0f, 0.0f, 0.0f,
                1.0f, 0.0f, 0.0f,
                1.0f, 1.0f, 0.0f,
                0.0f, 1.0f, 0.0f,
        };

        private float texture[] = {
                0.0f, 0.0f,
                0.25f, 0.0f,
                0.25f, 0.25f,
                0.0f, 0.25f,
        };

        private byte indices[] = {
                0,1,2,
                0,2,3,
        };

        public SFGoodGuy() {
                ByteBuffer byteBuf = ByteBuffer.allocateDirect(vertices.length * 4);
                byteBuf.order(ByteOrder.nativeOrder());
                vertexBuffer = byteBuf.asFloatBuffer();
                vertexBuffer.put(vertices);
                vertexBuffer.position(0);

                byteBuf = ByteBuffer.allocateDirect(texture.length * 4);
                byteBuf.order(ByteOrder.nativeOrder());
                textureBuffer = byteBuf.asFloatBuffer();
                textureBuffer.put(texture);
                textureBuffer.position(0);

                indexBuffer = ByteBuffer.allocateDirect(indices.length);
                indexBuffer.put(indices);
                indexBuffer.position(0);
        }

        public void draw(GL10 gl) {
                gl.glBindTexture(GL10.GL_TEXTURE_2D, textures[0]);
```

```
                    gl.glFrontFace(GL10.GL_CCW);
                    gl.glEnable(GL10.GL_CULL_FACE);
                    gl.glCullFace(GL10.GL_BACK);

                    gl.glEnableClientState(GL10.GL_VERTEX_ARRAY);
                    gl.glEnableClientState(GL10.GL_TEXTURE_COORD_ARRAY);

                    gl.glVertexPointer(3, GL10.GL_FLOAT, 0, vertexBuffer);
                    gl.glTexCoordPointer(2, GL10.GL_FLOAT, 0, textureBuffer);

                    gl.glDrawElements(GL10.GL_TRIANGLES, indices.length,
        GL10.GL_UNSIGNED_BYTE, indexBuffer);

                    gl.glDisableClientState(GL10.GL_VERTEX_ARRAY);
                    gl.glDisableClientState(GL10.GL_TEXTURE_COORD_ARRAY);
                    gl.glDisable(GL10.GL_CULL_FACE);
            }
        public void loadTexture(GL10 gl,int texture, Context context) {

            }
        }
```

There is one more change that you need to make to the SFGoodGuy() class before it is
finished. In the class for loadTexture() method of the background, you set the
glTexParameterf to GL_REPEAT to enable the repeating of the texture as you moved it on
the vertices. This is not really necessary for the playable character; therefore, you are
going to set this parameter to GL_CLAMP_TO_EDGE.

Finish your SFGoodGuy() class with the following loadTexture() method:

...

```
        public void loadTexture(GL10 gl,int texture, Context context) {
                InputStream imagestream =
        context.getResources().openRawResource(texture);
                Bitmap bitmap = null;
                try {

                        bitmap = BitmapFactory.decodeStream(imagestream);

                }catch(Exception e){

                }finally {
                        try {

                                imagestream.close();
                                imagestream = null;

                        } catch (IOException e) {
                        }
                }

                gl.glGenTextures(1, textures, 0);
                gl.glBindTexture(GL10.GL_TEXTURE_2D, textures[0]);
```

```
                gl.glTexParameterf(GL10.GL_TEXTURE_2D, GL10.GL_TEXTURE_MIN_FILTER,
GL10.GL_NEAREST);
                gl.glTexParameterf(GL10.GL_TEXTURE_2D, GL10.GL_TEXTURE_MAG_FILTER,
GL10.GL_LINEAR);

                gl.glTexParameterf(GL10.GL_TEXTURE_2D, GL10.GL_TEXTURE_WRAP_S,
GL10.GL_REPEAT);
                gl.glTexParameterf(GL10.GL_TEXTURE_2D, GL10.GL_TEXTURE_WRAP_T,
GL10.GL_REPEAT);

                GLUtils.texImage2D(GL10.GL_TEXTURE_2D, 0, bitmap, 0);

                bitmap.recycle();

        }
}
```

You now have a functional class that will load your playable character texture as a sprite sheet, display the first sprite in the sprite sheet, and not wrap the texture when it is moved.

Loading a Texture onto Your Character

The next step to loading a playable character is to instantiate a copy of the SFGoodGuy() and load a texture. Save and close the SFGoodGuy() class; you will not be needing to add any more code to it right now.

Let's add a few quick variables and constants to SFEngine. You will need these in your game loop.

First, you will add a variable called playerFlightAction. This is going to be used to track what action the player has taken so that you can respond appropriately in the game loop.

```
package com.proandroidgames;

import android.content.Context;
import android.content.Intent;
import android.view.Display;
import android.view.View;

public class SFEngine {

...


        public static int playerFlightAction = 0;

        /*Kill game and exit*/
        public boolean onExit(View v) {
        try
        {
                Intent bgmusic = new Intent(context, SFMusic.class);
```

```
                    context.stopService(bgmusic);
                    musicThread.stop();
                    return true;
            }catch(Exception e){
                    return false;
            }

            }
    }
```

Next, add in a constant that points to the sprite sheet from the last section of this chapter.

```
package com.proandroidgames;

import android.content.Context;
import android.content.Intent;
import android.view.Display;
import android.view.View;

public class SFEngine {

    ...


            public static int playerFlightAction = 0;
            public static final int PLAYER_SHIP = R.drawable.good_sprite;

            /*Kill game and exit*/
            public boolean onExit(View v) {
            try
            {
                    Intent bgmusic = new Intent(context, SFMusic.class);
                    context.stopService(bgmusic);
                    musicThread.stop();
                    return true;
            }catch(Exception e){
                    return false;
            }

            }
    }
```

The next three constants are going to indicate what action the player has taken. These will be assigned to the playerFlightAction variable when the player tries to move the character.

```
package com.proandroidgames;

import android.content.Context;
import android.content.Intent;
import android.view.Display;
import android.view.View;

public class SFEngine {

    ...


            public static int playerFlightAction = 0;
```

```
       public static final int PLAYER_SHIP = R.drawable.good_sprite;
       public static final int PLAYER_BANK_LEFT_1 = 1;
       public static final int PLAYER_RELEASE = 3;
       public static final int PLAYER_BANK_RIGHT_1 = 4;

       /*Kill game and exit*/
       public boolean onExit(View v) {
       try
       {
               Intent bgmusic = new Intent(context, SFMusic.class);
               context.stopService(bgmusic);
               musicThread.stop();
               return true;
       }catch(Exception e){
               return false;
       }

       }
}
```

Depending on how observant you are concerning the constants that you just added to SFEngine, you may be wondering why PLAYER_BANK_LEFT_1 has a value of 1 and PLAYER_RELEASE has a value of 3. These values are going to represent stages of your sprite animation. On the sprite sheet, there are two stages in the left-banking animation and two stages in the right-banking animation. However, in the code for the loop, you are going to be able to infer that between PLAYER_BANK_LEFT_1 and PLAYER_RELEASE is a PLAYER_BANK_LEFT_2 with a value of 2, and this constant will not have to be expressed in the SFEngine. This concept will definitely make more sense when you see it in action later in this section.

The next constant that you need will indicate how many loop iterations will equal one frame of sprite animation. Remember, the big difference between the playable character and the background of the game is that you are going to animate the character as it is moved across the screen. Keeping track of this animation is going to be a tricky thing. The game loop is running at 60 frames per second. If you ran a new frame of sprite animation for every iteration of the loop, your animation would be over before the player even had a chance to admire it. The constant PLAYER_FRAMES_BETWEEN_ANI will be set to 9, indicating that for every nine iterations of the main game loop, there will be one frame of sprite animation drawn.

```
package com.proandroidgames;

import android.content.Context;
import android.content.Intent;
import android.view.Display;
import android.view.View;

public class SFEngine {

...

       public static int playerFlightAction = 0;
       public static final int PLAYER_SHIP = R.drawable.good_sprite;
       public static final int PLAYER_BANK_LEFT_1 = 1;
```

```
        public static final int PLAYER_RELEASE = 3;
        public static final int PLAYER_BANK_RIGHT_1 = 4;
        public static final int PLAYER_FRAMES_BETWEEN_ANI = 9;

        /*Kill game and exit*/
        public boolean onExit(View v) {
        try
        {
                Intent bgmusic = new Intent(context, SFMusic.class);
                context.stopService(bgmusic);
                musicThread.stop();
                return true;
        }catch(Exception e){
                return false;
        }

        }
}
```

Finally, add one more constant and one more variable. These will represent the speed at which the player's ship will move from left to right and the current position of the player's ship on the x axis.

```
package com.proandroidgames;

import android.content.Context;
import android.content.Intent;
import android.view.Display;
import android.view.View;

public class SFEngine {

...

        public static int playerFlightAction = 0;
        public static final int PLAYER_SHIP = R.drawable.good_sprite;
        public static final int PLAYER_BANK_LEFT_1 = 1;
        public static final int PLAYER_RELEASE = 3;
        public static final int PLAYER_BANK_RIGHT_1 = 4;
        public static final int PLAYER_FRAMES_BETWEEN_ANI = 9;
        public static final float PLAYER_BANK_SPEED = .1f;
        public static float playerBankPosX = 1.75f;

        /*Kill game and exit*/
        public boolean onExit(View v) {
        try
        {
                Intent bgmusic = new Intent(context, SFMusic.class);
                context.stopService(bgmusic);
                musicThread.stop();
                return true;
        }catch(Exception e){
                return false;
        }

        }
}
```

SFEngine now has all of the code needed to help you implement your playable character. Save and close the file.

Open the SFGameRenderer.java file. This file is the home to your game loop. In the previous chapter, you created the game loop and added two methods for drawing and scrolling the different layers of the background. Now, you are going to add code to your loop that will draw and move the playable character.

Setting Up the Game Loop

The first step is to instantiate a new SFGoodGuy() called player1:

```
public class SFGameRenderer implements Renderer{
        private SFBackground background = new SFBackground();
        private SFBackground background2 = new SFBackground();
        private SFGoodGuy player1 = new SFGoodGuy();

        private float bgScroll1;
        private float bgScroll2;
    ...
}
```

The player1 object is going to be used in the same way as background and background2. You will call the loadTexture() and draw() methods from player1 to load your character into the game.

You need to create a variable that will track how many iterations of the game loop have passed, so you will know when you flip frames in your sprite animation.

```
public class SFGameRenderer implements Renderer{
        private SFBackground background = new SFBackground();
        private SFBackground background2 = new SFBackground();
        private SFGoodGuy player1 = new SFGoodGuy();
        private int goodGuyBankFrames = 0;

        private float bgScroll1;
        private float bgScroll2;
    ...
}
```

Next, locate the onSurfaceCreated() method of the SFGameRenderer Renderer. This method handles the loading of game textures. In the last chapter, you called the loading methods of background and background2 in this method. Now, you need to add a call to the loadTexture() method of player1.

```
package com.proandroidgames;

import javax.microedition.khronos.egl.EGLConfig;
import javax.microedition.khronos.opengles.GL10;

import android.opengl.GLSurfaceView.Renderer;

public class SFGameRenderer implements Renderer{
        private SFBackground background = new SFBackground();
        private SFBackground background2 = new SFBackground();
```

```
            private SFGoodGuy player1 = new SFGoodGuy();
            private int goodGuyBankFrames = 0;

...


            @Override
            public void onSurfaceCreated(GL10 gl, EGLConfig config) {
                    // TODO Auto-generated method stub
                     gl.glEnable(GL10.GL_TEXTURE_2D);
                    gl.glClearDepthf(1.0f);
                    gl.glEnable(GL10.GL_DEPTH_TEST);
                    gl.glDepthFunc(GL10.GL_LEQUAL);

                    background.loadTexture(gl,SFEngine.BACKGROUND_LAYER_ONE,
SFEngine.context);
                    background2.loadTexture(gl,SFEngine.BACKGROUND_LAYER_TWO,
SFEngine.context);

                    player1.loadTexture(gl, SFEngine.PLAYER_SHIP, SFEngine.context);
            }

}
```

So far, this code has all been pretty basic: create the texture, and load the texture. Now, it is time for the real meat of the chapter. It is time to write the method that will control the moving of your player's character.

Moving the Character

This section will help you create the code necessary to move your player's character on the screen. To do this, you will create a new method that will server as your core game loop. Finally, you will call methods from this loop that will perform the task of moving your character. Create a new method in SFGameRenderer SFGameRenderer that takes in a GL10.

```
package com.proandroidgames;

import javax.microedition.khronos.egl.EGLConfig;
import javax.microedition.khronos.opengles.GL10;

import android.opengl.GLSurfaceView.Renderer;

public class SFGameRenderer implements Renderer{

...


        private void movePlayer1(GL10 gl){

        }

...


}
```

Within the movePlayer1() method, you are going to run a switch statement on the playerFlightAction int that you added to SFEngine earlier in this chapter. Just in case you have never used one, a switch statement will examine the input object (playerFlightAction) and execute specific code based on the value of the input. The cases for this switch statement are PLAYER_BANK_LEFT_1, PLAYER_RELEASE, PLAYER_BANK_RIGHT_1, and default.

```
package com.proandroidgames;

import javax.microedition.khronos.egl.EGLConfig;
import javax.microedition.khronos.opengles.GL10;

import android.opengl.GLSurfaceView.Renderer;

public class SFGameRenderer implements Renderer{

...

        private void movePlayer1(GL10 gl){
                switch (SFEngine.playerFlightAction){
                case SFEngine.PLAYER_BANK_LEFT_1:

                        break;
                case SFEngine.PLAYER_BANK_RIGHT_1:

                        break;
                case SFEngine.PLAYER_RELEASE:

                        break;
                default:

                        break;
                }

        }

...

}
```

Let's start with the default case. The default case is going to be called when the player has taken no action at all with the character.

Drawing the Default State of the Character

Right now, the vertices are the same size as the screen. Therefore, if you were to just draw the playable character to the screen now, it would fill the entire screen. You will need to scale the game character by about 75 percent so that it looks good in the game.

To do this you are going to use glScalef(). Multiplying the scale by .25 will reduce the size of the ship to a quarter of its original size. This has one very important after effect that you need to understand.

In the last chapter, you briefly discovered that to scale or translate the vertices you need to work in the model matrix mode. Any operation that you do in any matrix mode affects *all* items in that matrix mode. Therefore, when you scale the vertices for the player ship by .25, you also scale the x and y axes that it occupies. In other words, whereas the x and y axis start at 0 and end at 1 when the scale is defaulted to 0 (full screen), the x and y axes will run for 0 to 4 when the scale is multiplied by .25.

This is important to you, because when you are trying to keep track of the player's location, you need to realize that the background may scroll from 0 to 1 but the player can scroll from 0 to 4.

Load the model matrix view, and scale the player by .25 on the x and y axes.

```
package com.proandroidgames;

import javax.microedition.khronos.egl.EGLConfig;
import javax.microedition.khronos.opengles.GL10;

import android.opengl.GLSurfaceView.Renderer;

public class SFGameRenderer implements Renderer{

...

        private void movePlayer1(GL10 gl){
                switch (SFEngine.playerFlightAction){
                case SFEngine.PLAYER_BANK_LEFT_1:

                        break;
                case SFEngine.PLAYER_BANK_RIGHT_1:

                        break;
                case SFEngine.PLAYER_RELEASE:

                        break;
                default:
                        gl.glMatrixMode(GL10.GL_MODELVIEW);
                        gl.glLoadIdentity();
                        gl.glPushMatrix();
                        gl.glScalef(.25f, .25f, 1f);

                        break;
                }

        }

...

}
```

Next, translate the model matrix on the x axis by the value in the variable playerBankPosX. The variable playerBankPosX is going to hold the player's current position on the x axis. Therefore, whenever the player is taking no action, the character will be right at the last place it was left.

```
package com.proandroidgames;

import javax.microedition.khronos.egl.EGLConfig;
import javax.microedition.khronos.opengles.GL10;

import android.opengl.GLSurfaceView.Renderer;

public class SFGameRenderer implements Renderer{

...

        private void movePlayer1(GL10 gl){
...

                default:
                        gl.glMatrixMode(GL10.GL_MODELVIEW);
                        gl.glLoadIdentity();
                        gl.glPushMatrix();
                        gl.glScalef(.25f, .25f, 1f);
                        gl.glTranslatef(SFEngine.playerBankPosX, 0f, 0f);

                        break;
                }

        }

...

}
```

When the player is at rest, no other action needs to be taken, so load the texture matrix, and make sure it is at the default position, which is the first sprite in the sprite sheet. Remember, the texture matrix mode will be the mode that you use to shift the position of the sprite sheet texture to *flip* the animation. If the player is not moving the character, there should be no animation—hence, the texture matrix should default to the first position.

```
package com.proandroidgames;

import javax.microedition.khronos.egl.EGLConfig;
import javax.microedition.khronos.opengles.GL10;

import android.opengl.GLSurfaceView.Renderer;

public class SFGameRenderer implements Renderer{

...

        private void movePlayer1(GL10 gl){
...

                default:
                        gl.glMatrixMode(GL10.GL_MODELVIEW);
                        gl.glLoadIdentity();
                        gl.glPushMatrix();
```

```
                        gl.glScalef(.25f, .25f, 1f);
                        gl.glTranslatef(SFEngine.playerBankPosX, 0f, 0f);
                        gl.glMatrixMode(GL10.GL_TEXTURE);
                        gl.glLoadIdentity();
                        gl.glTranslatef(0.0f,0.0f, 0.0f);
                        player1.draw(gl);
                        gl.glPopMatrix();
                        gl.glLoadIdentity();

                        break;
                }

        }

...

}
```

The next case in the switch statement that you code is for PLAYER_RELEASE. The
PLAYER_RELEASE action will be called when the player releases the control after moving
the character. While you have not yet coded the actual controls for the game, the player
will touch a control telling the character to move. When the player releases this control,
thus telling the character to stop moving, the PLAYER_RELEASE action will be called.

Coding the PLAYER_RELEASE Action

For now, the case for PLAYER_RELEASE will perform the same action as the default case.
That is, the character will stay where it has been left on the screen, and no matter what
texture was being displayer from the sprite sheet, it will be returned to the first texture
on the sheet. Copy and paste the entire code block from default into the case for
PLAYER_RELEASE.

```
package com.proandroidgames;

import javax.microedition.khronos.egl.EGLConfig;
import javax.microedition.khronos.opengles.GL10;

import android.opengl.GLSurfaceView.Renderer;

public class SFGameRenderer implements Renderer{

...

        private void movePlayer1(GL10 gl){
                switch (SFEngine.playerFlightAction){
                case SFEngine.PLAYER_BANK_LEFT_1:

                        break;
                case SFEngine.PLAYER_BANK_RIGHT_1:

                        break;
                case SFEngine.PLAYER_RELEASE:
                        gl.glMatrixMode(GL10.GL_MODELVIEW);
```

```
                            gl.glLoadIdentity();
                            gl.glPushMatrix();
                            gl.glScalef(.25f, .25f, 1f);
                            gl.glTranslatef(SFEngine.playerBankPosX, 0f, 0f);
                            gl.glMatrixMode(GL10.GL_TEXTURE);
                            gl.glLoadIdentity();
                            gl.glTranslatef(0.0f,0.0f, 0.0f);
                            player1.draw(gl);
                            gl.glPopMatrix();
                            gl.glLoadIdentity();

                            break;

...

                    }

            }

...

}
```

Before you are finished with the PLAYER_RELEASE case, you need to add one more line of code. Earlier in this chapter, you learned that you cannot flip the animation for your sprite at the same rate as your game loop (60 frames per second), because with only two frames in your sprite animation, it would be over before the player realized it happened. Therefore, you need a variable to hold the number of game loops that have passed. By knowing the number of game loops that have passed, you can compare that number to the PLAYER_FRAMES_BETWEEN_ANI constant to determine when you need to flip the sprite animation frames. The goodGuyBankFrames variable that you created earlier in this chapter will be used to track the number of game loops that have been executed.

In the PLAYER_RELEASE case, add the following lines of code to increment goodGuyBankFrames by one every time a loop is executed.

```
package com.proandroidgames;

import javax.microedition.khronos.egl.EGLConfig;
import javax.microedition.khronos.opengles.GL10;

import android.opengl.GLSurfaceView.Renderer;

public class SFGameRenderer implements Renderer{

...

        private void movePlayer1(GL10 gl){
                switch (SFEngine.playerFlightAction){
                case SFEngine.PLAYER_BANK_LEFT_1:

                        break;
                case SFEngine.PLAYER_BANK_RIGHT_1:
```

```
                              break;
                    case SFEngine.PLAYER_RELEASE:
                              gl.glMatrixMode(GL10.GL_MODELVIEW);
                              gl.glLoadIdentity();
                              gl.glPushMatrix();
                              gl.glScalef(.25f, .25f, 1f);
                              gl.glTranslatef(SFEngine.playerBankPosX, 0f, 0f);
                              gl.glMatrixMode(GL10.GL_TEXTURE);
                              gl.glLoadIdentity();
                              gl.glTranslatef(0.0f,0.0f, 0.0f);
                              player1.draw(gl);
                              gl.glPopMatrix();
                              gl.glLoadIdentity();
                              goodGuyBankFrames += 1;

                              break;

         ...
                    }

         }

    ...

}
```

The PLAYER_RELEASE and default cases were the easiest of the four cases in your
movePlayer1() method. Now, you need to code what will happen when the
PLAYER_BANK_LEFT_1 action is called.

The PLAYER_BANK_LEFT_1 action is called when the player uses the controls to bank the
character ship to the left. This means that not only do you need to not only move the
character along the x axis to the left but you also need to animate the character using
the two sprites on the sprite sheet that represent a bank to the left.

Moving the Character to the Left

As far as OpenGL is concerned, the operations of moving the character along the x axis
and changing the position of the sprite sheet utilize two different matrix modes. You will
need to use the model matrix mode to move the character along the x axis, and you will
need to use the texture matrix mode to move the sprite sheet texture—creating the
banking animation. Let's tackle the model matrix mode operation first.

The first step is to load up the model matrix mode and set the scale to .25 on the x and
y axes.

```
package com.proandroidgames;

import javax.microedition.khronos.egl.EGLConfig;
import javax.microedition.khronos.opengles.GL10;

import android.opengl.GLSurfaceView.Renderer;
```

```java
public class SFGameRenderer implements Renderer{

...

        private void movePlayer1(GL10 gl){
                switch (SFEngine.playerFlightAction){
                case SFEngine.PLAYER_BANK_LEFT_1:
                        gl.glMatrixMode(GL10.GL_MODELVIEW);
                        gl.glLoadIdentity();
                        gl.glPushMatrix();
                        gl.glScalef(.25f, .25f, 1f);

                        break;

...

                }

        }

...

}
```

Next, you are going to move the vertices along the x axis using glTranslatef(). You subtract the PLAYER_BANK_SPEED from the current x axis position, which is stored in playerBankPosX. (You are subtracting to get the position that you need to move to, because you are trying to move the character to the left along the x axis. If you were trying to move to the right, you would be adding.) Then, you use glTranslatef() to move the vertices to the position in playerBankPosX.

```java
package com.proandroidgames;

import javax.microedition.khronos.egl.EGLConfig;
import javax.microedition.khronos.opengles.GL10;

import android.opengl.GLSurfaceView.Renderer;

public class SFGameRenderer implements Renderer{

...

        private void movePlayer1(GL10 gl){
                switch (SFEngine.playerFlightAction){
                case SFEngine.PLAYER_BANK_LEFT_1:
                        gl.glMatrixMode(GL10.GL_MODELVIEW);
                        gl.glLoadIdentity();
                        gl.glPushMatrix();
                        gl.glScalef(.25f, .25f, 1f);
                        SFEngine.playerBankPosX -= SFEngine.PLAYER_BANK_SPEED;
                        gl.glTranslatef(SFEngine.playerBankPosX, 0f, 0f);

                        break;

...
```

```
                          }

                 }

      . . .

      }
```

Now that you are moving the character along the x axis, you need to flip to the next frame of animation.

Loading the Correct Sprite

Take a look, once again, at the sprite sheet in Figure 5–1. Notice that the two frames of animation that correspond to the left-banking motion are the fourth frame on the first line and the first frame on the second line (keep in mind that the sheet is inverted if it looks backward to you, so the frames that appear to be banking right will bank left when they are rendered).

Load the texture matrix mode, and translate the texture to display the fourth image on the first row. Because textures are translated in percentages, you have to do a little math. Then again, with only four images on a line, the math is pretty easy.

The x axis of the sprite sheet goes from 0 to 1. If you divide that by 4, each sprite on the sheet occupies .25 of the x axis. Therefore, to move the sprite sheet to the fourth sprite on the line, you need to translate it by .75. (The first sprite occupies x values 0 to .24, the second sprite occupies .25 to .49, the third sprite occupies .50 to .74, and the fourth sprite occupies .75 to 1.)

```java
package com.proandroidgames;

import javax.microedition.khronos.egl.EGLConfig;
import javax.microedition.khronos.opengles.GL10;

import android.opengl.GLSurfaceView.Renderer;

public class SFGameRenderer implements Renderer{

    ...

        private void movePlayer1(GL10 gl){
                switch (SFEngine.playerFlightAction){
                case SFEngine.PLAYER_BANK_LEFT_1:
                        gl.glMatrixMode(GL10.GL_MODELVIEW);
                        gl.glLoadIdentity();
                        gl.glPushMatrix();
                        gl.glScalef(.25f, .25f, 1f);
                        SFEngine.playerBankPosX -= SFEngine.PLAYER_BANK_SPEED;
                        gl.glTranslatef(SFEngine.playerBankPosX, 0f, 0f);
                        gl.glMatrixMode(GL10.GL_TEXTURE);
                        gl.glLoadIdentity();
                        gl.glTranslatef(0.75f,0.0f, 0.0f);
```

```
                    break;

...
              }

      }

...

}
```

The last step before you draw out the ship is to increment goodGuyBankFrames, so you can start tracking when to flip to the second frame in the script sheet.

```
package com.proandroidgames;

import javax.microedition.khronos.egl.EGLConfig;
import javax.microedition.khronos.opengles.GL10;

import android.opengl.GLSurfaceView.Renderer;

public class SFGameRenderer implements Renderer{

...

      private void movePlayer1(GL10 gl){
            switch (SFEngine.playerFlightAction){
            case SFEngine.PLAYER_BANK_LEFT_1:
                  gl.glMatrixMode(GL10.GL_MODELVIEW);
                  gl.glLoadIdentity();
                  gl.glPushMatrix();
                  gl.glScalef(.25f, .25f, 1f);
                  SFEngine.playerBankPosX -= SFEngine.PLAYER_BANK_SPEED;
                  gl.glTranslatef(SFEngine.playerBankPosX, 0f, 0f);
                  gl.glMatrixMode(GL10.GL_TEXTURE);
                  gl.glLoadIdentity();
                  gl.glTranslatef(0.75f,0.0f, 0.0f);
                  goodGuyBankFrames += 1;

                  break;

...
              }

      }

...

}
```

This code has one major problem. The player can now move the character to the left along the x axis, and the sprite of the ship will change to the first sprite of the left bank animation. The problem is that as the code is written right now, the sprite will move to the left to infinity. You need to wrap the block of code that moves the character in an if

. . . `else` statement that tests to see if the character has reached 0 on the x axis. If the character is at the 0 position, indicating that they are at the left edge of the screen, stop moving the character and return the animation to the default sprite.

```
package com.proandroidgames;

import javax.microedition.khronos.egl.EGLConfig;
import javax.microedition.khronos.opengles.GL10;

import android.opengl.GLSurfaceView.Renderer;

public class SFGameRenderer implements Renderer{

...

        private void movePlayer1(GL10 gl){
                switch (SFEngine.playerFlightAction){
                case SFEngine.PLAYER_BANK_LEFT_1:
                        gl.glMatrixMode(GL10.GL_MODELVIEW);
                        gl.glLoadIdentity();
                        gl.glPushMatrix();
                        gl.glScalef(.25f, .25f, 1f);
                        if (SFEngine.playerBankPosX > 0){
                                SFEngine.playerBankPosX -= SFEngine.PLAYER_BANK_SPEED;
                                gl.glTranslatef(SFEngine.playerBankPosX, 0f, 0f);
                                gl.glMatrixMode(GL10.GL_TEXTURE);
                                gl.glLoadIdentity();
                                gl.glTranslatef(0.75f,0.0f, 0.0f);
                                goodGuyBankFrames += 1;
                        }else{
                                gl.glTranslatef(SFEngine.playerBankPosX, 0f, 0f);
                                gl.glMatrixMode(GL10.GL_TEXTURE);
                                gl.glLoadIdentity();
                                gl.glTranslatef(0.0f,0.0f, 0.0f);
                        }

                        break;

...

                }

        }

...

}
```

Now, draw the character by calling the `draw()` method, and pop the matrix back on the stack. This step in the process should be the same as with the two background layers. In fact, this step in the process is going to be common across almost all OpenGL operations in this game.

```
package com.proandroidgames;

import javax.microedition.khronos.egl.EGLConfig;
```

```
import javax.microedition.khronos.opengles.GL10;

import android.opengl.GLSurfaceView.Renderer;

public class SFGameRenderer implements Renderer{

...

        private void movePlayer1(GL10 gl){
                switch (SFEngine.playerFlightAction){
                case SFEngine.PLAYER_BANK_LEFT_1:
                        gl.glMatrixMode(GL10.GL_MODELVIEW);
                        gl.glLoadIdentity();
                        gl.glPushMatrix();
                        gl.glScalef(.25f, .25f, 1f);
                        if (SFEngine.playerBankPosX > 0){
                                SFEngine.playerBankPosX -= SFEngine.PLAYER_BANK_SPEED;
                                gl.glTranslatef(SFEngine.playerBankPosX, 0f, 0f);
                                gl.glMatrixMode(GL10.GL_TEXTURE);
                                gl.glLoadIdentity();
                                gl.glTranslatef(0.75f,0.0f, 0.0f);
                                goodGuyBankFrames += 1;
                        }else{
                                gl.glTranslatef(SFEngine.playerBankPosX, 0f, 0f);
                                gl.glMatrixMode(GL10.GL_TEXTURE);
                                gl.glLoadIdentity();
                                gl.glTranslatef(0.0f,0.0f, 0.0f);
                        }
                        player1.draw(gl);
                        gl.glPopMatrix();
                        gl.glLoadIdentity();

                        break;

...

                }

        }

...

}
```

Now you have a case whereby, if the player is moving the character to the left, the vertices are moved along the x axis to the left until they hit zero. Also, the texture starts off at the default (top-down view) sprite, and when the player moves to the left, the sprite is changed to the first frame of left banking animation.

Loading the Second Frame of Animation

You need to flip the animation to the second frame of the left-banking animation if the player moves to the left far enough. Looking at the sprite sheet in Figure 5–1, the second frame of left-banking animation is the first frame on the second row. This will be easy enough to navigate to using glTranslatef(). The question is, how do you know when to flip the sprite?

Earlier in this chapter, you created a constant in SFEngine named PLAYER_FRAMES_BETWEEN_ANI and set it to 9. This constant says that you want to flip the player's character animation every nine frames of game animation (i.e., of the game loop). You also created a variable named goodGuyBankFrames that is being incremented by 1 every time the player's character is drawn.

You need to compare the current value of goodGuyBankFrames to PLAYER_FRAMES_BETWEEN_ANI. If goodGuyBankFrames is less, draw the first frame of animation. If goodGuyBankFrames is greater, draw the second frame of animation. Here is what your if . . . then statement should look like.

```
package com.proandroidgames;

import javax.microedition.khronos.egl.EGLConfig;
import javax.microedition.khronos.opengles.GL10;

import android.opengl.GLSurfaceView.Renderer;

public class SFGameRenderer implements Renderer{

...

        private void movePlayer1(GL10 gl){
                switch (SFEngine.playerFlightAction){
                case SFEngine.PLAYER_BANK_LEFT_1:
                        gl.glMatrixMode(GL10.GL_MODELVIEW);
                        gl.glLoadIdentity();
                        gl.glPushMatrix();
                        gl.glScalef(.25f, .25f, 1f);
                        if (goodGuyBankFrames < SFEngine.PLAYER_FRAMES_BETWEEN_ANI &&
SFEngine.playerBankPosX > 0){
                                SFEngine.playerBankPosX -= SFEngine.PLAYER_BANK_SPEED;
                                gl.glTranslatef(SFEngine.playerBankPosX, 0f, 0f);
                                gl.glMatrixMode(GL10.GL_TEXTURE);
                                gl.glLoadIdentity();
                                gl.glTranslatef(0.75f,0.0f, 0.0f);
                                goodGuyBankFrames += 1;
                        }else if (goodGuyBankFrames >=
SFEngine.PLAYER_FRAMES_BETWEEN_ANI && SFEngine.playerBankPosX > 0){
                                SFEngine.playerBankPosX -= SFEngine.PLAYER_BANK_SPEED;

                        }else{
                                gl.glTranslatef(SFEngine.playerBankPosX, 0f, 0f);
                                gl.glMatrixMode(GL10.GL_TEXTURE);
                                gl.glLoadIdentity();
                                gl.glTranslatef(0.0f,0.0f, 0.0f);
                        }
                        player1.draw(gl);
                        gl.glPopMatrix();
                        gl.glLoadIdentity();
```

```
                break;

...

            }

        }

...

}
```

In the if . . . else if condition, you test if the value of goodGuyBankFrames is greater than PLAYER_FRAMES_BETWEEN_ANI, indicating that you should flip to the next frame of left-banking animation. Let's write the code block to flip the animation.

In Figure 5–1, the second frame of left banking animation is on the second row in the first position. That means that the upper-left corner of that sprite is at the 0 position on the x axis (furthest to the left) and then a quarter of the way down the sheet on the y axis (.25). Simply use the glTranslatef() method to move the texture to this position.

NOTE: Before you move the texture you need to load the texture matrix mode.

```java
package com.proandroidgames;

import javax.microedition.khronos.egl.EGLConfig;
import javax.microedition.khronos.opengles.GL10;

import android.opengl.GLSurfaceView.Renderer;

public class SFGameRenderer implements Renderer{

...

        private void movePlayer1(GL10 gl){
                switch (SFEngine.playerFlightAction){
                case SFEngine.PLAYER_BANK_LEFT_1:
                        gl.glMatrixMode(GL10.GL_MODELVIEW);
                        gl.glLoadIdentity();
                        gl.glPushMatrix();
                        gl.glScalef(.25f, .25f, 1f);
                        if (goodGuyBankFrames < SFEngine.PLAYER_FRAMES_BETWEEN_ANI &&
SFEngine.playerBankPosX > 0){
                                SFEngine.playerBankPosX -= SFEngine.PLAYER_BANK_SPEED;
                                gl.glTranslatef(SFEngine.playerBankPosX, 0f, 0f);
                                gl.glMatrixMode(GL10.GL_TEXTURE);
                                gl.glLoadIdentity();
                                gl.glTranslatef(0.75f,0.0f, 0.0f);
                                goodGuyBankFrames += 1;
                        }else if (goodGuyBankFrames >=
SFEngine.PLAYER_FRAMES_BETWEEN_ANI && SFEngine.playerBankPosX > 0){
                                SFEngine.playerBankPosX -= SFEngine.PLAYER_BANK_SPEED;
```

```
                                    gl.glTranslatef(SFEngine.playerBankPosX, 0f, 0f);
                                    gl.glMatrixMode(GL10.GL_TEXTURE);
                                    gl.glLoadIdentity();
                                    gl.glTranslatef(0.0f,0.25f, 0.0f);
                      }else{
                                    gl.glTranslatef(SFEngine.playerBankPosX, 0f, 0f);
                                    gl.glMatrixMode(GL10.GL_TEXTURE);
                                    gl.glLoadIdentity();
                                    gl.glTranslatef(0.0f,0.0f, 0.0f);
                      }
                      player1.draw(gl);
                      gl.glPopMatrix();
                      gl.glLoadIdentity();

                      break;

      ...

                  }

          }

      ...

      }
```

Your switch statement for moving the character to the left and implementing two frames of sprite animation is complete.

Moving the Character to the Right

The last case statement you need to complete before the movePlayer1() method is finished is for PLAYER_BANK_RIGHT_1. This case is called when the player wants to move the character to the right-hand side of the screen, in the positive direction of the x axis.

The layout of the case is going to look the same, but you will need to load up different frames from the sprite sheet. First, lay out your model matrix, scale the character vertices, and set up the if . . . else if statement like you did in the PLAYER_BANK_LEFT_1 case.

This if . . . else if statement will have one difference from the statement in the PLAYER_BANK_LEFT_1 case. In the PLAYER_BANK_LEFT_1 case, you tested to see if the current position on the x axis of the vertices was greater than 0, indicating that the character had not gone off the left-hand side of the screen. For the PLAYER_BANK_RIGHT_1 case, you will need to test if the character has reached the furthest right-hand side of the screen.

Under default circumstances, the x axis starts at 0 and ends at 1. However, to make the playable character appear smaller on the screen, you have scaled the x axis to .25. This means the x axis now goes from 0 to 4. You need to test that the playable character has not scrolled further than 4 units to the right. Correct?

No, not entirely.

OpenGL tracks the upper-left corner of the vertices. Therefore, the character would already be off the screen if you tested for the case when it hit 4. You need to take into account the width of the character vertices. The character vertices are 1 unit wide. Testing that the character has not exceeded an x axis value of 3 will keep it on the screen where the player can see it.

```
package com.proandroidgames;

import javax.microedition.khronos.egl.EGLConfig;
import javax.microedition.khronos.opengles.GL10;

import android.opengl.GLSurfaceView.Renderer;

public class SFGameRenderer implements Renderer{

...

        private void movePlayer1(GL10 gl){
                switch (SFEngine.playerFlightAction){

...


                case SFEngine.PLAYER_BANK_RIGHT_1:
                        gl.glMatrixMode(GL10.GL_MODELVIEW);
                        gl.glLoadIdentity();
                        gl.glPushMatrix();
                        gl.glScalef(.25f, .25f, 1f);
                        if (goodGuyBankFrames < SFEngine.PLAYER_FRAMES_BETWEEN_ANI &&
SFEngine.playerBankPosX < 3){

                        }else if (goodGuyBankFrames >=
SFEngine.PLAYER_FRAMES_BETWEEN_ANI && SFEngine.playerBankPosX < 3){

                        }else{
                                gl.glTranslatef(SFEngine.playerBankPosX, 0f, 0f);
                                gl.glMatrixMode(GL10.GL_TEXTURE);
                                gl.glLoadIdentity();
                                gl.glTranslatef(0.0f,0.0f, 0.0f);
                        }
                        player1.draw(gl);
                        gl.glPopMatrix();
                        gl.glLoadIdentity();

                        break;

...
                }

        }

...

}
```

This initial block of code in the PLAYER_BANK_RIGHT_1 case is almost the same as in the PLAYER_BANK_LEFT_1. You are adjusting the model matrix, testing the position of the character on the x axis, and testing the number of game loops frames that have run to tell which frame of sprite animation needs to be displayed.

Now, you can display the first and second frames of right-banking animation in the appropriate places.

Loading the Right-Banking Animation

The first frame of animation that should be displayed when the player banks to the right is in the first row, second position (referring to the sprite sheet in Figure 5–1). Therefore, you need to translate the texture matrix by .25 on the x axis and 0 on the y axis to display this frame.

```
package com.proandroidgames;

import javax.microedition.khronos.egl.EGLConfig;
import javax.microedition.khronos.opengles.GL10;

import android.opengl.GLSurfaceView.Renderer;

public class SFGameRenderer implements Renderer{

...

        private void movePlayer1(GL10 gl){
                switch (SFEngine.playerFlightAction){
...

                case SFEngine.PLAYER_BANK_RIGHT_1:
                        gl.glMatrixMode(GL10.GL_MODELVIEW);
                        gl.glLoadIdentity();
                        gl.glPushMatrix();
                        gl.glScalef(.25f, .25f, 1f);
                        if (goodGuyBankFrames < SFEngine.PLAYER_FRAMES_BETWEEN_ANI &&
SFEngine.playerBankPosX < 3){
                                SFEngine.playerBankPosX += SFEngine.PLAYER_BANK_SPEED;
                                gl.glTranslatef(SFEngine.playerBankPosX, 0f, 0f);
                                gl.glMatrixMode(GL10.GL_TEXTURE);
                                gl.glLoadIdentity();
                                gl.glTranslatef(0.25f,0.0f, 0.0f);
                                goodGuyBankFrames += 1;
                        }else if (goodGuyBankFrames >=
SFEngine.PLAYER_FRAMES_BETWEEN_ANI && SFEngine.playerBankPosX < 3){

                        }else{
                                gl.glTranslatef(SFEngine.playerBankPosX, 0f, 0f);
                                gl.glMatrixMode(GL10.GL_TEXTURE);
                                gl.glLoadIdentity();
                                gl.glTranslatef(0.0f,0.0f, 0.0f);
                        }
                        player1.draw(gl);
```

```
                    gl.glPopMatrix();
                    gl.glLoadIdentity();

                    break;

...
                }

        }

...

}
```

Notice is this code block that the value of PLAYER_BANK_SPEED is added to, rather than subtracted from, the player's current position. This is the key to moving the vertices to the right, rather than the left, on the x axis.

Repeating this code, you need to translate the texture to .50 on the x axis to display the second frame of sprite animation for the right-hand bank.

```
package com.proandroidgames;

import javax.microedition.khronos.egl.EGLConfig;
import javax.microedition.khronos.opengles.GL10;

import android.opengl.GLSurfaceView.Renderer;

public class SFGameRenderer implements Renderer{

...

        private void movePlayer1(GL10 gl){
                switch (SFEngine.playerFlightAction){

...


                case SFEngine.PLAYER_BANK_RIGHT_1:
                        gl.glMatrixMode(GL10.GL_MODELVIEW);
                        gl.glLoadIdentity();
                        gl.glPushMatrix();
                        gl.glScalef(.25f, .25f, 1f);
                        if (goodGuyBankFrames < SFEngine.PLAYER_FRAMES_BETWEEN_ANI &&
SFEngine.playerBankPosX < 3){
                                SFEngine.playerBankPosX += SFEngine.PLAYER_BANK_SPEED;
                                gl.glTranslatef(SFEngine.playerBankPosX, 0f, 0f);
                                gl.glMatrixMode(GL10.GL_TEXTURE);
                                gl.glLoadIdentity();
                                gl.glTranslatef(0.25f,0.0f, 0.0f);
                                goodGuyBankFrames += 1;
                        }else if (goodGuyBankFrames >=
SFEngine.PLAYER_FRAMES_BETWEEN_ANI && SFEngine.playerBankPosX < 3){
                                SFEngine.playerBankPosX += SFEngine.PLAYER_BANK_SPEED;
                                gl.glTranslatef(SFEngine.playerBankPosX, 0f, 0f);
                                gl.glMatrixMode(GL10.GL_TEXTURE);
```

```
                                        gl.glLoadIdentity();
                                        gl.glTranslatef(0.50f,0.0f, 0.0f);
                                }else{

                                        gl.glTranslatef(SFEngine.playerBankPosX, 0f, 0f);
                                        gl.glMatrixMode(GL10.GL_TEXTURE);
                                        gl.glLoadIdentity();
                                        gl.glTranslatef(0.0f,0.0f, 0.0f);
                                }
                                player1.draw(gl);
                                gl.glPopMatrix();
                                gl.glLoadIdentity();

                                break;

        ...

                        }

                }

        ...

        }
```

Your movePlayer1() method is now finished. Your playable character will successfully
move to the left and to the right when the correct action is applied. All you have to do
now is to call the movePlayer1() method from the game loop and create a process to
allow the player to actually move the character.

```java
package com.proandroidgames;

import javax.microedition.khronos.egl.EGLConfig;
import javax.microedition.khronos.opengles.GL10;

import android.opengl.GLSurfaceView.Renderer;

public class SFGameRenderer implements Renderer{


        ...

        @Override
        public void onDrawFrame(GL10 gl) {
                try {
                        Thread.sleep(SFEngine.GAME_THREAD_FPS_SLEEP - loopRunTime);
                } catch (InterruptedException e) {
                        // TODO Auto-generated catch block
                        e.printStackTrace();
                }
                gl.glClear(GL10.GL_COLOR_BUFFER_BIT | GL10.GL_DEPTH_BUFFER_BIT);

                scrollBackground1(gl);
                scrollBackground2(gl);

                movePlayer1(gl);
```

```
                //All other game drawing will be called here

                gl.glEnable(GL10.GL_BLEND);
                gl.glBlendFunc(GL10.GL_ONE, GL10.GL_ONE_MINUS_SRC_ALPHA);

        }
...

}
```

Save and close SFGameRenderer.

In the next section of this chapter, you are going to learn how to listen for a TouchEvent on the screen of an Android device. You will then use that TouchEvent to set the player action, thus moving the character on the screen to the left or to the right.

Moving Your Character Using a Touch Event

You have created the necessary method and calls to move your playable character across the screen. However, as of right now, the player has no way to interact with the game and tell the game loop to make the calls that move the character.

In this section, you will code a simple touch listener that will detect if the player has touched either the right- or left-hand side of the screen. The player will move the character to the left or to the right by touching that side of the screen. The listener will go in the activity that is hosting your game loop, in this case, SFGame.java.

Open SFGame.java, and add an override for the onTouchEvent() method.

```
package com.proandroidgames;

import android.app.Activity;
import android.os.Bundle;
import android.view.MotionEvent;

public class SFGame extends Activity {


...

        @Override
        public boolean onTouchEvent(MotionEvent event) {

        return false;
        }
}
```

The onTouchEvent() is a standard Android event listener that will listen for any touch event occurring within the activity. Because your game is run from the SFGame activity, this is the activity that you must listen for touch events on.

> **TIP:** Don't confuse the game's activity with the game's loop. The game loop is the SFGameRenderer; the Activity that launches it is SFGame.

The onTouchEvent() listener will fire only when a device's screen is touched, swiped, dragged, or released. For this game, you are concerned with only a touch or a release and which side of the screen it happened on. To help you determine this, Android sends a MotionEvent view to the onTouchEvent() listener; it will have everything that you need to determine what kind of touch event fired the listener and where the touch happened on the screen.

Parsing MotionEvent

Your first concern within the onTouchEvent() listener is to get the x and y coordinates of the touch, so you can determine if the touch occurred on the left- or right-hand side of the device screen. The MotionEvent that is passed to the onTouchEvent() listener has getX() and getY() methods that you can use to determine the x and y coordinates of the touch event.

> **NOTE:** The x and y coordinates that you are dealing with in the onTouchEvent() listener are screen coordinates, *not* OpenGL coordinates.

```
package com.proandroidgames;

import android.app.Activity;
import android.os.Bundle;
import android.view.MotionEvent;

public class SFGame extends Activity {

...

        @Override
        public boolean onTouchEvent(MotionEvent event) {
                float x = event.getX();
                float y = event.getY();

                return false;
        }

}
```

Next, you are going to set up a playable area on the screen. That is, you do not want to react to touch events from just anywhere on the screen, so you are going to set up an area at the bottom of the screen that you will react to. The touchable area will be low on the screen, so players can touch it with their thumbs as they hold their devices.

Since the playable character occupies roughly the lower fourth of the device screen, you will set that area up as the area that you will react to.

```
package com.proandroidgames;

import android.app.Activity;
import android.os.Bundle;
import android.view.MotionEvent;

public class SFGame extends Activity {

...

        @Override
        public boolean onTouchEvent(MotionEvent event) {
                float x = event.getX();
                float y = event.getY();
                int height = SFEngine.display.getHeight() / 4;
                int playableArea = SFEngine.display.getHeight() - height;

                return false;
        }

}
```

You now have the location of the touch event and the area in which you want to react to touch events. Use a simple if statement to determine whether or not you should react to this event.

```
package com.proandroidgames;

import android.app.Activity;
import android.os.Bundle;
import android.view.MotionEvent;

public class SFGame extends Activity {

...

        @Override
        public boolean onTouchEvent(MotionEvent event) {
                float x = event.getX();
                float y = event.getY();
                int height = SFEngine.display.getHeight() / 4;
                int playableArea = SFEngine.display.getHeight() - height;
                if (y > playableArea){

                }
                return false;
        }

}
```

MotionEvent has a very useful method called getAction(), which returns to you the type of action that was detected on the screen. For the purposes of this game, you are concerned with the ACTION_UP and ACTION_DOWN actions. These actions indicate the moments when the player's finger initially touched the screen (ACTION_DOWN) and then came back off the screen (ACTION_UP).

Trapping ACTION_UP and ACTION_DOWN

Set up a simple switch statement to act on the ACTION_UP and ACTION_DOWN actions. Be sure to leave out the default case, because you only want to react to these two specific cases.

```
package com.proandroidgames;

import android.app.Activity;
import android.os.Bundle;
import android.view.MotionEvent;

public class SFGame extends Activity {

...

        @Override
        public boolean onTouchEvent(MotionEvent event) {
                float x = event.getX();
                float y = event.getY();
                int height = SFEngine.display.getHeight() / 4;
                int playableArea = SFEngine.display.getHeight() - height;
                if (y > playableArea){
                        switch (event.getAction()){
                        case MotionEvent.ACTION_DOWN:

                                break;
                        case MotionEvent.ACTION_UP:

                                break;
                        }
                }
                return false;
        }

}
```

Earlier in this chapter, you wrote the code to move the character on the screen. This code reacted to three action constants that you created: PLAYER_BANK_LEFT_1, PLAYER_BANK_RIGHT_1, and PLAYER_RELEASE. These actions will be set in the appropriate cases in the onTechEvent().

Let's start with the PLAYER_RELEASE. This case will be set when the player lifts a finger back off the screen, thus triggering an ACTION_UP event.

```
package com.proandroidgames;

import android.app.Activity;
import android.os.Bundle;
import android.view.MotionEvent;
```

```
public class SFGame extends Activity {

...

        @Override
        public boolean onTouchEvent(MotionEvent event) {
                float x = event.getX();
                float y = event.getY();
                int height = SFEngine.display.getHeight() / 4;
                int playableArea = SFEngine.display.getHeight() - height;
                if (y > playableArea){
                        switch (event.getAction()){
                                case MotionEvent.ACTION_DOWN:

                                        break;
                                case MotionEvent.ACTION_UP:
                                        SFEngine.playerFlightAction =
SFEngine.PLAYER_RELEASE;
                                        break;
                        }
                }
                return false;
        }

}
```

Finally, set the `PLAYER_BANK_LEFT_1` and `PLAYER_BANK_RIGHT_1` actions. To do this, you still need to determine if the player touched the right- or left-hand side of the screen. This can easily be determined by comparing the `getX()` value of the `MotionEvent` to the midpoint of the x axis. If the `getX()` is less than the midpoint, the action was on the left; if the `getX()` value is greater than the midpoint, the event happened on the right.

```
package com.proandroidgames;

import android.app.Activity;
import android.os.Bundle;
import android.view.MotionEvent;

public class SFGame extends Activity {

...

        @Override
        public boolean onTouchEvent(MotionEvent event) {
                float x = event.getX();
                float y = event.getY();
                int height = SFEngine.display.getHeight() / 4;
                int playableArea = SFEngine.display.getHeight() - height;
                if (y > playableArea){
                        switch (event.getAction()){
                        case MotionEvent.ACTION_DOWN:
                                if(x < SFEngine.display.getWidth() / 2){
                                        SFEngine.playerFlightAction =
SFEngine.PLAYER_BANK_LEFT_1;
```

```
                               }else{
                                       SFEngine.playerFlightAction =
SFEngine.PLAYER_BANK_RIGHT_1;
                               }
                               break;
                       case MotionEvent.ACTION_UP:
                               SFEngine.playerFlightAction = SFEngine.PLAYER_RELEASE;
                               break;
               }
        }
        return false;
    }

}
```

Save and close your SFGame.java class. You have just completed the user interface (UI) for this game. The player can now touch the right- or left-hand side of the screen to move the character to the left or to the right.

In the final section of this chapter, we will revisit the game thread and the calculation for frames per second.

Adjusting the FPS Delay

In the previous chapter, you created a delay to slow down your game loop and force it to run at 60 frames per second (FPS). This speed is the most desirable one for developers' games to run. However, you may have already begun to realize that this speed is not always achievable.

The more functions that you perform in your game loop, the longer the loop will take to finish, and the slower the game will run. This means that the delay that you created needs to be adjusted or turned off altogether, depending on how slowly the game is running.

Just for comparison, running the game in its current state, with two backgrounds and a playable character, I am achieving about 10 frames per second on the Windows emulator, about 35 frames per second on the Droid X, and roughly 43 frames per second on the Motorola Xoom.

One of the problems is that you are delaying the thread indiscriminately. You need to adjust the thread delay of the game loop to account for the amount of time it takes to run the loop. The following code will determine how long it takes for the loop to run and then subtract that amount from the delay. If the loop takes longer to run than the amount of the delay, the delay is turned off.

```
package com.proandroidgames;

import javax.microedition.khronos.egl.EGLConfig;
import javax.microedition.khronos.opengles.GL10;

import android.opengl.GLSurfaceView.Renderer;
```

```java
public class SFGameRenderer implements Renderer{

        private SFBackground background = new SFBackground();
        private SFBackground background2 = new SFBackground();
        private SFGoodGuy player1 = new SFGoodGuy();

        private int goodGuyBankFrames = 0;
        private long loopStart = 0;
        private long loopEnd = 0;
        private long loopRunTime = 0 ;

        private float bgScroll1;
        private float bgScroll2;

        @Override
        public void onDrawFrame(GL10 gl) {
                loopStart = System.currentTimeMillis();
                try {
                        if (loopRunTime < SFEngine.GAME_THREAD_FPS_SLEEP){
                                Thread.sleep(SFEngine.GAME_THREAD_FPS_SLEEP -
loopRunTime);
                        }
                } catch (InterruptedException e) {
                        // TODO Auto-generated catch block
                        e.printStackTrace();
                }
                gl.glClear(GL10.GL_COLOR_BUFFER_BIT | GL10.GL_DEPTH_BUFFER_BIT);

                scrollBackground1(gl);
                scrollBackground2(gl);

                movePlayer1(gl);

                //All other game drawing will be called here

                gl.glEnable(GL10.GL_BLEND);
                gl.glBlendFunc(GL10.GL_ONE, GL10.GL_ONE_MINUS_SRC_ALPHA);
                loopEnd = System.currentTimeMillis();
                loopRunTime = ((loopEnd - loopStart));

        }
...
```

Compile and run your game. Try to move the character across the screen, and watch for the change in animation.

Summary

In this chapter, you took another big step forward in the *Star Fighter* game. You can now add the following skills to your list of accomplishments:

▪ Create a playable character.

▪ Animate a character with textures from a sprite sheet.

- Detect a touch input on the device's screen.

- Move and animate the character based on a player's touch event.

- Adjusted the FPS rate to get the game to run as quickly as possible.

Chapter 6

Adding the Enemies

Your skill set as an Android game developer is getting much broader. In the previous chapter alone, you added your first playable character, worked with sprite animation, and created a basic listener to allow the player to control the character; for a basic 2-D shooter, your game is really shaping up.

In this chapter, you will be creating a class to help you manage your textures. You will also be creating an enemy class that will be used to create the three different types of enemies in *Star Fighter*. In the next chapter, you will create a basic AI system for these enemies.

Midgame Housekeeping

Remember, the point of this book is to help you through the process of creating a game, from beginning to end. Game creation is not always a linear process. Sometimes, you need to go back and reevaluate things that you have done to optimize the way your game works.

The preceding two chapters focused on teaching you how to load and deal with sprites and sprite sheets. However, with your current code, you are loading a separate sprite sheet for each character. This was the easiest way to *learn* how to use the sprite sheet, but it is by no means the best way to *use* a sprite sheet. In fact, by creating a separate sprite sheet for each character you are almost going against the purpose of a sprite sheet—that is, you should load all of the images for all of characters on to one sprite sheet.

> **TIP:** You can, of course, still use multiple sprite sheets if you have too many sprites to fit on one image. But that should not be a problem with the limited number of characters in this game.

By loading all of the images for all of your game's characters onto one sprite sheet, you will drastically reduce the amount of memory consumed by your game and the amount of processing that OpenGL will have to do to render the game.

That being said, it is time to perform some minor housekeeping in your game code to adapt it to use a common sprite sheet

Creating a Texture Class

You are going to create a common texture class with a loadTexture() method. The loadTexture() method will perform the same function as the loadTexture() method in the SFGoodGuy() class. The difference being that this common class will return an int array that you will be able to pass to all of the instantiated characters.

The first step is to open the SFGoodGuy() class and remove the loadTexture() method (and any variable that supported it). The modified SFGoodGuy() class should look like this when you are finished:

```
package com.proandroidgames;

import java.nio.ByteBuffer;
import java.nio.ByteOrder;
import java.nio.FloatBuffer;

import javax.microedition.khronos.opengles.GL10;

public class SFGoodGuy {

        private FloatBuffer vertexBuffer;
        private FloatBuffer textureBuffer;
        private ByteBuffer indexBuffer;

        private float vertices[] = {
                0.0f, 0.0f, 0.0f,
                1.0f, 0.0f, 0.0f,
                1.0f, 1.0f, 0.0f,
                0.0f, 1.0f, 0.0f,
        };

        private float texture[] = {
                0.0f, 0.0f,
                0.25f, 0.0f,
                0.25f, 0.25f,
                0.0f, 0.25f,
        };

        private byte indices[] = {
                0,1,2,
                0,2,3,
        };

        public SFGoodGuy() {
                ByteBuffer byteBuf = ByteBuffer.allocateDirect(vertices.length * 4);
                byteBuf.order(ByteOrder.nativeOrder());
                vertexBuffer = byteBuf.asFloatBuffer();
                vertexBuffer.put(vertices);
                vertexBuffer.position(0);
                byteBuf = ByteBuffer.allocateDirect(texture.length * 4);
```

```
                byteBuf.order(ByteOrder.nativeOrder());
                textureBuffer = byteBuf.asFloatBuffer();
                textureBuffer.put(texture);
                textureBuffer.position(0);

                indexBuffer = ByteBuffer.allocateDirect(indices.length);
                indexBuffer.put(indices);
                indexBuffer.position(0);
        }

        public void draw(GL10 gl, int[] spriteSheet) {
                gl.glBindTexture(GL10.GL_TEXTURE_2D, spriteSheet[0]);

                gl.glFrontFace(GL10.GL_CCW);
                gl.glEnable(GL10.GL_CULL_FACE);
                gl.glCullFace(GL10.GL_BACK);

                gl.glEnableClientState(GL10.GL_VERTEX_ARRAY);
                gl.glEnableClientState(GL10.GL_TEXTURE_COORD_ARRAY);

                gl.glVertexPointer(3, GL10.GL_FLOAT, 0, vertexBuffer);
                gl.glTexCoordPointer(2, GL10.GL_FLOAT, 0, textureBuffer);

                gl.glDrawElements(GL10.GL_TRIANGLES, indices.length,
GL10.GL_UNSIGNED_BYTE, indexBuffer);

                gl.glDisableClientState(GL10.GL_VERTEX_ARRAY);
                gl.glDisableClientState(GL10.GL_TEXTURE_COORD_ARRAY);
                gl.glDisable(GL10.GL_CULL_FACE);
        }

}
```

> **CAUTION:** When you finish making these changes, depending on the IDE you are using, you will
> begin to get some errors from other areas of your code. Don't worry about them now; you will
> address the errors later in this chapter.

Next, let's create a new common class to load your texture into OpenGL and return an int array. Create a new class in your main package named SFTextures().

```
package com.proandroidgames;

public class SFTextures {

}
```

Now, create a constructor for SFTextures() that accepts a GL10 instance. This instance will be used to initialize the textures. You will also need a textures variable that initializes an int array of two elements.

```
package com.proandroidgames;

import javax.microedition.khronos.opengles.GL10;
```

```
public class SFTextures {

        private int[] textures = new int[1];

        public SFTextures(GL10 gl){


        }

}
```

You need to let OpenGL generate some names for the textures that you are loading. Previously, this was done in the loadTexture() method of the SFGoodGuy() class using the glGenTextures() method. However, because you plan on calling this common textures class multiple times, OpenGL would assign new names to the textures every time you call the load method, which would make keeping track of your textures difficult, if not impossible.

To avoid assigning multiple names to the same textures, you are going to move the glGenTextures() method call to the SFTextures() constructor:

```
package com.proandroidgames;

import javax.microedition.khronos.opengles.GL10;

public class SFTextures {

        private int[] textures = new int[1];

                gl.glGenTextures(1, textures, 0);

        public SFTextures(GL10 gl){

        }

}
```

You need to create a loadTexture() method for SFTextures(). In the SFGoodGuy() and SFBackground() classes, the loadTexture() method was a simple method with no return. To allow you a better way to control the access of your textures, especially when you start loading multiple sprite sheets, create the loadTexture() method of SFTextures() to return an int array.

```
package com.proandroidgames;

import javax.microedition.khronos.opengles.GL10;

public class SFTextures {

        private int[] textures = new int[1];

                gl.glGenTextures(1, textures, 0);
```

```
        public SFTextures(GL10 gl){

        }

        public int[] loadTexture(GL10 gl,int texture, Context context,int textureNumber)
{

        }


}
```

Notice the addition of the textureNumber parameter. While this will be a 1 for now, in the next chapter when you start using this class to load multiple sprite sheets, this will be used to indicate which sheet is being loaded.

The core of the loadTexture() method looks otherwise identical to its counterpart in the SFGoodGuy() class. The only changes—other than the call to glGenTextures() being removed— are that the textureNumber parameter is now used as an array pointed in the glBindTextures() call and loadTextures() now returns the texture's int array when it is finished.

```
package com.proandroidgames;

import java.io.IOException;
import java.io.InputStream;

import javax.microedition.khronos.opengles.GL10;

import android.content.Context;
import android.graphics.Bitmap;
import android.graphics.BitmapFactory;
import android.opengl.GLUtils;


public class SFTextures {

        private int[] textures = new int[1];

                gl.glGenTextures(1, textures, 0);

        public SFTextures(GL10 gl){

        }

        public int[] loadTexture(GL10 gl,int texture, Context context,int textureNumber)
{
                InputStream imagestream =
context.getResources().openRawResource(texture);
                Bitmap bitmap = null;
                try {

                        bitmap = BitmapFactory.decodeStream(imagestream);
```

```
            }catch(Exception e){

            }finally {

                    try {
                            imagestream.close();
                            imagestream = null;
                    } catch (IOException e) {
                    }

            }

            gl.glBindTexture(GL10.GL_TEXTURE_2D, textures[textureNumber - 1]);

            gl.glTexParameterf(GL10.GL_TEXTURE_2D, GL10.GL_TEXTURE_MIN_FILTER,
GL10.GL_NEAREST);
            gl.glTexParameterf(GL10.GL_TEXTURE_2D, GL10.GL_TEXTURE_MAG_FILTER,
GL10.GL_LINEAR);

            gl.glTexParameterf(GL10.GL_TEXTURE_2D, GL10.GL_TEXTURE_WRAP_S,
GL10.GL_CLAMP_TO_EDGE);
            gl.glTexParameterf(GL10.GL_TEXTURE_2D, GL10.GL_TEXTURE_WRAP_T,
GL10.GL_CLAMP_TO_EDGE);

            GLUtils.texImage2D(GL10.GL_TEXTURE_2D, 0, bitmap, 0);

            bitmap.recycle();

            return textures;

    }

}
```

Your common texture class is finished and ready to use. Save SFTextures() and
SFGoodGuy(), and close them for now. Again, you should now see errors coming from
the SFGameSFGameRenderer() class. Ignore these errors for now; you will take care of
them as you move through this chapter.

In the next section, you will be creating the class that will load up your enemy ships and
prepare them for battle against the player.

Creating the Enemy Class

No matter what games you may have played, there is surely one thing in common with
all of them: there is never just one enemy to fight. Having a single enemy to fight in a
game would result in a very quick and very boring game.

In *Star Fighter*, you will be creating 30 enemies for the player to fight on the screen. We
outlined the story that *Star Fighter* is based on in Chapter 2. According to this story,
three different types of enemies are mentioned. In this section of the chapter, you will

create the class that these three types of enemies will be based on and the 30 enemies instantiated from.

Adding a New Sprite Sheet

The first thing that you need to add to your project is a new sprite sheet. You learned about the importance and purpose of sprite sheets to 2-D gaming in the previous chapter. Now that you have made provisions in your code to use a common sprite sheet for all of the character sprites, you can add it to your project. Figure 6–1 illustrates the common sprite sheet.

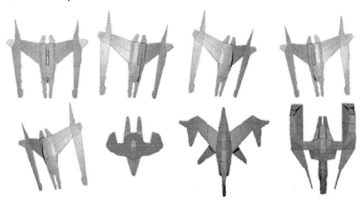

Figure 6–1. *The common sprite sheet*

Simply remove the good_guy sprite sheet that was in the drawable folder and add this one.

> **NOTE:** Notice that the player's characters are in the same position on this sprite sheet as they were on the last. Therefore, you will not have to change any of the texture positioning for the player's character.

Next, you need to edit the SFEngine class to add the constants and variables that you will be using in this chapter. There are quite a few of them this time. You will need 17 constants to help you control the enemy AI alone. Some of these you may not use until the next chapter, but adding them now is a good idea:

```
public static int CHARACTER_SHEET = R.drawable.character_sprite;
public static int TOTAL_INTERCEPTORS = 10;
public static int TOTAL_SCOUTS = 15;
public static int TOTAL_WARSHIPS = 5;
public static float INTERCEPTOR_SPEED = SCROLL_BACKGROUND_1 * 4f;
public static float SCOUT_SPEED = SCROLL_BACKGROUND_1 * 6f;
public static float WARSHIP_SPEED = SCROLL_BACKGROUND_2 * 4f;
public static final int TYPE_INTERCEPTOR = 1;
public static final int TYPE_SCOUT = 2;
public static final int TYPE_WARSHIP = 3;
```

```java
public static final int ATTACK_RANDOM = 0;
public static final int ATTACK_RIGHT = 1;
public static final int ATTACK_LEFT = 2;
public static final float BEZIER_X_1 = 0f;
public static final float BEZIER_X_2 = 1f;
public static final float BEZIER_X_3 = 2.5f;
public static final float BEZIER_X_4 = 3f;
public static final float BEZIER_Y_1 = 0f;
public static final float BEZIER_Y_2 = 2.4f;
public static final float BEZIER_Y_3 = 1.5f;
public static final float BEZIER_Y_4 = 2.6f;
```

Since the enemies that you add to the screen will start off as a class, much like the background and the playable character, add a new class to your main package named SFEnemy(). This class will be used to bring your enemies into the game.

> **TIP:** Even though you will have 30 total enemies of three different types, they will all be instantiated from the same SFEnemy() class.

Creating the SFEnemy Class

In this section, you will create the class that will be used to spawn all three types of enemies in the *Star Fighter* game. Add a new class to your project named SFEnemy():

```java
package com.proandroidgames;

public class SFEnemy {

}
```

Your enemy needs some properties that will help you as you begin to create the AI logic. You will need properties that you can use to set or get the enemy's current x and y positions, the t factor (used to fly the enemy in a curve), and the x and y increments to reach a target.

```java
package com.proandroidgames;

public class SFEnemy {
        public float posY = 0f; //the x position of the enemy
        public float posX = 0f; //the y position of the enemy
        public float posT = 0f; //the t used in calculating a Bezier curve
        public float incrementXToTarget = 0f; //the x increment to reach a potential
target
        public float incrementYToTarget = 0f; //the y increment to reach a potential
target

}
```

You will also need properties that will let you set or get the direction from which the enemy will attack, whether or not the enemy has been destroyed, and what type of enemy this instantiation represents.

```
package com.proandroidgames;

public class SFEnemy {
        public float posY = 0f; //the x position of the enemy
        public float posX = 0f; //the y position of the enemy
        public float posT = 0f; //the t used in calculating a Bezier curve
        public float posXToTarget = 0f; //the x increment to reach a potential target
        public float posYToTarget = 0f; //the y increment to reach a potential target

        public int attackDirection = 0; //the attack direction of the ship
        public boolean isDestroyed = false; //has this ship been destroyed?
        public int enemyType = 0; //what type of enemy is this?


}
```

The next three properties that your enemy class needs are an indicator to let you know if
it has locked on to a target (this will be crucial to your AI logic) and two coordinates that
will represent the lock on position of the target.

```
package com.proandroidgames;

public class SFEnemy {
        public float posY = 0f; //the x position of the enemy
        public float posX = 0f; //the y position of the enemy
        public float posT = 0f; //the t used in calculating a Bezier curve
        public float posXToTarget = 0f; //the x increment to reach a potential target
        public float posYToTarget = 0f; //the y increment to reach a potential target
        public int attackDirection = 0; //the attack direction of the ship
        public boolean isDestroyed = false; //has this ship been destroyed?
        public int enemyType = 0; //what type of enemy is this
        public boolean isLockedOn = false; //had the enemy locked on to a target?
        public float lockOnPosX = 0f; //x position of the target
        public float lockOnPosY = 0f; //y position of the target
}
```

Next, give your SFEnemy() class a constructor that takes in two int parameters. The first
parameter will be used to represent the type of enemy that should be
created:TYPE_INTERCEPTOR,TYPE_SCOUT, or TYPE_WARSHIP. The second parameter will be
used to indicate from which direction on the screen the particular enemy will be
attacking: ATTACK_RANDOM,ATTACK_RIGHT, or ATTACK_LEFT.

```
package com.proandroidgames;

public class SFEnemy {

...

        public SFEnemy(int type, int direction) {

        }

}
```

In the constructor for SFEnemy(), you need to set the enemy type based on the type int that is passed in to the constructor. You will also set the direction. Seeing these parameters will let you make decisions in your game loop based on the enemy's type and direction of motion.

```
 package com.proandroidgames;

public class SFEnemy {

    ...

        public SFEnemy(int type, int direction) {
            enemyType = type;
            attackDirection = direction;


        }

    }
```

The story for *Star Fighter* (in Chapter 2) described the attack characteristics for the three different enemies. The scout flies in a swift but predictable pattern, the interceptor locks onto and flies directly at the player's character, and the warship maneuvers in a random pattern. Each of these ships is going to need to start from a specific point on the screen.

Typically in scrolling shooters, the enemies start from a point on the y axis that is off the screen and then scroll down toward the player. Therefore, the next thing you will do in your constructor is to establish a y axis starting point for the enemies.

Android's random number generator is a great way to pick that starting point. The Android random number generator will generate a number between 0 and 1. Your enemy's y axis, however, is from 0 to 4. Multiply the number created by the random number generator by 4, and the result will be a valid y axis position on the screen. Add 4 to the valid y position to then push that starting point off the screen.

```
package com.proandroidgames;

public class SFEnemy {

    ...


private Random randomPos = new Random();
        public SFEnemy(int type, int direction) {
            enemyType = type;
            attackDirection = direction;
            posY = (randomPos.nextFloat() * 4) + 4;

        }

    }
```

That takes care of the y axis; now, you need to establish an x axis position. Take a look at the constants that you created in SFEngine. Three represent from where on the x axis an enemy could be attacking: ATTACK_LEFT, ATTACK_RANDOM, and ATTACK_RIGHT. The left-hand x-axis value is 0. The right-hand x-axis value is 3 (subtract 1 unit from 4 to account for the size of the sprite).

You can use a case statement to assign the x-axis starting point based on what attack direction is passed into the constructor.

```
package com.proandroidgames;

public class SFEnemy {

    ...

        public SFEnemy(int type, int direction) {
                enemyType = type;
                attackDirection = direction;
                posY = (randomPos.nextFloat() * 4) + 4;
                switch(attackDirection){
                        case SFEngine.ATTACK_LEFT:
                                posX = 0;
                                break;
                        case SFEngine.ATTACK_RANDOM:
                                posX = randomPos.nextFloat() * 3;
                                break;
                        case SFEngine.ATTACK_RIGHT:
                                posX = 3;
                                break;
                }


        }


}
```

The last variable that you need to establish is the posT. Don't worry about what posT does right now; you will discover that later in this chapter. Set posT to the value of SFEngine.SCOUT_SPEED.

```
package com.proandroidgames;

public class SFEnemy {

    ...

        public SFEnemy(int type, int direction) {
                enemyType = type;
                attackDirection = direction;
                posY = (randomPos.nextFloat() * 4) + 4;
                switch(attackDirection){
                        case SFEngine.ATTACK_LEFT:
                                posX = 0;
                                break;
                        case SFEngine.ATTACK_RANDOM:
                                posX = randomPos.nextFloat() * 3;
                                break;
                        case SFEngine.ATTACK_RIGHT:
                                posX = 3;
```

```
                                    break;
                        }
                posT = SFEngine.SCOUT_SPEED;

            }

    }
```

Two of the enemy types that you can create, the interceptor and the warship, will travel in diagonal, but straight, lines. The code to generate those attack paths will be handled in the game loop, because it is relatively easy to guide an object in a straight line. The scout enemy type, on the other hand, will move in a pattern known as a Bezier curve. In the next section, you will create the methods that help the enemy fly in a curve.

The Bezier Curve

While you may not know it by name, you will most likely have seen a Bezier curve before. Figure 6–2 illustrates what a Bezier curve looks like.

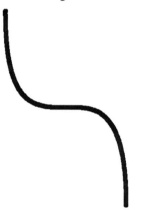

Figure 6–2. *A quadratic Bezier curve*

For the scout to fly in a quadratic Bezier curve from the top to the bottom of the screen, you will need two methods: one to get you the next x axis value on the Bezier curve and one to give you the next y axis value on the Bezier curve. Each time you call these methods, you will be give the next point on the x and y axes that the particular enemy needs to be moved to.

Luckily, plotting points on a Bezier curve is fairly simple. To construct a quadratic Bezier curve, you need four Cartesian points: a start, an end, and two points somewhere in between for the curve to wrap around. These points will never change in the *Star Fighter* game. Every scout will follow the same curve, from either the left or right. Therefore, eight constants were created in SFEngine to represent the four quadratic Bezier curve points on each axis.

The key value in plotting the points is the t factor The t factor tells the formula where on the curve you are, thus allowing the formula to calculate the x or y coordinate for that single position. Because your ships will be moving at a predefined speed, you will use that value as the seed value for t.

> **TIP:** If you do not understand the math behind the formulas in this section, there are many great resources for Bezier curves, including the following Wikipedia page:
> http://en.wikipedia.org/wiki/Bézier_curve.

Create two methods in your SFEnemy() class: one to get the next x axis value and one to get the next y axis value.

```
package com.proandroidgames;

public class SFEnemy {

...

        public SFEnemy(int type, int direction) {

...

        }

        public float getNextScoutX(){

        }
        public float getNextScoutY(){

        }

}
```

Here is the formula to find a point on a quadratic Bezier curve on the y axis (replace the y with x to find the values on the x axis):

$$(y_1*(t^3)) + (y_2 * 3 * (t^2) * (1-t)) + (y_3 * 3 * t * (1-t)^2) + (y_4* (1-t)^3)$$

Use this formula in your getNextScoutY() method with the correct variables.

```
package com.proandroidgames;

public class SFEnemy {

...

        public SFEnemy(int type, int direction) {

...

        }

        public float getNextScoutX(){

        }

        public float getNextScoutY(){
```

```
                return (float)((SFEngine.BEZIER_Y_1*(posT*posT*posT)) +
(SFEngine.BEZIER_Y_2 * 3 * (posT * posT) * (1-posT)) + (SFEngine.BEZIER_Y_3 * 3 * posT *
((1-posT) * (1-posT))) + (SFEngine.BEZIER_Y_4 * ((1-posT) * (1-posT) * (1-posT))));

        }

}
```

Use this same formula for the x axis, with one minor change. You will need to reverse the formula if the enemy is attacking from the left-hand side of the screen as opposed to the right.

```
package com.proandroidgames;

public class SFEnemy {

    …

        public SFEnemy(int type, int direction) {

        …

        }

        public float getNextScoutX(){
                if (attackDirection == SFEngine.ATTACK_LEFT){
                        return (float)((SFEngine.BEZIER_X_4*(posT*posT*posT)) +
(SFEngine.BEZIER_X_3 * 3 * (posT * posT) * (1-posT)) + (SFEngine.BEZIER_X_2 * 3 * posT *
((1-posT) * (1-posT))) + (SFEngine.BEZIER_X_1 * ((1-posT) * (1-posT) * (1-posT))));
                }else{
                        return (float)((SFEngine.BEZIER_X_1*(posT*posT*posT)) +
(SFEngine.BEZIER_X_2 * 3 * (posT * posT) * (1-posT)) + (SFEngine.BEZIER_X_3 * 3 * posT *
((1-posT) * (1-posT))) + (SFEngine.BEZIER_X_4 * ((1-posT) * (1-posT) * (1-posT))));
                }

        }

        public float getNextScoutY(){
                return (float)((SFEngine.BEZIER_Y_1*(posT*posT*posT)) +
(SFEngine.BEZIER_Y_2 * 3 * (posT * posT) * (1-posT)) + (SFEngine.BEZIER_Y_3 * 3 * posT *
((1-posT) * (1-posT))) + (SFEngine.BEZIER_Y_4 * ((1-posT) * (1-posT) * (1-posT))));
        }

}
```

Notice, when calculating for the right-hand side of the x axis, that the values are x_1, x_2, x_3, and x_4— from the left, the points are used in the opposite order: x_4, x_3, x_2, and x_1.

The remainder of the SFEnemy class should look the same as the SFGoodGuy class, taking into account the changes made to use the new common sprite sheets.

```
package com.proandroidgames;

import java.nio.ByteBuffer;
import java.nio.ByteOrder;
import java.nio.FloatBuffer;
import java.util.Random;
```

```java
import javax.microedition.khronos.opengles.GL10;

public class SFEnemy {

        public float posY = 0f;
        public float posX = 0f;
        public float posT = 0f;
        public float incrementXToTarget = 0f;
        public float incrementYToTarget = 0f;
        public int attackDirection = 0;
        public boolean isDestroyed = false;

        public int enemyType = 0;

        public boolean isLockedOn = false;
        public float lockOnPosX = 0f;
        public float lockOnPosY = 0f;

        private Random randomPos = new Random();

        private FloatBuffer vertexBuffer;
        private FloatBuffer textureBuffer;
        private ByteBuffer indexBuffer;

        private float vertices[] = {
                0.0f, 0.0f, 0.0f,
                1.0f, 0.0f, 0.0f,
                1.0f, 1.0f, 0.0f,
                0.0f, 1.0f, 0.0f,
        };

        private float texture[] = {
                0.0f, 0.0f,
                0.25f, 0.0f,
                0.25f, 0.25f,
                0.0f, 0.25f,
        };

        private byte indices[] = {
                0,1,2,
                0,2,3,
        };

        public SFEnemy(int type, int direction) {
                enemyType = type;
                attackDirection = direction;
                posY = (randomPos.nextFloat() * 4) + 4;
                switch(attackDirection){
                        case SFEngine.ATTACK_LEFT:
                                posX = 0;
                        break;
                        case SFEngine.ATTACK_RANDOM:
                                posX = randomPos.nextFloat() * 3;
                        break;
                        case SFEngine.ATTACK_RIGHT:
```

```java
                            posX = 3;
                    break;
            }
            posT = SFEngine.SCOUT_SPEED;

            ByteBuffer byteBuf = ByteBuffer.allocateDirect(vertices.length * 4);
            byteBuf.order(ByteOrder.nativeOrder());
            vertexBuffer = byteBuf.asFloatBuffer();
            vertexBuffer.put(vertices);
            vertexBuffer.position(0);

            byteBuf = ByteBuffer.allocateDirect(texture.length * 4);
            byteBuf.order(ByteOrder.nativeOrder());
            textureBuffer = byteBuf.asFloatBuffer();
            textureBuffer.put(texture);
            textureBuffer.position(0);

            indexBuffer = ByteBuffer.allocateDirect(indices.length);
            indexBuffer.put(indices);
            indexBuffer.position(0);
    }

    public float getNextScoutX(){
            if (attackDirection == SFEngine.ATTACK_LEFT){
                    return (float)((SFEngine.BEZIER_X_4*(posT*posT*posT)) +
(SFEngine.BEZIER_X_3 * 3 * (posT * posT) * (1-posT)) + (SFEngine.BEZIER_X_2 * 3 * posT *
((1-posT) * (1-posT))) + (SFEngine.BEZIER_X_1 * ((1-posT) * (1-posT) * (1-posT))));
            }else{
                    return (float)((SFEngine.BEZIER_X_1*(posT*posT*posT)) +
(SFEngine.BEZIER_X_2 * 3 * (posT * posT) * (1-posT)) + (SFEngine.BEZIER_X_3 * 3 * posT *
((1-posT) * (1-posT))) + (SFEngine.BEZIER_X_4 * ((1-posT) * (1-posT) * (1-posT))));
            }

    }

    public float getNextScoutY(){
            return (float)((SFEngine.BEZIER_Y_1*(posT*posT*posT)) +
(SFEngine.BEZIER_Y_2 * 3 * (posT * posT) * (1-posT)) + (SFEngine.BEZIER_Y_3 * 3 * posT *
((1-posT) * (1-posT))) + (SFEngine.BEZIER_Y_4 * ((1-posT) * (1-posT) * (1-posT))));
            }

    public void draw(GL10 gl, int[] spriteSheet) {
            gl.glBindTexture(GL10.GL_TEXTURE_2D, spriteSheet[0]);

            gl.glFrontFace(GL10.GL_CCW);
            gl.glEnable(GL10.GL_CULL_FACE);
            gl.glCullFace(GL10.GL_BACK);

            gl.glEnableClientState(GL10.GL_VERTEX_ARRAY);
            gl.glEnableClientState(GL10.GL_TEXTURE_COORD_ARRAY);

            gl.glVertexPointer(3, GL10.GL_FLOAT, 0, vertexBuffer);
            gl.glTexCoordPointer(2, GL10.GL_FLOAT, 0, textureBuffer);
```

```
            gl.glDrawElements(GL10.GL_TRIANGLES, indices.length,
GL10.GL_UNSIGNED_BYTE, indexBuffer);

            gl.glDisableClientState(GL10.GL_VERTEX_ARRAY);
            gl.glDisableClientState(GL10.GL_TEXTURE_COORD_ARRAY);
            gl.glDisable(GL10.GL_CULL_FACE);
        }


}
```

You now have a working class from which you can spawn all of the enemies in your game. Save the SFEnemy() class. In the next chapter, you will begin to create the AI for your enemies.

Summary

In this chapter, you took another major step forward in your skill set. A lot of work has gone into creating the enemies for your game, and there is still more to do. The following list describes what you have learned in this chapter, and you will expand on what you have learned in Chapter 7:

- Create a common texture class to hold a large sprite sheet.

- Create an array to hold all of the game's enemies for easier processing.

- Create the SFEnemy() class for spawning three different enemies.

- Create method for moving your enemy in a Bezier curve.

Adding Basic Enemy Artificial Intelligence

The artificial intelligence (AI) of the enemy will define how the enemy attacks the player and how easy or difficult the game is for the player to win. It would be easy to create an AI that anticipates every move of the player by intercepting the listener calls from the player to touchListener. However, that would not make a fun experience for the player, and your game would not be very fulfilling. The enemies that you created in the preceding chapter need some kind of plan of attack by which to engage the player and create a satisfying gaming experience.

In this chapter, you are going to add the three distinct AIs for the three different enemy types that were discussed in Chapter 2 and created in Chapter 6: the interceptors, scouts, and warships. On the surface this task may seem easy given what you learned in the last chapter, but the fact is that creating the enemies is more difficult than creating the playable character. Why? Playable characters do not have to think; that is what the player does. The enemies, on the other hand, need at least a basic AI to guide them through the game.

Getting the Enemies Ready for AI

You'll need to first initialize the enemies and their textures before you can deal with the AI. So, to begin, open and edit the game loop, SFGameRenderer(). You need to add an array that will hold all of the enemies in the game. To determine the number of enemies, add the values for TOTAL_INTECEPTORS, TOTAL_SCOUTS, and TOTAL_WARSHIPS (minus 1 to account for the zero-based array).

```
package com.proandroidgames;

import java.util.Random;

import javax.microedition.khronos.egl.EGLConfig;
import javax.microedition.khronos.opengles.GL10;
```

```
import android.opengl.GLSurfaceView.Renderer;

public class  SFGameRenderer implements Renderer{
        private SFBackground background = new SFBackground();
        private SFBackground background2 = new SFBackground();
        private SFGoodGuy player1 = new SFGoodGuy();

        private SFEnemy[] enemies = new SFEnemy[SFEngine.TOTAL_INTERCEPTORS +
SFEngine.TOTAL_SCOUTS + SFEngine.TOTAL_WARSHIPS - 1];

        private int goodGuyBankFrames = 0;
        private long loopStart = 0;
        private long loopEnd = 0;
        private long loopRunTime = 0 ;

        private float bgScroll1;
        private float bgScroll2;

    ...

}
```

Next, create a new instantiation of the SFTextures class and a new int array to hold the common sprite sheets. For now, the spriteSheets[] array will contain one element. In the next chapter, you will change this array so it holds more.

> **TIP:** You could go even further and modify the spriteSheets[] array and SFBackground()
> to hold the textures for the background as well as the sprite sheets. Doing so would be easy and
> will gain you more optimization.

```
public class  SFGameRenderer implements Renderer{

    ...


        private SFEnemy[] enemies = new SFEnemy[SFEngine.TOTAL_INTERCEPTORS +
SFEngine.TOTAL_SCOUTS + SFEngine.TOTAL_WARSHIPS - 1];
        private SFTextures textureLoader;
        private int[] spriteSheets = new int[1];

        private int goodGuyBankFrames = 0;
        private long loopStart = 0;
        private long loopEnd = 0;
        private long loopRunTime = 0 ;

        private float bgScroll1;
        private float bgScroll2;

    ...

}
```

Now, you have an array to hold your enemies but no enemies to put in it. You need three private methods to fill your array: one each for interceptors, scouts, and warships.

```
;


public class  SFGameRenderer implements Renderer{

…

        private SFEnemy[] enemies = new SFEnemy[SFEngine.TOTAL_INTERCEPTORS +
SFEngine.TOTAL_SCOUTS + SFEngine.TOTAL_WARSHIPS - 1];
        private SFTextures textureLoader;
        private int[] spriteSheets = new int[2];

...

        private void initializeInterceptors(){

        }

        private void initializeScouts(){

        }

        private void initializeWarships(){

        }

...

}
```

Creating Each Enemy's Logic

Use a simple for loop to instantiate a new enemy of the corresponding type, and add it to the array. For example, in the initializeInterceptors() method, create a for loop that counts up to the value of TOTAL_INTERCEPTORS. This loop will instantiate a new enemy of the type TYPE_INTERCEPTOR and add it to the array.

```
public class  SFGameRenderer implements Renderer{

…

        private SFEnemy[] enemies = new SFEnemy[SFEngine.TOTAL_INTERCEPTORS +
SFEngine.TOTAL_SCOUTS + SFEngine.TOTAL_WARSHIPS - 1];
        private SFTextures textureLoader;
        private int[] spriteSheets = new int[2];

;

...

        private void initializeInterceptors(){

                for (int x = 0; x<SFEngine.TOTAL_INTERCEPTORS -1 ; x++){
```

```
                                 SFEnemy interceptor = new SFEnemy(SFEngine.TYPE_INTERCEPTOR,
        SFEngine.ATTACK_RANDOM);
                                 enemies[x] = interceptor;
                        }

                }

            private void initializeScouts(){

            }

            private void initializeWarships(){

            }

...

}
```

Use this same loop logic on the warships.

```
public class  SFGameRenderer implements Renderer{

...

        private SFEnemy[] enemies = new SFEnemy[SFEngine.TOTAL_INTERCEPTORS +
        SFEngine.TOTAL_SCOUTS + SFEngine.TOTAL_WARSHIPS - 1];
        private SFTextures textureLoader;
        private int[] spriteSheets = new int[2];


...

        private void initializeInterceptors(){

                for (int x = 0; x<SFEngine.TOTAL_INTERCEPTORS -1 ; x++){
                        SFEnemy interceptor = new SFEnemy(SFEngine.TYPE_INTERCEPTOR,
        SFEngine.ATTACK_RANDOM);
                                enemies[x] = interceptor;
                        }

                }

            private void initializeScouts(){

            }

            private void initializeWarships(){

                        for (int x = SFEngine.TOTAL_INTERCEPTORS + SFEngine.TOTAL_SCOUTS -1;
        x<SFEngine.TOTAL_INTERCEPTORS + SFEngine.TOTAL_SCOUTS + SFEngine.TOTAL_WARSHIPS -1;
        x++){
                                SFEnemy interceptor = new SFEnemy(SFEngine.TYPE_WARSHIP,
        SFEngine.ATTACK_RANDOM);
                                enemies[x] = interceptor;
```

```
            }
        }

...

}
```

The interceptors and the warships both attack from random directions. However, the scouts will attack from either the right or left. Therefore, in the loop that instantiates the scouts, split the load in half, and instantiate half from the right and half from the left.

```
package com.proandroidgames;


public class  SFGameRenderer implements Renderer{

...
        private SFEnemy[] enemies = new SFEnemy[SFEngine.TOTAL_INTERCEPTORS +
SFEngine.TOTAL_SCOUTS + SFEngine.TOTAL_WARSHIPS - 1];
        private SFTextures textureLoader;
        private int[] spriteSheets = new int[2];


...

        private void initializeInterceptors(){

                for (int x = 0; x<SFEngine.TOTAL_INTERCEPTORS -1 ; x++){
                        SFEnemy interceptor = new SFEnemy(SFEngine.TYPE_INTERCEPTOR,
SFEngine.ATTACK_RANDOM);
                        enemies[x] = interceptor;
                }

        }

        private void initializeScouts(){

                for (int x = SFEngine.TOTAL_INTERCEPTORS -1;
x<SFEngine.TOTAL_INTERCEPTORS + SFEngine.TOTAL_SCOUTS -1; x++){
                        SFEnemy interceptor;
                        if (x>=(SFEngine.TOTAL_INTERCEPTORS + SFEngine.TOTAL_SCOUTS) / 2
){
                                interceptor = new SFEnemy(SFEngine.TYPE_SCOUT,
SFEngine.ATTACK_RIGHT);
                        }else{
                                interceptor = new SFEnemy(SFEngine.TYPE_SCOUT,
SFEngine.ATTACK_LEFT);
                        }
                        enemies[x] = interceptor;
                }

        }
```

```
        private void initializeWarships(){

                for (int x = SFEngine.TOTAL_INTERCEPTORS + SFEngine.TOTAL_SCOUTS -1;
x<SFEngine.TOTAL_INTERCEPTORS + SFEngine.TOTAL_SCOUTS + SFEngine.TOTAL_WARSHIPS -1;
x++){
                        SFEnemy interceptor = new SFEnemy(SFEngine.TYPE_WARSHIP,
SFEngine.ATTACK_RANDOM);
                        enemies[x] = interceptor;
                }

        }

...

}
```

Initializing the Enemies

You have your methods to initialize your enemies. All of your other game loop
initialization has taken place in the onSurfaceCreated() method of SFGameRenderer.
Therefore, it stands to reason that the new initialization methods you just created will
also be called from here.

```
public class  SFGameRenderer implements Renderer{

    ...

        private SFEnemy[] enemies = new SFEnemy[SFEngine.TOTAL_INTERCEPTORS +
SFEngine.TOTAL_SCOUTS + SFEngine.TOTAL_WARSHIPS - 1];
        private SFTextures textureLoader;
        private int[] spriteSheets = new int[2];


    ...

        private void initializeInterceptors(){

                for (int x = 0; x<SFEngine.TOTAL_INTERCEPTORS -1 ; x++){
                        SFEnemy interceptor = new SFEnemy(SFEngine.TYPE_INTERCEPTOR,
SFEngine.ATTACK_RANDOM);
                        enemies[x] = interceptor;
                }

        }

        private void initializeScouts(){

                for (int x = SFEngine.TOTAL_INTERCEPTORS -1;
x<SFEngine.TOTAL_INTERCEPTORS + SFEngine.TOTAL_SCOUTS -1; x++){
                        SFEnemy interceptor;
                        if (x>=(SFEngine.TOTAL_INTERCEPTORS + SFEngine.TOTAL_SCOUTS) / 2
){
```

```
                                interceptor = new SFEnemy(SFEngine.TYPE_SCOUT,
SFEngine.ATTACK_RIGHT);
                    }else{
                                interceptor = new SFEnemy(SFEngine.TYPE_SCOUT,
SFEngine.ATTACK_LEFT);
                    }
                    enemies[x] = interceptor;
                }

        }

        private void initializeWarships(){

                for (int x = SFEngine.TOTAL_INTERCEPTORS + SFEngine.TOTAL_SCOUTS -1;
x<SFEngine.TOTAL_INTERCEPTORS + SFEngine.TOTAL_SCOUTS + SFEngine.TOTAL_WARSHIPS -1;
x++){
                    SFEnemy interceptor = new SFEnemy(SFEngine.TYPE_WARSHIP,
SFEngine.ATTACK_RANDOM);
                    enemies[x] = interceptor;
                }

        }

...

        @Override
        public void onSurfaceCreated(GL10 gl, EGLConfig config) {
                initializeInterceptors();
                initializeScouts();
                initializeWarships();

                gl.glEnable(GL10.GL_TEXTURE_2D);
                gl.glClearDepthf(1.0f);
                gl.glEnable(GL10.GL_DEPTH_TEST);
                gl.glDepthFunc(GL10.GL_LEQUAL);

                background.loadTexture(gl,SFEngine.BACKGROUND_LAYER_ONE,
SFEngine.context);
                background2.loadTexture(gl,SFEngine.BACKGROUND_LAYER_TWO,
SFEngine.context);
        }

}
```

Loading the Sprite Sheet

With the enemies[] array initialized, you can focus on the sprite sheet. Recall that you created a common texture method that will return the OpenGL assigned names of all textures assigned in an int array. This int array of OpenGL names is going to be held in the spriteSheets[] array.

Instantiate your textureLoader() method. After textureLoader() is instantiated, call the loadTexture() method, passing it the CHARACTER_SHEET, and assign the return to the spriteSheets[] array.

```
public class  SFGameRenderer implements Renderer{

...

        @Override
        public void onSurfaceCreated(GL10 gl, EGLConfig config) {
                initializeInterceptors();
                initializeScouts();
                initializeWarships();
                textureLoader = new SFTextures(gl);
                spriteSheets = textureLoader.loadTexture(gl, SFEngine.CHARACTER_SHEET,
SFEngine.context, 1);

                gl.glEnable(GL10.GL_TEXTURE_2D);
                gl.glClearDepthf(1.0f);
                gl.glEnable(GL10.GL_DEPTH_TEST);
                gl.glDepthFunc(GL10.GL_LEQUAL);

                background.loadTexture(gl,SFEngine.BACKGROUND_LAYER_ONE,
SFEngine.context);
                background2.loadTexture(gl,SFEngine.BACKGROUND_LAYER_TWO,
SFEngine.context);
        }

}
```

Your initialization of the enemies and their textures is complete. 3+39.```

+It is time to move on to the AI logic. Let's start with the interceptors.

Reviewing the AI

The description of the interceptor AI sounds complicated, but in reality, it is the easiest of the three enemies. The interceptor will start off moving in a straight line down the y axis. At some point along the y axis, it will lock on to the player's ship and fly directly at those coordinates in an effort to ram the player's ship.

The way you will accomplish this is by subtracting a predefined amount, INTERCEPTOR_SPEED, from the y axis position to slowly move the interceptor down the screen. Because the interceptor could be at any random point above the visible edge of the screen, you have to wait for it to be visible before it can lock on to the enemy. Once the interceptor has reached this point, you will then pass it the x and y coordinates of the player's ship at that moment. Finally, you will use a simple slope formula to move the Interceptor toward these coordinates.

Creating the moveEnemy() Method

The first step to adding some enemy AI is to create a moveEnemy() method that will hold all of the AI logic for your enemies. Just like the movePlayer1() method, the moveEnemy() method will be called by the game loop to update the positions of the enemy ships.

```
package com.proandroidgames;

import java.util.Random;

import javax.microedition.khronos.egl.EGLConfig;
import javax.microedition.khronos.opengles.GL10;

import android.opengl.GLSurfaceView.Renderer;

public class  SFGameRenderer implements Renderer{

...

        private void moveEnemy(GL10 gl){

        }

...

}
```

The moveEnemy() method will update all of your enemies in one call. Addressing all of your enemies in one call is always the best way to approach updating a large amount of nonplayable characters. Doing so can save you precious processor cycles.

Creating an enemies[] Array Loop

You want to create a for loop within the moveEnemy() method that will be able to cycle through each live enemy in the enemies[] array. By limiting the core of your process to only those enemies that have not been destroyed, you take care of two things in your game. First, you ensure that you are not drawing enemies that should no longer be on the screen. Second, you ensure that you are not wasting cycles on enemies that would not have any moves to be processed.

```
public class  SFGameRenderer implements Renderer{

...

        private void moveEnemy(GL10 gl){

                for (int x = 0; x < SFEngine.TOTAL_INTERCEPTORS + SFEngine.TOTAL_SCOUTS
+ SFEngine.TOTAL_WARSHIPS - 1; x++){
                        if (!enemies[x].isDestroyed){

                        }
                }
```

```
        }

...

}
```

> **NOTE:** Don't worry too much about what actually sets the isDestroyed flag of the enemies. We
> will address this in a section about collision detection in the next chapter. You will also apply this
> logic to the player's character.

Now, you have a loop within your updating method that runs once for each enemy in
your game and skips those enemies that have been destroyed.

Moving Each Enemy Using Its AI Logic

You have to run this loop for three different kinds of enemies, each with its own AI. The
enemy class has an enemyType property that you set when you instantiated the enemy.
Therefore, you will need to set up a switch on the enemyType so that you will know which
AI to run for the enemy that is being updated.

```
public class  SFGameRenderer implements Renderer{

...

        private void moveEnemy(GL10 gl){

                for (int x = 0; x < SFEngine.TOTAL_INTERCEPTORS + SFEngine.TOTAL_SCOUTS
+ SFEngine.TOTAL_WARSHIPS - 1; x++){
                        if (!enemies[x].isDestroyed){

                                switch (enemies[x].enemyType){
                                case SFEngine.TYPE_INTERCEPTOR:

                                        break;
                                case SFEngine.TYPE_SCOUT:

                                        break;
                                case SFEngine.TYPE_WARSHIP

                                        break;

                                }

                        }
                }

        }

...

}
```

In the next section, you will create the interceptor AI, the logic that drives the interceptor enemies toward the player.

Creating the Interceptor AI

Let's now create the interceptor AI. The first thing that you are going to want to test for in this AI is whether or not the Interceptor has already moved off the screen. Recall that all of the enemies are going to move from the top to the bottom of the screen. Unless they are destroyed by the player, they will eventually reach the bottom of the screen.

You have a choice when you are designing a game like this. When an enemy reaches the bottom of the screen, you can either kill it to take it out of the rotation, or you can reset it to run again. For *Star Fighter*, you are going to reset the enemy to a random position above the top of the screen so that it will continue to attack the player until it is destroyed.

Test if the y axis position of the enemy is less than 0—below the bottom edge of the screen—and if so, reset its x and y positions to random positions. Also, you will want to clear any lock on positions and lock flags, just in case the enemy had previously locked onto the player.

```
public class  SFGameRenderer implements Renderer{

...

        private void moveEnemy(GL10 gl){

                for (int x = 0; x < SFEngine.TOTAL_INTERCEPTORS + SFEngine.TOTAL_SCOUTS
+ SFEngine.TOTAL_WARSHIPS - 1; x++){
                        if (!enemies[x].isDestroyed){

                            Random randomPos = new Random();

                            switch (enemies[x].enemyType){
                            case SFEngine.TYPE_INTERCEPTOR:

                                if (enemies[x].posY <= 0){
                                        enemies[x].posY = (randomPos.nextFloat()
* 4) + 4;

                                        enemies[x].posX = randomPos.nextFloat()
* 3;

                                        enemies[x].isLockedOn = false;
                                        enemies[x].lockOnPosX = 0;
                                }

                            break;
                            case SFEngine.TYPE_SCOUT:

                            break;
                            case SFEngine.TYPE_WARSHIP

                            break;
```

```
                                              }
                                    }
                           }
                  }

          ...

          }
```

In the next section, you will add the OpenGL code to the logic.

Adjusting the Vertices

The next step in the AI is some standard OpenGL work. You need to load the model matrix mode and adjust the vertices. This code should look very familiar to you, because it was already covered in the last chapter. In short, you are resizing the vertices so that the enemy ship is about the same size and the player—not the size of the entire screen.

```
package com.proandroidgames;

import java.util.Random;

import javax.microedition.khronos.egl.EGLConfig;
import javax.microedition.khronos.opengles.GL10;

import android.opengl.GLSurfaceView.Renderer;

public class  SFGameRenderer implements Renderer{

...

        private void moveEnemy(GL10 gl){

                for (int x = 0; x < SFEngine.TOTAL_INTERCEPTORS + SFEngine.TOTAL_SCOUTS
+ SFEngine.TOTAL_WARSHIPS - 1; x++){
                        if (!enemies[x].isDestroyed){

                                Random randomPos = new Random();

                                switch (enemies[x].enemyType){
                                case SFEngine.TYPE_INTERCEPTOR:

                                        if (enemies[x].posY <= 0){
                                                enemies[x].posY = (randomPos.nextFloat()
* 4) + 4;

                                                enemies[x].posX = randomPos.nextFloat()
* 3;

                                                enemies[x].isLockedOn = false;
                                                enemies[x].lockOnPosX = 0;
                                        }
                                        gl.glMatrixMode(GL10.GL_MODELVIEW);
```

```
                                gl.glLoadIdentity();
                                gl.glPushMatrix();
                                gl.glScalef(.25f, .25f, 1f);

                            break;
                    case SFEngine.TYPE_SCOUT:

                            break;
                    case SFEngine.TYPE_WARSHIP

                            break;

                    }

                }

            }

        }

...

}
```

At this point, the AI for the interceptor is going to be split into two different clauses. The first describes what happens before the interceptor locks onto the player's position, and the second describes what happens after the interceptor locks on to the player's position.

Locking on to the Player's Position

Before the Interceptor locks onto the player's position, it will simply travel down the screen in straight line. Pick an arbitrary position on the y axis; this will be the point at which the Interceptor locks onto the player's position. For *Star Fighter*, the interceptor's y axis position when it locks onto the player's position is 3, meaning the interceptor will start at a random position on the y axis and move down in a straight line until it reaches 3.

```
;

public class  SFGameRenderer implements Renderer{

...

        private void moveEnemy(GL10 gl){

                for (int x = 0; x < SFEngine.TOTAL_INTERCEPTORS + SFEngine.TOTAL_SCOUTS
+ SFEngine.TOTAL_WARSHIPS - 1; x++){
                        if (!enemies[x].isDestroyed){

                            Random randomPos = new Random();

                            switch (enemies[x].enemyType){
                            case SFEngine.TYPE_INTERCEPTOR:
```

```
                                        if (enemies[x].posY <= 0){
                                                enemies[x].posY = (randomPos.nextFloat()
* 4) + 4;
                                                enemies[x].posX = randomPos.nextFloat()
* 3;
                                                enemies[x].isLockedOn = false;
                                                enemies[x].lockOnPosX = 0;
                                        }
                                        gl.glMatrixMode(GL10.GL_MODELVIEW);
                                        gl.glLoadIdentity();
                                        gl.glPushMatrix();
                                        gl.glScalef(.25f, .25f, 1f);
                                        if (enemies[x].posY >= 3){

                                        }else{

                                        }

                                        break;
                                case SFEngine.TYPE_SCOUT:

                                        break;
                                case SFEngine.TYPE_WARSHIP

                                        break;

                                }

                        }
                }

        }

    ...

    }
```

Before the Interceptor reaches the lock on position, it will move in a straight line down the screen. This is accomplished by subtracting the INTERCEPTOR_SPEED value from the interceptor's current y axis position.

```
public class  SFGameRenderer implements Renderer{

...

        private void moveEnemy(GL10 gl){

                for (int x = 0; x < SFEngine.TOTAL_INTERCEPTORS + SFEngine.TOTAL_SCOUTS
+ SFEngine.TOTAL_WARSHIPS - 1; x++){
                        if (!enemies[x].isDestroyed){

                                Random randomPos = new Random();

                                switch (enemies[x].enemyType){
```

```
                                        case SFEngine.TYPE_INTERCEPTOR:

                                                if (enemies[x].posY <= 0){
                                                        enemies[x].posY = (randomPos.nextFloat()
* 4) + 4;

                                                        enemies[x].posX = randomPos.nextFloat()
* 3;

                                                        enemies[x].isLockedOn = false;
                                                        enemies[x].lockOnPosX = 0;
                                                }
                                                gl.glMatrixMode(GL10.GL_MODELVIEW);
                                                gl.glLoadIdentity();
                                                gl.glPushMatrix();
                                                gl.glScalef(.25f, .25f, 1f);
                                                if (enemies[x].posY >= 3){
                                                        enemies[x].posY -=
SFEngine.INTERCEPTOR_SPEED;

                                                }else{

                                                }

                                                break;
                                        case SFEngine.TYPE_SCOUT:

                                                break;
                                        case SFEngine.TYPE_WARSHIP

                                                break;

                                }

                        }
                }

        }

...

}
```

Now, you can program the second half of the interceptor's AI logic.

Implementing a Slope Formula

First, set the interceptor to locked on, and get the current position of the player.

```
public class  SFGameRenderer implements Renderer{

...

        private void moveEnemy(GL10 gl){

                for (int x = 0; x < SFEngine.TOTAL_INTERCEPTORS + SFEngine.TOTAL_SCOUTS
+ SFEngine.TOTAL_WARSHIPS - 1; x++){
```

```
                    if (!enemies[x].isDestroyed){

                        Random randomPos = new Random();

                        switch (enemies[x].enemyType){
                        case SFEngine.TYPE_INTERCEPTOR:

                            if (enemies[x].posY <= 0){
                                enemies[x].posY = (randomPos.nextFloat()
* 4) + 4;

                                enemies[x].posX = randomPos.nextFloat()
* 3;

                                enemies[x].isLockedOn = false;
                                enemies[x].lockOnPosX = 0;
                            }
                            gl.glMatrixMode(GL10.GL_MODELVIEW);
                            gl.glLoadIdentity();
                            gl.glPushMatrix();
                            gl.glScalef(.25f, .25f, 1f);
                            if (enemies[x].posY >= 3){
                                enemies[x].posY -=
SFEngine.INTERCEPTOR_SPEED;

                            }else{
                                if (!enemies[x].isLockedOn){
                                        enemies[x].lockOnPosX =
SFEngine.playerBankPosX;

                                        enemies[x].isLockedOn = true;

                                }

                            }

                            break;
                        case SFEngine.TYPE_SCOUT:

                            break;
                        case SFEngine.TYPE_WARSHIP

                            break;

                        }

                    }
                }

        }
    ...

}
```

Next, you are going to use a simple slope formula to determine the increments at which the interceptor needs to move to reach the player. Slope can be determined by using this formula:

$(x_1 - x_2) / (y_1 - y_2)$

Just to make things a little more interesting, you want the Interceptor to speed up once it locks onto the target. Therefore, replace y_2 in the slope with INTERCEPTOR_SPEED. There is one modification you need to make to this formula before you can use it.

The formula as it is written will give you the full position directly to the player in one shot. However, you want to move in steady increments to the player. Therefore, you need to divide y_1 by y_2 rather than subtracting y_2. This will give you an incremental value that you can keep adding to itself to move the interceptor along.

```java
public class  SFGameRenderer implements Renderer{

...

        private void moveEnemy(GL10 gl){

                for (int x = 0; x < SFEngine.TOTAL_INTERCEPTORS + SFEngine.TOTAL_SCOUTS
+ SFEngine.TOTAL_WARSHIPS - 1; x++){
                        if (!enemies[x].isDestroyed){

                                Random randomPos = new Random();

                                switch (enemies[x].enemyType){
                                case SFEngine.TYPE_INTERCEPTOR:

                                        if (enemies[x].posY <= 0){
                                                enemies[x].posY = (randomPos.nextFloat()
* 4) + 4;
                                                enemies[x].posX = randomPos.nextFloat()
* 3;
                                                enemies[x].isLockedOn = false;
                                                enemies[x].lockOnPosX = 0;
                                        }
                                        gl.glMatrixMode(GL10.GL_MODELVIEW);
                                        gl.glLoadIdentity();
                                        gl.glPushMatrix();
                                        gl.glScalef(.25f, .25f, 1f);
                                        if (enemies[x].posY >= 3){
                                                enemies[x].posY -=
SFEngine.INTERCEPTOR_SPEED;
                                        }else{
                                                if (!enemies[x].isLockedOn){
                                                        enemies[x].lockOnPosX =
SFEngine.playerBankPosX;

                                                        enemies[x].isLockedOn = true;
                                                        enemies[x].incrementXToTarget =
(float) ((enemies[x].lockOnPosX - enemies[x].posX )/ (enemies[x].posY /
(SFEngine.INTERCEPTOR_SPEED * 4)));
                                                }

                                        }

                                        break;
```

```
                                       case SFEngine.TYPE_SCOUT:

                                           break;
                                       case SFEngine.TYPE_WARSHIP

                                           break;

                                   }

                          }
                      }

              }

    ...

    }
```

Finish the logic by setting the x and y positions of the interceptor.

```
public class  SFGameRenderer implements Renderer{

...

        private void moveEnemy(GL10 gl){

                   for (int x = 0; x < SFEngine.TOTAL_INTERCEPTORS + SFEngine.TOTAL_SCOUTS
+ SFEngine.TOTAL_WARSHIPS - 1; x++){
                          if (!enemies[x].isDestroyed){

                              Random randomPos = new Random();

                              switch (enemies[x].enemyType){
                              case SFEngine.TYPE_INTERCEPTOR:

                                  if (enemies[x].posY <= 0){
                                          enemies[x].posY = (randomPos.nextFloat()
* 4) + 4;

                                          enemies[x].posX = randomPos.nextFloat()
* 3;

                                          enemies[x].isLockedOn = false;
                                          enemies[x].lockOnPosX = 0;
                                  }
                                  gl.glMatrixMode(GL10.GL_MODELVIEW);
                                  gl.glLoadIdentity();
                                  gl.glPushMatrix();
                                  gl.glScalef(.25f, .25f, 1f);
                                  if (enemies[x].posY >= 3){
                                          enemies[x].posY -=
SFEngine.INTERCEPTOR_SPEED;

                                  }else{
                                          if (!enemies[x].isLockedOn){
                                                  enemies[x].lockOnPosX =
SFEngine.playerBankPosX;

                                                  enemies[x].isLockedOn = true;
```

```
                                                    enemies[x].incrementXToTarget =
(float) ((enemies[x].lockOnPosX - enemies[x].posX )/ (enemies[x].posY /
(SFEngine.INTERCEPTOR_SPEED * 4)));
                                        }
                                        enemies[x].posY -=
(SFEngine.INTERCEPTOR_SPEED * 4);

                                        enemies[x].posX +=
enemies[x].incrementXToTarget;

                            }

                        break;
                    case SFEngine.TYPE_SCOUT:

                        break;
                    case SFEngine.TYPE_WARSHIP

                        break;

                }

            }

        }

    }

...

}
```

Finally, you can update OpenGL with the position changes that you made to your
interceptor. You need to move the vertices according to the new x and y axis positions
of the Interceptor. Then, you need to push the texture matrix off the stack and set the
texture to the interceptor sprite on the common sprite sheet.

```
public class  SFGameRenderer implements Renderer{

...

        private void moveEnemy(GL10 gl){

                for (int x = 0; x < SFEngine.TOTAL_INTERCEPTORS + SFEngine.TOTAL_SCOUTS
+ SFEngine.TOTAL_WARSHIPS - 1; x++){
                        if (!enemies[x].isDestroyed){

                            Random randomPos = new Random();

                            switch (enemies[x].enemyType){
                            case SFEngine.TYPE_INTERCEPTOR:

                                if (enemies[x].posY <= 0){
                                        enemies[x].posY = (randomPos.nextFloat()
* 4) + 4;
```

```java
                                enemies[x].posX = randomPos.nextFloat()
* 3;
                                enemies[x].isLockedOn = false;
                                enemies[x].lockOnPosX = 0;
                        }
                        gl.glMatrixMode(GL10.GL_MODELVIEW);
                        gl.glLoadIdentity();
                        gl.glPushMatrix();
                        gl.glScalef(.25f, .25f, 1f);
                        if (enemies[x].posY >= 3){
                                enemies[x].posY -=
SFEngine.INTERCEPTOR_SPEED;
                        }else{
                                if (!enemies[x].isLockedOn){
                                        enemies[x].lockOnPosX =
SFEngine.playerBankPosX;
                                        enemies[x].isLockedOn = true;
                                        enemies[x].incrementXToTarget =
(float) ((enemies[x].lockOnPosX - enemies[x].posX )/ (enemies[x].posY /
(SFEngine.INTERCEPTOR_SPEED * 4)));
                                }
                                enemies[x].posY -=
(SFEngine.INTERCEPTOR_SPEED * 4);
                                enemies[x].posX +=
enemies[x].incrementXToTarget;
                                gl.glTranslatef(enemies[x].posX,
enemies[x].posY, 0f);
                                gl.glMatrixMode(GL10.GL_TEXTURE);
                                gl.glLoadIdentity();
                                gl.glTranslatef(0.25f, .25f , 0.0f);
                        }

                        break;
                case SFEngine.TYPE_SCOUT:

                        break;
                case SFEngine.TYPE_WARSHIP

                        break;

                }

            }
          }

      }

...

}
```

Draw the interceptor, and you are ready to tackle the scout AI.

```java
public class  SFGameRenderer implements Renderer{
```

...

```
        private void moveEnemy(GL10 gl){

                for (int x = 0; x < SFEngine.TOTAL_INTERCEPTORS + SFEngine.TOTAL_SCOUTS
+ SFEngine.TOTAL_WARSHIPS - 1; x++){
                        if (!enemies[x].isDestroyed){

                                Random randomPos = new Random();

                                switch (enemies[x].enemyType){
                                case SFEngine.TYPE_INTERCEPTOR:

                                        if (enemies[x].posY <= 0){
                                                enemies[x].posY = (randomPos.nextFloat()
* 4) + 4;

                                                enemies[x].posX = randomPos.nextFloat()
* 3;

                                                enemies[x].isLockedOn = false;
                                                enemies[x].lockOnPosX = 0;
                                        }
                                        gl.glMatrixMode(GL10.GL_MODELVIEW);
                                        gl.glLoadIdentity();
                                        gl.glPushMatrix();
                                        gl.glScalef(.25f, .25f, 1f);
                                        if (enemies[x].posY >= 3){
                                                enemies[x].posY -=
SFEngine.INTERCEPTOR_SPEED;
                                        }else{
                                                if (!enemies[x].isLockedOn){
                                                        enemies[x].lockOnPosX =
SFEngine.playerBankPosX;

                                                        enemies[x].isLockedOn = true;
                                                        enemies[x].incrementXToTarget =
(float) ((enemies[x].lockOnPosX - enemies[x].posX )/ (enemies[x].posY /
(SFEngine.INTERCEPTOR_SPEED * 4)));

                                                }
                                                enemies[x].posY -=
(SFEngine.INTERCEPTOR_SPEED * 4);

                                                enemies[x].posX +=
enemies[x].incrementXToTarget;

                                                gl.glTranslatef(enemies[x].posX,
enemies[x].posY, 0f);

                                                gl.glMatrixMode(GL10.GL_TEXTURE);
                                                gl.glLoadIdentity();
                                                gl.glTranslatef(0.25f, .25f , 0.0f);
                                        }
                                        enemies[x].draw(gl, spriteSheets);
                                        gl.glPopMatrix();
                                        gl.glLoadIdentity();

                                        break;
                                case SFEngine.TYPE_SCOUT:
```

```
                                    break;
                        case SFEngine.TYPE_WARSHIP

                                    break;

                                }

                        }
                }
        }
...

}
```

In the next section, you will create the AI logic for the scout enemy type.

Creating the Scout AI

Now that you have gotten your hands dirty with a little AI work, the remaining two enemies should be fairly easy. The only major difference between the scout and the interceptor is that the scout is going to move in a predefined pattern down the screen.

First, test to determine if the scout is off the bottom of the screen; if it is, reset it. In this same logic for the interceptor, you set both the x and y axis positions to random values. However, the scout will only attack from the extreme left or the extreme right of the screen. Therefore, set the x axis position to either 0 or 3 based on its direction of attack.

```
public class  SFGameRenderer implements Renderer{

...

        private void moveEnemy(GL10 gl){

                for (int x = 0; x < sfengine.TOTAL_INTERCEPTORS + sfengine.TOTAL_SCOUTS
+ sfengine.TOTAL_WARSHIPS - 1; x++){
                        if (!enemies[x].isDestroyed){

                                Random randomPos = new Random();

                                switch (enemies[x].enemyType){
                                case SFEngine.TYPE_INTERCEPTOR:

...

                                        break;
                                case SFEngine.TYPE_SCOUT:
                                        if (enemies[x].posY <= 0){
                                                enemies[x].posY = (randomPos.nextFloat()
* 4) + 4;

                                                enemies[x].isLockedOn = false;
                                                enemies[x].posT = SFEngine.SCOUT_SPEED;
```

```
enemies[x].getNextScoutX();

enemies[x].getNextScoutY();

SFEngine.ATTACK_LEFT){
```

```
                                        enemies[x].lockOnPosX =

                                        enemies[x].lockOnPosY =

                                        if(enemies[x].attackDirection ==

                                                    enemies[x].posX = 0;
                                        }else{
                                                    enemies[x].posX = 3f;
                                        }
                                }
                                gl.glMatrixMode(GL10.GL_MODELVIEW);
                                gl.glLoadIdentity();
                                gl.glPushMatrix();
                                gl.glScalef(.25f, .25f, 1f);

                                break;
                        case SFEngine.TYPE_WARSHIP

                                break;

                }

            }
        }
    }

...

}
```

Just like you did for the interceptor, you are going to slowly move the scout down the screen until it reaches the lock on point.

Setting a Random Point to Move the Scout

Since the action would look far too mechanical to the player if all of the enemies changed direction at the same point on the screen, you should set the lock-on point for the scout a little lower than that of the interceptor; otherwise, the code is the same.

```
public class  SFGameRenderer implements Renderer{

...

        private void moveEnemy(GL10 gl){

                for (int x = 0; x < sfengine.TOTAL_INTERCEPTORS + sfengine.TOTAL_SCOUTS
+ sfengine.TOTAL_WARSHIPS - 1; x++){
                        if (!enemies[x].isDestroyed){

                                Random randomPos = new Random();
```

```
                              switch (enemies[x].enemyType){
                              case SFEngine.TYPE_INTERCEPTOR:

...


                                  break;
                              case SFEngine.TYPE_SCOUT:
                                  if (enemies[x].posY <= 0){
                                      enemies[x].posY = (randomPos.nextFloat()
* 4) + 4;

                                      enemies[x].isLockedOn = false;
                                      enemies[x].posT = SFEngine.SCOUT_SPEED;
                                      enemies[x].lockOnPosX =
enemies[x].getNextScoutX();

                                      enemies[x].lockOnPosY =
enemies[x].getNextScoutY();

                                      if(enemies[x].attackDirection ==
SFEngine.ATTACK_LEFT){

                                          enemies[x].posX = 0;
                                      }else{
                                          enemies[x].posX = 3f;
                                      }
                                  }
                                  gl.glMatrixMode(GL10.GL_MODELVIEW);
                                  gl.glLoadIdentity();
                                  gl.glPushMatrix();
                                  gl.glScalef(.25f, .25f, 1f);
                                  if (enemies[x].posY >= 2.75f){
                                          enemies[x].posY -= SFEngine.SCOUT_SPEED;
                                  }else{

                                  }

                                  break;
                              case SFEngine.TYPE_WARSHIP

                                  break;

                              }

                      }
                  }

          }

...

}
```
In the next section, you will learn how to move the scout along a Bezier curve.

Moving Along a Bezier Curve

Luckily, you have already created methods to automatically supply you with the next x and y coordinates in a Bezier curve. All you have to do now is call the getNextScoutX() and getNextScoutY() methods to begin moving the scout along its curved path. Increment posT by the value of SCOUT_SPEED after you call these methods; otherwise, you will get the same values the next time you call them.

```
public class  SFGameRenderer implements Renderer{

...

        private void moveEnemy(GL10 gl){
                for (int x = 0; x < sfengine.TOTAL_INTERCEPTORS + sfengine.TOTAL_SCOUTS
+ sfengine.TOTAL_WARSHIPS - 1; x++){
                        if (!enemies[x].isDestroyed){
                                Random randomPos = new Random();

                                switch (enemies[x].enemyType){
                                case SFEngine.TYPE_INTERCEPTOR:

...

                                        break;
                                case SFEngine.TYPE_SCOUT:
                                        if (enemies[x].posY <= 0){
                                                enemies[x].posY = (randomPos.nextFloat()
* 4) + 4;

                                                enemies[x].isLockedOn = false;
                                                enemies[x].posT = SFEngine.SCOUT_SPEED;
                                                enemies[x].lockOnPosX =
enemies[x].getNextScoutX();

enemies[x].getNextScoutY();
                                                enemies[x].lockOnPosY =

                                                if(enemies[x].attackDirection ==
SFEngine.ATTACK_LEFT){
                                                        enemies[x].posX = 0;
                                                }else{
                                                        enemies[x].posX = 3f;
                                                }
                                        }
                                        gl.glMatrixMode(GL10.GL_MODELVIEW);
                                        gl.glLoadIdentity();
                                        gl.glPushMatrix();
                                        gl.glScalef(.25f, .25f, 1f);
                                        if (enemies[x].posY >= 2.75f){
                                                enemies[x].posY -= SFEngine.SCOUT_SPEED;
                                        }else{
                                                enemies[x].posX =
enemies[x].getNextScoutX();

                                                enemies[x].posY =
enemies[x].getNextScoutY();
```

```
                                              enemies[x].posT += SFEngine.SCOUT_SPEED;
                                }

                            break;
                        case SFEngine.TYPE_WARSHIP

                            break;

                    }

                }

            }

        }

    ...

    }
```

Believe it or not, that is all there is to the scout AI. Finish up this enemy's AI by performing your OpenGL procedure to translate the vertices and set the texture to the correct sprite for the scout.

```
public class  SFGameRenderer implements Renderer{

...

        private void moveEnemy(GL10 gl){

                for (int x = 0; x < SFEngine.TOTAL_INTERCEPTORS + SFEngine.TOTAL_SCOUTS
+ SFEngine.TOTAL_WARSHIPS - 1; x++){
                        if (!enemies[x].isDestroyed){

                            Random randomPos = new Random();

                            switch (enemies[x].enemyType){
                            case SFEngine.TYPE_INTERCEPTOR:

...

                                break;
                            case SFEngine.TYPE_SCOUT:
                                if (enemies[x].posY <= 0){
                                    enemies[x].posY = (randomPos.nextFloat()
* 4) + 4;

                                    enemies[x].isLockedOn = false;
                                    enemies[x].posT = SFEngine.SCOUT_SPEED;
                                    enemies[x].lockOnPosX =
enemies[x].getNextScoutX();

                                    enemies[x].lockOnPosY =
enemies[x].getNextScoutY();

                                    if(enemies[x].attackDirection ==
SFEngine.ATTACK_LEFT){

                                            enemies[x].posX = 0;
                                    }else{
```

```
                                                enemies[x].posX = 3f;
                                        }
                                }
                                gl.glMatrixMode(GL10.GL_MODELVIEW);
                                gl.glLoadIdentity();
                                gl.glPushMatrix();
                                gl.glScalef(.25f, .25f, 1f);
                                if (enemies[x].posY >= 2.75f){
                                        enemies[x].posY -= SFEngine.SCOUT_SPEED;
                                }else{
                                        enemies[x].posX =
enemies[x].getNextScoutX();

enemies[x].getNextScoutY();            enemies[x].posY =


enemies[x].posY, 0f);                  enemies[x].posT += SFEngine.SCOUT_SPEED;
                                }
                                gl.glTranslatef(enemies[x].posX,

                                gl.glMatrixMode(GL10.GL_TEXTURE);
                                gl.glLoadIdentity();
                                gl.glTranslatef(0.75f, .25f , 0.0f);
                                enemies[x].draw(gl, spriteSheets);
                                gl.glPopMatrix();
                                gl.glLoadIdentity();

                                break;
                        case SFEngine.TYPE_WARSHIP

                                break;

                        }

                        }
                  }

            }

...

}
```

The last bit of AI that you need to add to your moveEnemy() method is the warship.

Creating the Warship AI

In the story for *Star Fight*er, the warship moves in a random direction toward the player. You will accomplish this by selecting a random position on the x axis and, using the same logic as the interceptor, moving the warship toward the random point, rather than directly to the position of the player.

Moving the warship toward a random position will make the game less predictable and make the enemy harder to fight. However, the AI for the warship will be almost identical to that of the interceptor, except that you need to replace the player's locked-on x position with a random number between 0 and 3.

```java
public class  SFGameRenderer implements Renderer{

...

        private void moveEnemy(GL10 gl){

                for (int x = 0; x < SFEngine.TOTAL_INTERCEPTORS + SFEngine.TOTAL_SCOUTS
+ SFEngine.TOTAL_WARSHIPS - 1; x++){
                        if (!enemies[x].isDestroyed){

                                Random randomPos = new Random();

                                switch (enemies[x].enemyType){
                                case SFEngine.TYPE_INTERCEPTOR:

...

                                        break;

...

                                        break;
                                case SFEngine.TYPE_WARSHIP
                                        if (enemies[x].posY < 0){
                                                enemies[x].posY = (randomPos.nextFloat()
* 4) + 4;
                                                enemies[x].posX = randomPos.nextFloat()
* 3;

                                                enemies[x].isLockedOn = false;
                                                enemies[x].lockOnPosX = 0;
                                        }
                                        gl.glMatrixMode(GL10.GL_MODELVIEW);
                                        gl.glLoadIdentity();
                                        gl.glPushMatrix();
                                        gl.glScalef(.25f, .25f, 1f);

                                        if (enemies[x].posY >= 3){
                                                enemies[x].posY -=
SFEngine.WARSHIP_SPEED;
                                        }else{
                                                if (!enemies[x].isLockedOn){
                                                        enemies[x].lockOnPosX =
randomPos.nextFloat() * 3;
                                                        enemies[x].isLockedOn = true;
                                                        enemies[x].incrementXToTarget =
(float) ((enemies[x].lockOnPosX - enemies[x].posX )/ (enemies[x].posY /
(SFEngine.WARSHIP_SPEED * 4)));
                                                }
                                                enemies[x].posY -=
(SFEngine.WARSHIP_SPEED * 2);

                                                enemies[x].posX +=
enemies[x].incrementXToTarget;
```

```
                                                        }
                                                        gl.glTranslatef(enemies[x].posX,

enemies[x].posY, 0f);
                                                        gl.glMatrixMode(GL10.GL_TEXTURE);
                                                        gl.glLoadIdentity();
                                                        gl.glTranslatef(0.50f, .25f , 0.0f);

                                                        enemies[x].draw(gl,spriteSheets);
                                                        gl.glPopMatrix();
                                                        gl.glLoadIdentity();
                                                        break;

                                    }

                           }
                     }

           }

...

}
```

Finish your game loop by calling your new moveEnemy() method from the onDrawFrame()
method, right after you call movePlayer1().

Summary

In this chapter, you learned a great deal about creating three different, basic AI
structures for your enemies. You also

▪ Created the calls to load multiple textures

▪ Created methods to move your enemies

▪ Tested for the condition of your enemy before moving it

▪ Created logic for moving your enemies along paths

In the next chapter, you will finish your game by developing some weapons and
implementing collision detection.

Defend Yourself!

Your gaming development skills are coming along at a great pace now. While *Star Fighter* is not going to win any gaming awards, it is a perfect sandbox for you to hone your newly developed game-making skills.

Now, you find yourself at the last chapter of this book that will deal directly with the development of a 2-D sprite-based game. In this chapter, you are going to add a weapon for your playable character to use and create some basic 2-D collision detection. You will load a sprite sheet that contains some weapon images, write some AI logic for the bullets to follow a path, and create some collision detection to ensure you know when your weapons hit their targets.

If this were a going to be a full game that you were going to release to the public, you would want to add some score tracking, multiple levels, and possibly items such as power-ups and upgradeable weapons. However, the real purpose of this small 2-D project is to give you a proper base of knowledge and enough experience using the skills so that the chapters on 3-D game development (Chapters 10–12) will make sense to you. At the end of the chapter, you'll have the opportunity to review some of the key files that you've worked on thus far. This will ensure you have everything in place before moving on to the next stage of 3-D development.

Creating a Weapon Sprite Sheet

Your player would not last very long in the game without a way to defend against the onslaught of enemies that you set upon them in the last chapter. Therefore, you are going to arm your player with the standard space-fighting weapon—a blaster.

You first need to create a sprite sheet for your weapon, in the same way you created one for the enemies in Chapter 6 and for the playable character in Chapter 5.

> **NOTE:** Theoretically, the weapons could be included on the same sprite sheet as the player and the enemy ships. However, it is good practice for you to see how to juggle two textures in OpenGL.

Add the sprite sheet (it can be downloaded from this book's page on Apress.com, along with the code to this project) to your *Star Fighter* project. The sprite sheet in Figure 8–1 includes multiple weapons and character explosions.

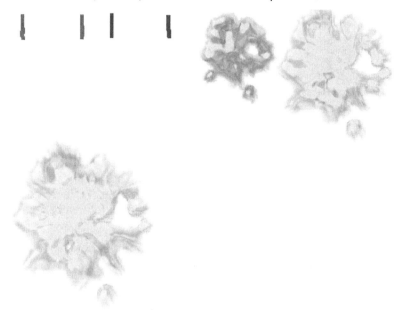

Figure 8–1. *Weapon sprite sheet*

Once you have added the sprite sheet to your project, open the SFEngine.java file and add the following constants to it:

```
SFEngine        public static final int WEAPONS_SHEET = R.drawable.destruction;
        public static final int PLAYER_SHIELDS = 5;
        public static final int SCOUT_SHIELDS = 3;
        public static final int INTERCEPTOR_SHIELDS = 1;
        public static final int WARSHIP_SHIELDS = 5;
        public static final float PLAYER_BULLET_SPEED = .125f;
SFMusic
```

The WEAPONS_SHEET constant is going to hold the pointer to your new sprite sheet. The SHOUT_SHIELDS, INTERCEPTOR_SHIELDS, and WARSHIP_SHIELDS constants will indicate how many hits the respective enemies can take before being destroyed, and the PLAYER_BULLET_SPEED constant will hold the speed at which the blaster fire will leave the playable character and travel up the screen.

Creating a Weapon Class

When you created the playable character and the enemies, you created a class to base them from. You are going to follow the same process for the weapon. Create a new class called SFWeapon for your weapons.

```
package com.proandroidgames;

public class SFWeapon {

}
```

You need to know three things about your weapons to draw them to the screen: the x and y positions of the sprite's vertex and whether the sprite is currently on the screen. The x and y positions are going to help you place the sprite on the correct point on the screen, and they will also help you in determining collisions.

Just as you might see multiple enemies, more than one blaster shot will be on the screen at a time. Therefore, you are going to have the weapons in an array. You will need to know, when you loop through your array, if the shot that you are looking at is currently on the screen or if it is free to be fired.

Add the following public properties to your class:

```
package com.proandroidgames;

public class SFWeapon {

        public float posY = 0f;
        public float posX = 0f;
        public boolean shotFired = false;


}
```

Create the vertices, indices, and texture arrays the same way you did in the enemy and playable character classes. These arrays, along with the constructor, will be used to set the data needed for OpenGL to draw your weapons to the screen.

```
public class SFWeapon {

        public float posY = 0f;
        public float posX = 0f;
        public boolean shotFired = false;

        private FloatBuffer vertexBuffer;
        private FloatBuffer textureBuffer;
        private ByteBuffer indexBuffer;

        private float vertices[] = {
                0.0f, 0.0f, 0.0f,
                1.0f, 0.0f, 0.0f,
                1.0f, 1.0f, 0.0f,
                0.0f, 1.0f, 0.0f,
```

```
        };

        private float texture[] = {
                0.0f, 0.0f,
                0.25f, 0.0f,
                0.25f, 0.25f,
                0.0f, 0.25f,
        };

        private byte indices[] = {
                0,1,2,
                0,2,3,
        };

        public SFWeapon() {

                ByteBuffer byteBuf = ByteBuffer.allocateDirect(vertices.length * 4);
                byteBuf.order(ByteOrder.nativeOrder());
                vertexBuffer = byteBuf.asFloatBuffer();
vertexBuffer.put(vertices);
                vertexBuffer.position(0);

byteBuf = ByteBuffer.allocateDirect(texture.length * 4);
                byteBuf.order(ByteOrder.nativeOrder());
                textureBuffer = byteBuf.asFloatBuffer();
                textureBuffer.put(texture);
                textureBuffer.position(0);

                indexBuffer = ByteBuffer.allocateDirect(indices.length);
                indexBuffer.put(indices);
                indexBuffer.position(0);
        }

}
```

The last step to creating a weapon class is to make an onDraw() method. Having
followed along with the previous chapters, you should be very familiar with the onDraw()
method. Just be aware that the weapon sprite sheet is going to be the second OpenGL
pointer in the spriteSheet array that you created for the game loop in the previous
chapter. Therefore, alter the onDraw() method appropriately so that you are pulling from
the correct sprite sheet when you call the method.

```
public class SFWeapon {

        ...

        public void draw(GL10 gl, int[] spriteSheet) {
                gl.glBindTexture(GL10.GL_TEXTURE_2D, spriteSheet[1]);

                gl.glFrontFace(GL10.GL_CCW);
                gl.glEnable(GL10.GL_CULL_FACE);
                gl.glCullFace(GL10.GL_BACK);
```

```
                gl.glEnableClientState(GL10.GL_VERTEX_ARRAY);
                gl.glEnableClientState(GL10.GL_TEXTURE_COORD_ARRAY);

                gl.glVertexPointer(3, GL10.GL_FLOAT, 0, vertexBuffer);
                gl.glTexCoordPointer(2, GL10.GL_FLOAT, 0, textureBuffer);

                gl.glDrawElements(GL10.GL_TRIANGLES, indices.length,
GL10.GL_UNSIGNED_BYTE, indexBuffer);

                gl.glDisableClientState(GL10.GL_VERTEX_ARRAY);
                gl.glDisableClientState(GL10.GL_TEXTURE_COORD_ARRAY);
                gl.glDisable(GL10.GL_CULL_FACE);
        }
}
```

With the class for your weapons created, you can now move over to the game loop and add the weapons. In the next section, you will create the automatic firing process for your playable character and let it fire the weapons from the weapon class that you created.

Giving Your Weapon a Trajectory

Now that you have your weapon class created, you're ready to instantiate it and create a method to allow the playable character to fire it. Recall that, in the story for *Star Fighter*, the playable character's weapon is autofired. Therefore, the method that you create to fire the weapon must do so without interaction from the player.

Creating a Weapon Array

Like you did for the enemy ships, you are going to create an array to hold all of the possible shots that your player could fire. Open SFGameRenderer, and create a new array of SFWeapon() in your game loop class.

```
package com.proandroidgames;

import java.util.Random;

import javax.microedition.khronos.egl.EGLConfig;
import javax.microedition.khronos.opengles.GL10;

import android.opengl.GLSurfaceView.Renderer;

public class SFGameRenderer implements Renderer{
        private SFBackGround background = new SFBackGround();
        private SFBackGround background2 = new SFBackGround();
        private SFGoodGuy player1 = new SFGoodGuy();
        private SFEnemy[] enemies = new SFEnemy[SFEngine.TOTAL_INTERCEPTORS +
SFEngine.TOTAL_SCOUTS + SFEngine.TOTAL_WARSHIPS - 1];
        private SFTextures textureLoader;
        private int[] spriteSheets = new int[2];
        private SFWeapon[] playerFire = new SFWeapon[4];
```

...

}

In the preceding chapter, you created a common texture class. Because the class is currently instantiated in your game loop, it will hold two textures. It is now time to add a second sprite sheet to this array.

Adding a Second Sprite Sheet

The second sprite sheet is the one that holds the weapons.

```
public class SFGameRenderer implements Renderer{

...

@Override
        public void onSurfaceCreated(GL10 gl, EGLConfig config) {
                initializeInterceptors();
                initializeScouts();
                initializeWarships();
                initializePlayerWeapons();
                textureLoader = new SFTextures(gl);
                spriteSheets = textureLoader.loadTexture(gl, SFEngine.CHARACTER_SHEET,
SFEngine.context, 1);
spriteSheets = textureLoader.loadTexture(gl, SFEngine.WEAPONS_SHEET, SFEngine.context,
2);

                gl.glEnable(GL10.GL_TEXTURE_2D);
                gl.glClearDepthf(1.0f);
                gl.glEnable(GL10.GL_DEPTH_TEST);
                gl.glDepthFunc(GL10.GL_LEQUAL);

                background.loadTexture(gl,SFEngine.BACKGROUND_LAYER_ONE,
SFEngine.context);
                background2.loadTexture(gl,SFEngine.BACKGROUND_LAYER_TWO,
SFEngine.context);

        }
```

> **CAUTION:** Be careful to label the new sheet as number 2, or you will just replace the previous sheet.

In the preceding chapter, you wrote an initialization method to instantiate new copies of the enemy class and added it to the enemies' array. You are going to follow the same process when creating the weapons for you playable character.

Initializing the Weapons

Start by creating an initialization class named initializePlayerWeapons() as follows:

```
public class SFGameRenderer implements Renderer{

    ...

        private void initializePlayerWeapons(){

        }

    ...

}
```

In the initializePlayerWeapons() method, you need to loop through the playerFire[] array that you created and add a new instantiation of the SFWeapon() class to it.

```
public class SFGameRenderer implements Renderer{

    ...

        private void initializePlayerWeapons(){
            for(int x = 0; x < 4; x++){
                SFWeapon weapon = new SFWeapon();
                playerFire[x] = weapon;
            }

        }

    ...

}
```

Finish off the initialization method by setting the initial properties of the first shot to be fired. Since the weapon is autofired, you can set the first shot as having been fired. The x axis position of the shot is going to be equal to the current x axis position of the player character.

As for the y axis position, set that to 1.25. This will set the y axis of the shot to be slightly above the player's ship, giving it the appearance of coming out of a forward-facing blaster cannon. If you set the y axis lower, the shot will be drawn over the ship and look like it is coming from somewhere on top of the ship.

```
public class SFGameRenderer implements Renderer{

    ...

        private void initializePlayerWeapons(){
```

```
            for(int x = 0; x < 4; x++){
                    SFWeapon weapon = new SFWeapon();
                    playerFire[x] = weapon;
            }
            playerFire[0].shotFired = true;
            playerFire[0].posX = SFEngine.playerBankPosX;
            playerFire[0].posY = 1.25f;
        }

    ...

    }
```

The array for the weapon shots is created, instantiated, and populated. In the previous chapters, you created private methods that could be called from the game loop to move players and enemies. Now, you need to create a private method to move the weapon shots up the screen.

Moving the Weapon Shots

The trajectory of each shot will be a straight line, and it will move from the player's x position at the time of the shot to the top of the screen. Create a method named firePlayerWeapon() to be used to move each shot in a straight line as it is fired.

```
public class SFGameRenderer implements Renderer{

    ...

        private void initializePlayerWeapons(){
                for(int x = 0; x < 4; x++){
                        SFWeapon weapon = new SFWeapon();
                        playerFire[x] = weapon;
                }
                playerFire[0].shotFired = true;
                playerFire[0].posX = SFEngine.playerBankPosX;
                playerFire[0].posY = 1.25f;
        }

    ...

        private void firePlayerWeapon(GL10 gl){

        }

    ...

    }
```

In the firePlayerWeapon() method, create a loop that will run only if the shot has been fired. This will save you from looping on shots that do not need to be drawn.

```
public class SFGameRenderer implements Renderer{

...


        private void firePlayerWeapon(GL10 gl){
               for(int x = 0; x < 4; x++ ){
                        if (playerFire[x].shotFired){

                              }
                     }

             }

...

}
```

The first thing that you are doing in this method is creating an int named nextShot. The autofire feature of the playable character fires each shot in succession. Therefore, one shot should not be fired until the shot before has traveled an acceptable distance away from the character. The nextShotint tracks the next shot to be fired so you can set some initial properties on it when the time is right.

```
public class SFGameRenderer implements Renderer{

...


        private void firePlayerWeapon(GL10 gl){
               for(int x = 0; x < 4; x++ ){
                        if (playerFire[x].shotFired){
                              int nextShot = 0;


                              }
                     }

             }

...

}
```

Detecting the Edge of the Screen

You need a way to determine if a shot has hit the edge of the viewable screen, so the cannon blast isn't drawn when the player can't see it, thus wasting valuable resources. Set up an ifstatement to test if the current shot has gone off the screen. If the shot has extended off the screen, set its shotFired property to false to prevent it from being drawn unnecessarily.

```
public class SFGameRenderer implements Renderer{

...
```

```
                    private void firePlayerWeapon(GL10 gl){
                        for(int x = 0; x < 4; x++ ){
                            if (playerFire[x].shotFired){
                                int nextShot = 0;
if (playerFire[x].posY > 4.25){
                                        playerFire[x].shotFired = false;
                                }else{

                                }

                            }
                        }
                    }

    ...

    }
```

Assuming the shot has not yet extended off the screen, it must still be in the player's view and must be dealt with. Because the shots fly in a straight trajectory, all you have to do to move the shot is continue to add PLAYER_BULLET_SPEED to the current y position of the shot. Then, you can call all of the OpenGL operations that you have been dealing with when drawing characters to the screen.

> **TIP:** If any of the OpenGL operations in the following code do not look familiar, review Chapters 4 and 5.

```
public class SFGameRenderer implements Renderer{


    ...

        private void firePlayerWeapon(GL10 gl){
            for(int x = 0; x < 4; x++ ){
                if (playerFire[x].shotFired){
                    int nextShot = 0;
                    if (playerFire[x].posY > 4.25){
                        playerFire[x].shotFired = false;
                    }else{

playerFire[x].posY += SFEngine.PLAYER_BULLET_SPEED;
gl.glMatrixMode(GL10.GL_MODELVIEW);
                                    gl.glLoadIdentity();
                                    gl.glPushMatrix();
                                    gl.glScalef(.25f, .25f, 0f);
gl.glTranslatef(playerFire[x].posX, playerFire[x].posY, 0f);

gl.glMatrixMode(GL10.GL_TEXTURE);
gl.glLoadIdentity();
                                    gl.glTranslatef(0.0f,0.0f, 0.0f);

                                    playerFire[x].draw(gl,spriteSheets);
```

```
                                        gl.glPopMatrix();
                                        gl.glLoadIdentity();


                          }
                    }
              }
        }

...

}
```

You need to take care of one last thing in this method. Once the current shot has moved along the y axis more than 1 unit away from the character, it is time to fire the next shot. Therefore, you need to test if the current shot is more than 1 y-axis unit away from the character and, if so, set the properties of the next shot to be fired.

Keep in mind that shots fire successively, so by the time the last shot has fired, the first shot should be off the screen and disabled. The first shot can then be fired again when the last shot has passed the firing threshold.

```
public class SFGameRenderer implements Renderer{


...

        private void firePlayerWeapon(GL10 gl){
              for(int x = 0; x < 4; x++ ){
                    if (playerFire[x].shotFired){
                          int nextShot = 0;
                          if (playerFire[x].posY > 4.25){
                                playerFire[x].shotFired = false;
                          }else{
                                if (playerFire[x].posY> 2){
                                      if (x == 3){
                                            nextShot = 0;
                                      }else{
                                            nextShot = x + 1;
                                      }
                                      if (playerFire[nextShot].shotFired ==
false){
                                            playerFire[nextShot].shotFired =
true;
                                            playerFire[nextShot].posX =
SFEngine.playerBankPosX;
                                            playerFire[nextShot].posY =
1.25f;
                                }
                          }
                          playerFire[x].posY +=
SFEngine.PLAYER_BULLET_SPEED;
gl.glMatrixMode(GL10.GL_MODELVIEW);
                                gl.glLoadIdentity();
                                gl.glPushMatrix();
```

```
                                        gl.glScalef(.25f, .25f, 0f);
gl.glTranslatef(playerFire[x].posX, playerFire[x].posY, 0f);

gl.glMatrixMode(GL10.GL_TEXTURE);
gl.glLoadIdentity();
                                        gl.glTranslatef(0.0f,0.0f, 0.0f);

                                        playerFire[x].draw(gl,spriteSheets);
                                        gl.glPopMatrix();
                                        gl.glLoadIdentity();


                                }
                        }
                }
        }

    ...

}
```

Calling the firePlayerWeapons() Method

When you were working on the playable character and the enemies, you called methods
to move them, in increments, from the main game loop. The problem with following this
process for the player's weapon is that you do not know if the player's character is
currently valid and ready for firing. To get around this, you are going to call the
firePlayerWeapons() method from the movePlayer1() method, rather than calling it from
the main game loop. Doing so will ensure that you move the weapons on the screen only
when they are eligible to be moved.

```
public class SFGameRenderer implements Renderer{

    ...

        private void movePlayer1(GL10 gl){
                if(!player1.isDestroyed){
                        switch (SFEngine.playerFlightAction){

    ...

                        }
                        firePlayerWeapon(gl);
                }
        }

    ...

}
```

Your player can now fire weapons at the enemies. However, the weapons do not
accomplish anything. If you were to compile and play the game right now, you would
see the shots simply fly through any enemies and continue until they reach the edge of

the screen. So too, the enemies would just continue in their descent, oblivious to any shots fired.

To make your shots effective, you need to create some collision detection. In the next section, you will create a method for simply 2-D collision detection that will be used to determine if an enemy should be destroyed.

Implementing Collision Detection

Collision detection determines if two objects on the screen have touched and is essential to any video game. In *Star Fighter*, you will use basic collision detection to destroy enemies. In other games, collision detection is used to keep a player from walking through walls, allow a player to pick up a new item, or even determine if an enemy can see the player from an obscured view.

In this section, you are going to create a method that will track the position each enemy on the screen, and each shot fired, to determine if any of the shots have hit any of the enemies. In a 2-D game like *Star Fighter*, this is process is made easier because you have to test on only two axes (you do not have to deal with the z axis in a 2-D game).

Applying Collision Damage

When a collision has been detected, you must apply the damage to the enemy that has been hit. Each enemy can take a certain amount of damage before it is destroyed. To track this damage, create a new method named applyDamage() in your SFEnemy() class. This method will simply increment an int each time the specific enemy is hit. When the int value reaches the predefined limit for that enemy, the isDestroyed flag will be flipped, and the enemy will no longer be drawn to the screen.

```
package com.proandroidgames;

...

import javax.microedition.khronos.opengles.GL10;

public class SFEnemy {

        public float posY = 0f;
        public float posX = 0f;
        public float posT = 0f;
        public float incrementXToTarget = 0f;
        public float incrementYToTarget = 0f;
        public int attackDirection = 0;
        public boolean isDestroyed = false;
        private int damage = 0;

...

        public void applyDamage(){
                damage++;
                switch(enemyType){
```

```
                    case SFEngine.TYPE_INTERCEPTOR:
                        if (damage == SFEngine.INTERCEPTOR_SHIELDS){
                            isDestroyed = true;
                        }
                        break;
                    case SFEngine.TYPE_SCOUT:
                        if (damage == SFEngine.SCOUT_SHIELDS){
                            isDestroyed = true;
                        }
                        break;
                    case SFEngine.TYPE_WARSHIP:
                        if (damage == SFEngine.WARSHIP_SHIELDS){
                            isDestroyed = true;
                        }
                        break;
                }
        }


...

}
```

Every time that your collision detection method determines that a collision has been made with an enemy ship, all you have to do is call the appyDamage() method of the enemy, and it will take care of the rest. Once the isDestroyed flag on the enemy is set to true, that enemy will no longer be processed in the moveEnemy() method or drawn to the screen. Save and close SFEnemy.java.

Creating the detectCollisions() Method

With collision damage calculations taken care of, continue to edit your renderer by creating a method named detectCollisions() in your SFGameRenderer.java file.

```
public class SFGameRenderer implements Renderer{
        private void initializePlayerWeapons(){
                for(int x = 0; x < 4; x++){
                        sfweapon weapon = new sfweapon();
                        playerFire[x] = weapon;
                }
                playerFire[0].shotFired = true;
                playerFire[0].posX = sfengine.playerBankPosX;
                playerFire[0].posY = 1.25f;
        }

...

        private void detectCollisions(){

        }


...
```

```
}
```

Within the detectCollisions() method, set up two loops, one to iterate through each fired shot and one to iterate through each enemy that has not already been destroyed. Remember, because the enemies start at random positions beyond the upper edge of the screen, they can be valid (isDestroyed == false) without being in the player's view. This means you also need to test if the enemy is in view of the player as well as whether or not it has been destroyed.

```
public class SFGameRenderer implements Renderer{

...

        private void detectCollisions(){
                for (int y = 0; y < 3; y ++){
if (playerFire[y].shotFired){
                                for (int x = 0; x < SFEngine.TOTAL_INTERCEPTORS +
SFEngine.TOTAL_SCOUTS + SFEngine.TOTAL_WARSHIPS - 1; x++ ){
                                        if(!enemies[x].isDestroyed && enemies[x].posY <
4.25 ){

                                        }
                                }
                        }
                }

...

}
```

Now comes the tricky part of the method. You know two pieces of information about each enemy and each shot fired: the x and y positions. You also know dimension of the vertices for the enemies and the shots; in this case, they are each 1 × 1 unit.

Detecting the Specific Collisions

Create an if statement to determine if a shot and an enemy collided based on their x and y positions and their respective dimensions.

```
public class SFGameRenderer implements Renderer{

...

        private void detectCollisions(){
                for (int y = 0; y < 3; y ++){
if (playerFire[y].shotFired){
                                for (int x = 0; x < SFEngine.TOTAL_INTERCEPTORS +
SFEngine.TOTAL_SCOUTS + SFEngine.TOTAL_WARSHIPS - 1; x++ ){
```

```
                                            if(!enemies[x].isDestroyed && enemies[x].posY <
4.25 ){
                                                if ((playerFire[y].posY >=
enemies[x].posY - 1
&& playerFire[y].posY <= enemies[x].posY )
&& (playerFire[y].posX <= enemies[x].posX + 1
&& playerFire[y].posX >= enemies[x].posX - 1)){

                                                    }
                                                }
                                            }
                                        }
                                    }
                                }

        ...


        ...

}
```

If both the enemy and the shot being tested make it passed this if statement, they have
collided. When and enemy and a shot collide, you need to call the applyDamage()
method on the enemy to either add to the damage of that enemy or destroy it
completely.

Removing Void Shots

Once a shot has hit an enemy, regardless of whether the enemy is completely
destroyed, the shot needs to be taken off the screen so that it cannot hit any other
enemies. Set the shotFiredflag on the shot to false to negate the shot.

> **NOTE:** Whether a shot hits an enemy or travels until it reaches the top on the screen, it will have
> the same result; the next shot in the array can be activated. Therefore, in your collision method, if
> a shot has hit an enemy, activate the next shot after you have deactivated the one that collided.

```
public class SFGameRenderer implements Renderer{


    ...

        private void detectCollisions(){
                for (int y = 0; y < 3; y ++){
if (playerFire[y].shotFired){
                                for (int x = 0; x < SFEngine.TOTAL_INTERCEPTORS +
SFEngine.TOTAL_SCOUTS + SFEngine.TOTAL_WARSHIPS - 1; x++ ){
                                    if(!enemies[x].isDestroyed && enemies[x].posY <
4.25 ){
```

```
                                                  if ((playerFire[y].posY >=
enemies[x].posY - 1
&& playerFire[y].posY <= enemies[x].posY )
&& (playerFire[y].posX <= enemies[x].posX + 1
&& playerFire[y].posX >= enemies[x].posX - 1)){
                                                          int nextShot = 0;
enemies[x].applyDamage();
                                                          playerFire[y].shotFired = false;
                                                          if (y == 3){
                                                                  nextShot = 0;
                                                          }else{
                                                                  nextShot = y + 1;
                                                          }
                                                          if
(playerFire[nextShot].shotFired == false){

playerFire[nextShot].shotFired = true;

playerFire[nextShot].posX = SFEngine.playerBankPosX;

playerFire[nextShot].posY = 1.25f;
                                                          }
                                                  }
                                          }
                                  }
                          }
                  }
          }

...


...

}
```

That is a fairly simple version of 2-D collision detection that should get you well on your path to creating an entertaining game. Now, all you have to do is call the collision detection method from the main game loop.

...

```
public void onDrawFrame(GL10 gl) {
        loopStart = System.currentTimeMillis();
        try {
                if (loopRunTime < SFEngine.GAME_THREAD_FPS_SLEEP){
                        Thread.sleep(SFEngine.GAME_THREAD_FPS_SLEEP - loopRunTime);
                }
        } catch (InterruptedException e) {
                e.printStackTrace();
        }
        gl.glClear(GL10.GL_COLOR_BUFFER_BIT | GL10.GL_DEPTH_BUFFER_BIT);

        scrollBackground1(gl);
        scrollBackground2(gl);
```

```
        movePlayer1(gl);
        moveEnemy(gl);

        detectCollisions();


        gl.glEnable(GL10.GL_BLEND);
        gl.glBlendFunc(GL10.GL_ONE, GL10.GL_ONE_MINUS_SRC_ALPHA);
        loopEnd = System.currentTimeMillis();
        loopRunTime = ((loopEnd - loopStart));

}

...
```

Save and compile your game. You can now move your playable character and take out enemies as they try to attack you. This is the final chapter that deals directly with 2-D graphics and the *Star Fighter* game. In the next section, you will find some suggestions for expanding on what you learned in the chapters that led you here before progressing into the realm of 3-D gaming.

Expanding on What You Learned

If you want to really expand on your *Star Fighter* game, you can add several key elements to your code that will make a major difference to the game play.

- Expand the weapons so that they are also fired from the scouts and warships.

- Expand the collision detection to include shot impacts on the player and collisions between the payer and enemies.

- Add a three- or four-sprite animation sequence of an explosion that can be triggered when a ship is destroyed.

- Give the player more than one life to work with.

All of these items can easily be accomplished with the skills that you have obtained to this point in this book.

Summary

In this chapter, you learned how to create weapons that can be autofired by the player. You also added some basic 2-D collision detection to destroy enemies as they are hit by the player.

In the next chapter, you will learn how to publish your game on the Android Marketplace before moving on to 3-D game programming.

But before we move on, please review the full source code for the keys files of Star Fighter I have provided in the next section. I selected the files that have either had the most changes to them, or have the most code. The code listings for these files are provided so that you can compare your code against the code from the project.

This is designed to help you along should you have problems compiling or running your project. Given that games can be complicate to create from scratch, and because some code can be overlooked when you are following through the chapters, you may discover that you cannot correctly run or compile the game the way it appears in the book. Being the last chapter in which you will learn 2D gaming, this is a good spot to stop and review your code.

Reviewing the Key 2-D Code

The first file that you should check— if you are having problems running your Star Fighter game—is the SFEngine.java. This file contains settings that are used throughout the game, and in almost every class in the project. You first created this file back in Chapter 3, and continued to edit it thoughout Part 1. Therefore it is the most likely place that you may have missed something. The source for the SFEngine.java is shown in the Listing 8–1.

Listing 8–1. *SFEngine.java*

```
package com.proandroidgames;

import android.content.Context;
import android.content.Intent;
import android.view.Display;
import android.view.View;

public class SFEngine {
        /*Constants that will be used in the game*/
        public static final int GAME_THREAD_DELAY = 4000;
        public static final int MENU_BUTTON_ALPHA = 0;
        public static final boolean HAPTIC_BUTTON_FEEDBACK = true;
        public static final int SPLASH_SCREEN_MUSIC = R.raw.warfieldedit;
        public static final int R_VOLUME = 100;
        public static final int L_VOLUME = 100;
        public static final boolean LOOP_BACKGROUND_MUSIC = true;
        public static final int GAME_THREAD_FPS_SLEEP = (1000/60);
        public static float SCROLL_BACKGROUND_1  = .002f;
        public static float SCROLL_BACKGROUND_2  = .007f;
        public static final int BACKGROUND_LAYER_ONE = R.drawable.backgroundstars;
        public static final int BACKGROUND_LAYER_TWO = R.drawable.debris;
        public static final int PLAYER_BANK_LEFT_1 = 1;
        public static final int PLAYER_RELEASE = 3;
        public static final int PLAYER_BANK_RIGHT_1 = 4;
        public static final int PLAYER_FRAMES_BETWEEN_ANI = 9;
        public static final float PLAYER_BANK_SPEED = .1f;
        public static int CHARACTER_SHEET = R.drawable.character_sprite;
        public static int TOTAL_INTERCEPTORS = 10;
        public static int TOTAL_SCOUTS = 15;
        public static int TOTAL_WARSHIPS = 5;
        public static float INTERCEPTOR_SPEED = SCROLL_BACKGROUND_1 * 4f;
```

```
        public static float SCOUT_SPEED = SCROLL_BACKGROUND_1 * 6f;
        public static float WARSHIP_SPEED = SCROLL_BACKGROUND_2 * 4f;
        public static final int TYPE_INTERCEPTOR = 1;
        public static final int TYPE_SCOUT = 2;
        public static final int TYPE_WARSHIP = 3;
        public static final int ATTACK_RANDOM = 0;
        public static final int ATTACK_RIGHT = 1;
        public static final int ATTACK_LEFT = 2;
        public static final float BEZIER_X_1 = 0f;
        public static final float BEZIER_X_2 = 1f;
        public static final float BEZIER_X_3 = 2.5f;
        public static final float BEZIER_X_4 = 3f;
        public static final float BEZIER_Y_1 = 0f;
        public static final float BEZIER_Y_2 = 2.4f;
        public static final float BEZIER_Y_3 = 1.5f;
        public static final float BEZIER_Y_4 = 2.6f;
        public static final int WEAPONS_SHEET = R.drawable.destruction;
        public static final int PLAYER_SHIELDS = 5;
        public static final int SCOUT_SHIELDS = 3;
        public static final int INTERCEPTOR_SHIELDS = 1;
        public static final int WARSHIP_SHIELDS = 5;
        public static final float PLAYER_BULLET_SPEED = .125f;
        /*Game Variables*/

        public static Context context;
        public static Thread musicThread;
        public static Display display;
        public static int playerFlightAction = 0;
        public static float playerBankPosX = 1.75f;
        /*Kill game and exit*/
        public boolean onExit(View v) {
                try
                {
                        Intent bgmusic = new Intent(context, SFMusic.class);
                        context.stopService(bgmusic);
                        musicThread.stop();

                        return true;
                }catch(Exception e){
                        return false;
                }
        }
}
```

The next file (Listing 8–2) is the class used to create your weapons. This file was created earlier and therefore may have been overlooked. Pay attention to the onDraw() method when you are checking this file against yours – if you coppied the contents of this file from a similar one, like SFBackground.java, you may have missed some changes.

Listing 8–2. *SFWeapon.java*

```
package com.proandroidgames;

import java.nio.ByteBuffer;
import java.nio.ByteOrder;
import java.nio.FloatBuffer;

import javax.microedition.khronos.opengles.GL10;
```

```java
public class SFWeapon {

        public float posY = 0f;
        public float posX = 0f;
        public boolean shotFired = false;

        private FloatBuffer vertexBuffer;
        private FloatBuffer textureBuffer;
        private ByteBuffer indexBuffer;

        private float vertices[] = {
        0.0f, 0.0f, 0.0f,
        1.0f, 0.0f, 0.0f,
        1.0f, 1.0f, 0.0f,
        0.0f, 1.0f, 0.0f,
        };

        private float texture[] = {
        0.0f, 0.0f,
        0.25f, 0.0f,
        0.25f, 0.25f,
        0.0f, 0.25f,
        };

        private byte indices[] = {
         0,1,2,
        0,2,3,
        };

        public SFWeapon() {

                ByteBuffer byteBuf = ByteBuffer.allocateDirect(vertices.length * 4);
                byteBuf.order(ByteOrder.nativeOrder());
                vertexBuffer = byteBuf.asFloatBuffer();
                vertexBuffer.put(vertices);
                vertexBuffer.position(0);

                byteBuf = ByteBuffer.allocateDirect(texture.length * 4);
                byteBuf.order(ByteOrder.nativeOrder());
                textureBuffer = byteBuf.asFloatBuffer();
                textureBuffer.put(texture);
                textureBuffer.position(0);

                indexBuffer = ByteBuffer.allocateDirect(indices.length);
                indexBuffer.put(indices);
                 indexBuffer.position(0);
        }

        public void draw(GL10 gl, int[] spriteSheet) {
                gl.glBindTexture(GL10.GL_TEXTURE_2D, spriteSheet[1]);

                gl.glFrontFace(GL10.GL_CCW);
                gl.glEnable(GL10.GL_CULL_FACE);
                 gl.glCullFace(GL10.GL_BACK);

                 gl.glEnableClientState(GL10.GL_VERTEX_ARRAY);
```

```
                    gl.glEnableClientState(GL10.GL_TEXTURE_COORD_ARRAY);

                    gl.glVertexPointer(3, GL10.GL_FLOAT, 0, vertexBuffer);
                    gl.glTexCoordPointer(2, GL10.GL_FLOAT, 0, textureBuffer);

                    gl.glDrawElements(GL10.GL_TRIANGLES, indices.length,
        GL10.GL_UNSIGNED_BYTE, indexBuffer);

                    gl.glDisableClientState(GL10.GL_VERTEX_ARRAY);
                    gl.glDisableClientState(GL10.GL_TEXTURE_COORD_ARRAY);
                    gl.glDisable(GL10.GL_CULL_FACE);
                }

        }
```

The SFTextures file was also a relatively new file to the code, therefore it is possible for problems to show up here as well. This code was used to expand update an existing process for calling textures. If you were not paying attention it would have been very easy to overlook an important part of this. When you are checking the code in Listing 8–3, be sure to check that your arrays are instantiated correctly.

Listing 8–3. *SFTextures.java*

```java
package com.proandroidgames;

import java.io.IOException;
import java.io.InputStream;

import javax.microedition.khronos.opengles.GL10;

import android.content.Context;
import android.graphics.Bitmap;
import android.graphics.BitmapFactory;
import android.opengl.GLUtils;

public class SFTextures {

        private int[] textures = new int[2];

        public SFTextures(GL10 gl){

        gl.glGenTextures(2, textures, 0);

        }
        public int[] loadTexture(GL10 gl,int texture, Context context,int
textureNumber) {
        InputStream imagestream = context.getResources().openRawResource(texture);
        Bitmap bitmap = null;
        try {

                bitmap = BitmapFactory.decodeStream(imagestream);

        }catch(Exception e){

        }finally {
        //Always clear and close
```

```
        try {
                imagestream.close();
                imagestream = null;
        } catch (IOException e) {
        }
    }

    gl.glBindTexture(GL10.GL_TEXTURE_2D, textures[textureNumber - 1]);

    gl.glTexParameterf(GL10.GL_TEXTURE_2D, GL10.GL_TEXTURE_MIN_FILTER,
GL10.GL_NEAREST);
    gl.glTexParameterf(GL10.GL_TEXTURE_2D, GL10.GL_TEXTURE_MAG_FILTER,
GL10.GL_LINEAR);

    gl.glTexParameterf(GL10.GL_TEXTURE_2D, GL10.GL_TEXTURE_WRAP_S,
GL10.GL_CLAMP_TO_EDGE);
    gl.glTexParameterf(GL10.GL_TEXTURE_2D, GL10.GL_TEXTURE_WRAP_T,
GL10.GL_CLAMP_TO_EDGE);

    GLUtils.texImage2D(GL10.GL_TEXTURE_2D, 0, bitmap, 0);

    bitmap.recycle();

    return textures;
    }
}
```

If your files appear to match those in the previous listings, and you are still having
problems, then it is time to dive into the game loop. The SFGameRenderer.java contains
the main game loop for Star Fighter and is the most likely place for a problem to
happen. Unfortunately, being the largest file in the game, it is also the hardest file to
troubleshoot. Listing 8–4 shows the source code for the SFGameRenderer.java. Pay
special attention to the onDrawFrame() method.

Listing 8–4. *SFGameRenderer.java*

```
package com.proandroidgames;

import java.util.Random;

import javax.microedition.khronos.egl.EGLConfig;
import javax.microedition.khronos.opengles.GL10;

import android.opengl.GLSurfaceView.Renderer;

public class SFGameRenderer implements Renderer{
        private SFBackGround background = new SFBackGround();
        private SFBackGround background2 = new SFBackGround();
        private SFGoodGuy player1 = new SFGoodGuy();
        private SFEnemy[] enemies = new SFEnemy[SFEngine.TOTAL_INTERCEPTORS +
SFEngine.TOTAL_SCOUTS + SFEngine.TOTAL_WARSHIPS - 1];
        private SFTextures textureLoader;
        private int[] spriteSheets = new int[2];
        private SFWeapon[] playerFire = new SFWeapon[4];

        private int goodGuyBankFrames = 0;
        private long loopStart = 0;
```

```java
            private long loopEnd = 0;
            private long loopRunTime = 0 ;

            private float bgScroll1;
            private float bgScroll2;

            @Override
            public void onDrawFrame(GL10 gl) {
                    loopStart = System.currentTimeMillis();
                    // TODO Auto-generated method stub
                    try {
                            if (loopRunTime < SFEngine.GAME_THREAD_FPS_SLEEP){
                                    Thread.sleep(SFEngine.GAME_THREAD_FPS_SLEEP -
loopRunTime);
                            }
                    } catch (InterruptedException e) {
                            // TODO Auto-generated catch block
                            e.printStackTrace();
                    }
                    gl.glClear(GL10.GL_COLOR_BUFFER_BIT | GL10.GL_DEPTH_BUFFER_BIT);

                    scrollBackground1(gl);
                    scrollBackground2(gl);

                    movePlayer1(gl);
                    moveEnemy(gl);

                    detectCollisions();

                    gl.glEnable(GL10.GL_BLEND);
            gl.glBlendFunc(GL10.GL_ONE, GL10.GL_ONE_MINUS_SRC_ALPHA);
            loopEnd = System.currentTimeMillis();
            loopRunTime = ((loopEnd - loopStart));

            }
            private void initializeInterceptors(){
                    for (int x = 0; x<SFEngine.TOTAL_INTERCEPTORS -1 ; x++){
                            SFEnemy interceptor = new SFEnemy(SFEngine.TYPE_INTERCEPTOR,
SFEngine.ATTACK_RANDOM);
                            enemies[x] = interceptor;
                    }
            }
            private void initializeScouts(){
                    for (int x = SFEngine.TOTAL_INTERCEPTORS -1;
x<SFEngine.TOTAL_INTERCEPTORS + SFEngine.TOTAL_SCOUTS -1; x++){
                            SFEnemy interceptor;
                            if (x>=(SFEngine.TOTAL_INTERCEPTORS + SFEngine.TOTAL_SCOUTS) / 2
){
                                    interceptor = new SFEnemy(SFEngine.TYPE_SCOUT,
SFEngine.ATTACK_RIGHT);
                            }else{
                                    interceptor = new SFEnemy(SFEngine.TYPE_SCOUT,
SFEngine.ATTACK_LEFT);
                            }
                            enemies[x] = interceptor;
                    }
            }
```

```
        private void initializeWarships(){
                for (int x = SFEngine.TOTAL_INTERCEPTORS + SFEngine.TOTAL_SCOUTS -1;
x<SFEngine.TOTAL_INTERCEPTORS + SFEngine.TOTAL_SCOUTS + SFEngine.TOTAL_WARSHIPS -1;
x++){
                        SFEnemy interceptor = new SFEnemy(SFEngine.TYPE_WARSHIP,
SFEngine.ATTACK_RANDOM);
                        enemies[x] = interceptor;
                }
        }
        private void initializePlayerWeapons(){
                for(int x = 0; x < 4; x++){
                        SFWeapon weapon = new SFWeapon();
                        playerFire[x] = weapon;
                }
                playerFire[0].shotFired = true;
                playerFire[0].posX = SFEngine.playerBankPosX;
                playerFire[0].posY = 1.25f;
        }
        private void moveEnemy(GL10 gl){
                for (int x = 0; x < SFEngine.TOTAL_INTERCEPTORS + SFEngine.TOTAL_SCOUTS
+ SFEngine.TOTAL_WARSHIPS - 1; x++){
                        if (!enemies[x].isDestroyed){
                                Random randomPos = new Random();
                                switch (enemies[x].enemyType){
                                case SFEngine.TYPE_INTERCEPTOR:
                                    if (enemies[x].posY < 0){
                                            enemies[x].posY = (randomPos.nextFloat()
* 4) + 4;

                                            enemies[x].posX = randomPos.nextFloat()
* 3;

                                            enemies[x].isLockedOn = false;
                                            enemies[x].lockOnPosX = 0;
                                    }
                                    gl.glMatrixMode(GL10.GL_MODELVIEW);
                                    gl.glLoadIdentity();
                                    gl.glPushMatrix();
                                    gl.glScalef(.25f, .25f, 1f);

                                    if (enemies[x].posY >= 3){
                                            enemies[x].posY -=
SFEngine.INTERCEPTOR_SPEED;
                                    }else{
                                            if (!enemies[x].isLockedOn){
                                                    enemies[x].lockOnPosX =
SFEngine.playerBankPosX;

                                                    enemies[x].isLockedOn = true;
                                                    enemies[x].incrementXToTarget
=(float) ((enemies[x].lockOnPosX - enemies[x].posX )/ (enemies[x].posY /
(SFEngine.INTERCEPTOR_SPEED* 4)));
                                            }
                                            enemies[x].posY -=
(SFEngine.INTERCEPTOR_SPEED* 4);

                                            enemies[x].posX +=
enemies[x].incrementXToTarget;

                                    }
```

```
                                        gl.glTranslatef(enemies[x].posX,
enemies[x].posY, 0f);

                                        gl.glMatrixMode(GL10.GL_TEXTURE);
                                        gl.glLoadIdentity();
                                        gl.glTranslatef(0.25f, .25f , 0.0f);
                                 enemies[x].draw(gl, spriteSheets);
                                 gl.glPopMatrix();
                                 gl.glLoadIdentity();

                                 break;
                         case SFEngine.TYPE_SCOUT:
                                 if (enemies[x].posY <= 0){
                                        enemies[x].posY = (randomPos.nextFloat()
* 4) + 4;

                                        enemies[x].isLockedOn = false;
                                        enemies[x].posT = SFEngine.SCOUT_SPEED;
                                        enemies[x].lockOnPosX =
enemies[x].getNextScoutX();
                                        enemies[x].lockOnPosY =
enemies[x].getNextScoutY();
                                        if(enemies[x].attackDirection ==
SFEngine.ATTACK_LEFT){
                                                enemies[x].posX = 0;
                                        }else{
                                                enemies[x].posX = 3f;
                                        }
                                 }
                                 gl.glMatrixMode(GL10.GL_MODELVIEW);
                                 gl.glLoadIdentity();
                                 gl.glPushMatrix();
                                 gl.glScalef(.25f, .25f, 1f);

                                 if (enemies[x].posY >= 2.75f){
                                        enemies[x].posY -= SFEngine.SCOUT_SPEED;

                                 }else{
                                        enemies[x].posX =
enemies[x].getNextScoutX();
                                        enemies[x].posY =
enemies[x].getNextScoutY();
                                        enemies[x].posT += SFEngine.SCOUT_SPEED;


                                 }
                                        gl.glTranslatef(enemies[x].posX,
enemies[x].posY, 0f);

                                        gl.glMatrixMode(GL10.GL_TEXTURE);
                                        gl.glLoadIdentity();
                                        gl.glTranslatef(0.50f, .25f , 0.0f);
                                 enemies[x].draw(gl, spriteSheets);
                                 gl.glPopMatrix();
                                 gl.glLoadIdentity();

                                 break;
                         case SFEngine.TYPE_WARSHIP:
                                 if (enemies[x].posY < 0){
```

```java
                                              enemies[x].posY = (randomPos.nextFloat()
* 4) + 4;
                                              enemies[x].posX = randomPos.nextFloat()
* 3;
                                              enemies[x].isLockedOn = false;
                                              enemies[x].lockOnPosX = 0;
                                    }
                                    gl.glMatrixMode(GL10.GL_MODELVIEW);
                                    gl.glLoadIdentity();
                                    gl.glPushMatrix();
                                    gl.glScalef(.25f, .25f, 1f);

                                    if (enemies[x].posY >= 3){
                                            enemies[x].posY -=
SFEngine.WARSHIP_SPEED;

                                    }else{
                                            if (!enemies[x].isLockedOn){
                                                    enemies[x].lockOnPosX =
randomPos.nextFloat() * 3;

                                                    enemies[x].isLockedOn = true;
                                                    enemies[x].incrementXToTarget
=(float) ((enemies[x].lockOnPosX - enemies[x].posX )/ (enemies[x].posY /
(SFEngine.WARSHIP_SPEED* 4)));

                                            }
                                            enemies[x].posY -=
(SFEngine.WARSHIP_SPEED* 2);

                                            enemies[x].posX +=
enemies[x].incrementXToTarget;


                                    }
                                            gl.glTranslatef(enemies[x].posX,
enemies[x].posY, 0f);

                                            gl.glMatrixMode(GL10.GL_TEXTURE);
                                            gl.glLoadIdentity();
                                            gl.glTranslatef(0.75f, .25f , 0.0f);
                                    enemies[x].draw(gl,spriteSheets);
                                    gl.glPopMatrix();
                                    gl.glLoadIdentity();

                                    break;

                        }
                    }
                }
        }


        private void movePlayer1(GL10 gl){
                if(!player1.isDestroyed){
                        switch (SFEngine.playerFlightAction){
                        case SFEngine.PLAYER_BANK_LEFT_1:
                                gl.glMatrixMode(GL10.GL_MODELVIEW);
                                gl.glLoadIdentity();
                                gl.glPushMatrix();
```

```
                                        gl.glScalef(.25f, .25f, 1f);
                                        if (goodGuyBankFrames <
SFEngine.PLAYER_FRAMES_BETWEEN_ANI && SFEngine.playerBankPosX > 0){
                                                SFEngine.playerBankPosX -=
SFEngine.PLAYER_BANK_SPEED;
                                            gl.glTranslatef(SFEngine.playerBankPosX, 0f,
0f);

                                            gl.glMatrixMode(GL10.GL_TEXTURE);
                                            gl.glLoadIdentity();
                                            gl.glTranslatef(0.75f,0.0f, 0.0f);
                                            goodGuyBankFrames += 1;
                                        }else if (goodGuyBankFrames >=
SFEngine.PLAYER_FRAMES_BETWEEN_ANI && SFEngine.playerBankPosX > 0){
                                                SFEngine.playerBankPosX -=
SFEngine.PLAYER_BANK_SPEED;
                                            gl.glTranslatef(SFEngine.playerBankPosX, 0f,
0f);

                                            gl.glMatrixMode(GL10.GL_TEXTURE);
                                            gl.glLoadIdentity();
                                            gl.glTranslatef(0.0f,0.25f, 0.0f);
                                        }else{
                                            gl.glTranslatef(SFEngine.playerBankPosX, 0f,
0f);

                                            gl.glMatrixMode(GL10.GL_TEXTURE);
                                            gl.glLoadIdentity();
                                            gl.glTranslatef(0.0f,0.0f, 0.0f);
                                        }
                                        player1.draw(gl,spriteSheets);
                                        gl.glPopMatrix();
                                        gl.glLoadIdentity();

                                        break;
                                case SFEngine.PLAYER_BANK_RIGHT_1:
                                        gl.glMatrixMode(GL10.GL_MODELVIEW);
                                        gl.glLoadIdentity();
                                        gl.glPushMatrix();
                                        gl.glScalef(.25f, .25f, 1f);
                                        if (goodGuyBankFrames <
SFEngine.PLAYER_FRAMES_BETWEEN_ANI && SFEngine.playerBankPosX < 3){
                                                SFEngine.playerBankPosX +=
SFEngine.PLAYER_BANK_SPEED;
                                            gl.glTranslatef(SFEngine.playerBankPosX, 0f,
0f);

                                            gl.glMatrixMode(GL10.GL_TEXTURE);
                                            gl.glLoadIdentity();
                                            gl.glTranslatef(0.25f,0.0f, 0.0f);
                                            goodGuyBankFrames += 1;
                                        }else if (goodGuyBankFrames >=
SFEngine.PLAYER_FRAMES_BETWEEN_ANI && SFEngine.playerBankPosX < 3){
                                            gl.glTranslatef(SFEngine.playerBankPosX, 0f,
0f);

                                            gl.glMatrixMode(GL10.GL_TEXTURE);
                                            gl.glLoadIdentity();
                                            gl.glTranslatef(0.50f,0.0f, 0.0f);
                                                SFEngine.playerBankPosX +=
SFEngine.PLAYER_BANK_SPEED;
                                        }else{
```

```
                                          gl.glTranslatef(SFEngine.playerBankPosX, 0f,
0f);

                                          gl.glMatrixMode(GL10.GL_TEXTURE);
                                          gl.glLoadIdentity();
                                          gl.glTranslatef(0.0f,0.0f, 0.0f);
                                  }
                                  player1.draw(gl,spriteSheets);
                                  gl.glPopMatrix();
                                  gl.glLoadIdentity();
                                  break;
                          case SFEngine.PLAYER_RELEASE:
                                  gl.glMatrixMode(GL10.GL_MODELVIEW);
                                  gl.glLoadIdentity();
                                  gl.glPushMatrix();
                                  gl.glScalef(.25f, .25f, 1f);
                                  gl.glTranslatef(SFEngine.playerBankPosX, 0f, 0f);
                                  gl.glMatrixMode(GL10.GL_TEXTURE);
                                  gl.glLoadIdentity();
                                  gl.glTranslatef(0.0f,0.0f, 0.0f);
                                  goodGuyBankFrames = 0;
                                  player1.draw(gl,spriteSheets);
                                  gl.glPopMatrix();
                                  gl.glLoadIdentity();
                                  break;
                          default:
                                  gl.glMatrixMode(GL10.GL_MODELVIEW);
                                  gl.glLoadIdentity();
                                  gl.glPushMatrix();
                                  gl.glScalef(.25f, .25f, 1f);
                                  gl.glTranslatef(SFEngine.playerBankPosX, 0f, 0f);
                                  gl.glMatrixMode(GL10.GL_TEXTURE);
                                  gl.glLoadIdentity();
                                  gl.glTranslatef(0.0f,0.0f, 0.0f);
                                  player1.draw(gl,spriteSheets);
                                  gl.glPopMatrix();
                                  gl.glLoadIdentity();
                                  break;
                          }
                          firePlayerWeapon(gl);
                  }


        }
        private void detectCollisions(){
                  for (int y = 0; y < 3; y ++){
                          if (playerFire[y].shotFired){
                                  for (int x = 0; x < SFEngine.TOTAL_INTERCEPTORS +
SFEngine.TOTAL_SCOUTS + SFEngine.TOTAL_WARSHIPS - 1; x++ ){
                                          if(!enemies[x].isDestroyed && enemies[x].posY <
4.25 ){
                                                  if ((playerFire[y].posY >=
enemies[x].posY - 1
                                                          && playerFire[y].posY <=
enemies[x].posY )
                                                          && (playerFire[y].posX
<= enemies[x].posX + 1
```

```java
                                              && playerFire[y].posX >=
enemies[x].posX - 1)){
                                          int nextShot = 0;
                                          enemies[x].applyDamage();
                                          playerFire[y].shotFired = false;
                                          if (y == 3){
                                              nextShot = 0;
                                          }else{
                                              nextShot = y + 1;
                                          }
                                          if
(playerFire[nextShot].shotFired == false){

playerFire[nextShot].shotFired = true;

playerFire[nextShot].posX = SFEngine.playerBankPosX;

playerFire[nextShot].posY = 1.25f;
                                              }
                                          }
                                      }
                                  }
                              }
                          }
                      }
                  }
    private void firePlayerWeapon(GL10 gl){
        for(int x = 0; x < 4; x++){
            if (playerFire[x].shotFired){
                int nextShot = 0;
                if (playerFire[x].posY > 4.25){
                    playerFire[x].shotFired = false;
                }else{
                    if (playerFire[x].posY> 2){
                        if (x == 3){
                            nextShot = 0;
                        }else{
                            nextShot = x + 1;
                        }
                        if (playerFire[nextShot].shotFired ==
false){
                                          playerFire[nextShot].shotFired =
true;
                                          playerFire[nextShot].posX =
SFEngine.playerBankPosX;
                                          playerFire[nextShot].posY =
1.25f;
                        }
                    }
                }
                playerFire[x].posY +=
SFEngine.PLAYER_BULLET_SPEED;

                gl.glMatrixMode(GL10.GL_MODELVIEW);
                gl.glLoadIdentity();
                gl.glPushMatrix();
                gl.glScalef(.25f, .25f, 0f);
                gl.glTranslatef(playerFire[x].posX,
playerFire[x].posY, 0f);
```

```
                              gl.glMatrixMode(GL10.GL_TEXTURE);
                              gl.glLoadIdentity();
                              gl.glTranslatef(0.0f,0.0f, 0.0f);

                              playerFire[x].draw(gl,spriteSheets);
                              gl.glPopMatrix();
                              gl.glLoadIdentity();

                    }
              }
         }
}
private void scrollBackground1(GL10 gl){
        if (bgScroll1 == Float.MAX_VALUE){
                bgScroll1 = 0f;
        }


gl.glMatrixMode(GL10.GL_MODELVIEW);
gl.glLoadIdentity();
gl.glPushMatrix();
gl.glScalef(1f, 1f, 1f);
gl.glTranslatef(0f, 0f, 0f);

        gl.glMatrixMode(GL10.GL_TEXTURE);
        gl.glLoadIdentity();
gl.glTranslatef(0.0f,bgScroll1, 0.0f);

background.draw(gl);
gl.glPopMatrix();
bgScroll1 +=SFEngine.SCROLL_BACKGROUND_1;
gl.glLoadIdentity();


}
private void scrollBackground2(GL10 gl){
        if (bgScroll2 == Float.MAX_VALUE){
                bgScroll2 = 0f;
        }
gl.glMatrixMode(GL10.GL_MODELVIEW);
gl.glLoadIdentity();
gl.glPushMatrix();
gl.glScalef(.5f, 1f, 1f);
gl.glTranslatef(1.5f, 0f, 0f);

gl.glMatrixMode(GL10.GL_TEXTURE);
        gl.glLoadIdentity();
gl.glTranslatef( 0.0f,bgScroll2, 0.0f);

background2.draw(gl);
gl.glPopMatrix();
bgScroll2 +=SFEngine.SCROLL_BACKGROUND_2;
gl.glLoadIdentity();
}
@Override
public void onSurfaceChanged(GL10 gl, int width, int height) {
```

```
                        // TODO Auto-generated method stub

                        gl.glViewport(0, 0, width,height);

                        gl.glMatrixMode(GL10.GL_PROJECTION);
                        gl.glLoadIdentity();

                        gl.glOrthof(0f, 1f, 0f, 1f, -1f, 1f);

                }

        @Override
        public void onSurfaceCreated(GL10 gl, EGLConfig config) {
                        // TODO Auto-generated method stub
                        initializeInterceptors();
                        initializeScouts();
                        initializeWarships();
                        initializePlayerWeapons();
                        textureLoader = new SFTextures(gl);
                        spriteSheets = textureLoader.loadTexture(gl, SFEngine.CHARACTER_SHEET,
SFEngine.context, 1);
                        spriteSheets = textureLoader.loadTexture(gl, SFEngine.WEAPONS_SHEET,
SFEngine.context, 2);

                        gl.glEnable(GL10.GL_TEXTURE_2D);
                        gl.glClearDepthf(1.0f);
                        gl.glEnable(GL10.GL_DEPTH_TEST);
                        gl.glDepthFunc(GL10.GL_LEQUAL);

                        background.loadTexture(gl,SFEngine.BACKGROUND_LAYER_ONE,
SFEngine.context);
                        background2.loadTexture(gl,SFEngine.BACKGROUND_LAYER_TWO,
SFEngine.context);
                }

        }
```

Finally, Listings 8–5 and 8–6 show the last two key files in this project. The SFGoodGuy.java and SFBadGuy.java contain the code for the player and enemy classes. While you shouldn't have noticed any problems in these files early on in the writing of this game, it can never hurt to double check your work.

When looking at the SFEnemy.java, check the formulas for the Bezier curves.

Listing 8–5. *SFGoodGuy.java*

```
package com.proandroidgames;

import java.nio.ByteBuffer;
import java.nio.ByteOrder;
import java.nio.FloatBuffer;

import javax.microedition.khronos.opengles.GL10;

public class SFGoodGuy {
        public boolean isDestroyed = false;
        private int damage = 0;
```

```java
private FloatBuffer vertexBuffer;
private FloatBuffer textureBuffer;
private ByteBuffer indexBuffer;

private float vertices[] = {
0.0f, 0.0f, 0.0f,
1.0f, 0.0f, 0.0f,
1.0f, 1.0f, 0.0f,
0.0f, 1.0f, 0.0f,
};

private float texture[] = {
0.0f, 0.0f,
0.25f, 0.0f,
0.25f, 0.25f,
0.0f, 0.25f,
};

private byte indices[] = {
0,1,2,
0,2,3,
};

public void applyDamage(){
        damage++;
        if (damage == SFEngine.PLAYER_SHIELDS){
                isDestroyed = true;
        }

}
 public SFGoodGuy() {
ByteBuffer byteBuf = ByteBuffer.allocateDirect(vertices.length * 4);
byteBuf.order(ByteOrder.nativeOrder());
vertexBuffer = byteBuf.asFloatBuffer();
vertexBuffer.put(vertices);
vertexBuffer.position(0);

byteBuf = ByteBuffer.allocateDirect(texture.length * 4);
byteBuf.order(ByteOrder.nativeOrder());
textureBuffer = byteBuf.asFloatBuffer();
textureBuffer.put(texture);
textureBuffer.position(0);

indexBuffer = ByteBuffer.allocateDirect(indices.length);
indexBuffer.put(indices);
indexBuffer.position(0);
 }

public void draw(GL10 gl, int[] spriteSheet) {
gl.glBindTexture(GL10.GL_TEXTURE_2D, spriteSheet[0]);

gl.glFrontFace(GL10.GL_CCW);
gl.glEnable(GL10.GL_CULL_FACE);
gl.glCullFace(GL10.GL_BACK);

gl.glEnableClientState(GL10.GL_VERTEX_ARRAY);
```

```
        gl.glEnableClientState(GL10.GL_TEXTURE_COORD_ARRAY);

        gl.glVertexPointer(3, GL10.GL_FLOAT, 0, vertexBuffer);
        gl.glTexCoordPointer(2, GL10.GL_FLOAT, 0, textureBuffer);

        gl.glDrawElements(GL10.GL_TRIANGLES, indices.length, GL10.GL_UNSIGNED_BYTE,
indexBuffer);

        gl.glDisableClientState(GL10.GL_VERTEX_ARRAY);
        gl.glDisableClientState(GL10.GL_TEXTURE_COORD_ARRAY);
        gl.glDisable(GL10.GL_CULL_FACE);
         }

    }
```

Listing 8–6. *SFEnemy.java*

```
package com.proandroidgames;

import java.nio.ByteBuffer;
import java.nio.ByteOrder;
import java.nio.FloatBuffer;
import java.util.Random;

import javax.microedition.khronos.opengles.GL10;

public class SFEnemy {

                public float posY = 0f;
                public float posX = 0f;
                public float posT = 0f;
                public float incrementXToTarget = 0f;
                public float incrementYToTarget = 0f;
                public int attackDirection = 0;
                public boolean isDestroyed = false;
                private int damage = 0;

                public int enemyType = 0;

                public boolean isLockedOn = false;
                public float lockOnPosX = 0f;
                public float lockOnPosY = 0f;

                private Random randomPos = new Random();

        private FloatBuffer vertexBuffer;
        private FloatBuffer textureBuffer;
        private ByteBuffer indexBuffer;

        private float vertices[] = {
        0.0f, 0.0f, 0.0f,
        1.0f, 0.0f, 0.0f,
        1.0f, 1.0f, 0.0f,
        0.0f, 1.0f, 0.0f,
        };

        private float texture[] = {
```

```
 0.0f, 0.0f,
 0.25f, 0.0f,
 0.25f, 0.25f,
 0.0f, 0.25f,
};

private byte indices[] = {
 0,1,2,
 0,2,3,
};
public void applyDamage(){
        damage++;
        switch(enemyType){
        case SFEngine.TYPE_INTERCEPTOR:
                if (damage == SFEngine.INTERCEPTOR_SHIELDS){
                        isDestroyed = true;
                }
                break;
        case SFEngine.TYPE_SCOUT:
                if (damage == SFEngine.SCOUT_SHIELDS){
                        isDestroyed = true;
                }
                break;
        case SFEngine.TYPE_WARSHIP:
                if (damage == SFEngine.WARSHIP_SHIELDS){
                        isDestroyed = true;
                }
                break;
        }
}

 public SFEnemy(int type, int direction) {
        enemyType = type;
        attackDirection = direction;
        posY = (randomPos.nextFloat() * 4) + 4;
        switch(attackDirection){
        case SFEngine.ATTACK_LEFT:
                posX = 0;
                break;
        case SFEngine.ATTACK_RANDOM:
                posX = randomPos.nextFloat() * 3;
                break;
        case SFEngine.ATTACK_RIGHT:
                posX = 3;
                break;
        }
        posT = SFEngine.SCOUT_SPEED;

ByteBuffer byteBuf = ByteBuffer.allocateDirect(vertices.length * 4);
byteBuf.order(ByteOrder.nativeOrder());
vertexBuffer = byteBuf.asFloatBuffer();
vertexBuffer.put(vertices);
vertexBuffer.position(0);

byteBuf = ByteBuffer.allocateDirect(texture.length * 4);
byteBuf.order(ByteOrder.nativeOrder());
textureBuffer = byteBuf.asFloatBuffer();
```

```
            textureBuffer.put(texture);
            textureBuffer.position(0);

            indexBuffer = ByteBuffer.allocateDirect(indices.length);
            indexBuffer.put(indices);
            indexBuffer.position(0);
        }
        public float getNextScoutX(){
                if (attackDirection == SFEngine.ATTACK_LEFT){
                        return (float)((SFEngine.BEZIER_X_4*(posT*posT*posT)) +
(SFEngine.BEZIER_X_3 * 3 * (posT * posT) * (1-posT)) + (SFEngine.BEZIER_X_2 * 3 * posT *
((1-posT) * (1-posT))) + (SFEngine.BEZIER_X_1 * ((1-posT) * (1-posT) * (1-posT))));
                }else{
                        return (float)((SFEngine.BEZIER_X_1*(posT*posT*posT)) +
(SFEngine.BEZIER_X_2 * 3 * (posT * posT) * (1-posT)) + (SFEngine.BEZIER_X_3 * 3 * posT *
((1-posT) * (1-posT))) + (SFEngine.BEZIER_X_4 * ((1-posT) * (1-posT) * (1-posT))));
                }


        }
        public float getNextScoutY(){
                return (float)((SFEngine.BEZIER_Y_1*(posT*posT*posT)) +
(SFEngine.BEZIER_Y_2 * 3 * (posT * posT) * (1-posT)) + (SFEngine.BEZIER_Y_3 * 3 * posT *
((1-posT) * (1-posT))) + (SFEngine.BEZIER_Y_4 * ((1-posT) * (1-posT) * (1-posT))));
        }

        public void draw(GL10 gl, int[] spriteSheet) {
                gl.glBindTexture(GL10.GL_TEXTURE_2D, spriteSheet[0]);

                gl.glFrontFace(GL10.GL_CCW);
                gl.glEnable(GL10.GL_CULL_FACE);
                gl.glCullFace(GL10.GL_BACK);

                gl.glEnableClientState(GL10.GL_VERTEX_ARRAY);
                gl.glEnableClientState(GL10.GL_TEXTURE_COORD_ARRAY);

                gl.glVertexPointer(3, GL10.GL_FLOAT, 0, vertexBuffer);
                gl.glTexCoordPointer(2, GL10.GL_FLOAT, 0, textureBuffer);

                gl.glDrawElements(GL10.GL_TRIANGLES, indices.length,
GL10.GL_UNSIGNED_BYTE, indexBuffer);

                gl.glDisableClientState(GL10.GL_VERTEX_ARRAY);
                gl.glDisableClientState(GL10.GL_TEXTURE_COORD_ARRAY);
                gl.glDisable(GL10.GL_CULL_FACE);
        }

}
```

Publishing Your Game

You may have, by now, a pretty enjoyable 2-D game. Like most casual game developers, you probably want to share your creation with the rest of the world. The way to get your game into the hands, and onto the devices, of the masses is to publish it to the Android Marketplace. This chapter is going to outline the process of publishing your game on the Android Marketplace.

Before you can publish your masterpiece, you must do a few things to prepare your code to be compiled for release. This chapter will walk you through the steps to ready your game to be published. You must prepare your AndroidManifest file and sign and align your code.

> **NOTE:** There are many resources on the Net, including the Android Developer Forums, for instructions on the actual upload process to the Marketplace. This chapter will not cover the upload process, just the preparation steps that may be overlooked otherwise.

This is your last chance to work with the 2-D code that you've created thus far. In the remainder of this book, you will be working on skills to create 3-D games. However, the steps outlined herein will hold true no matter what kind of game or application you are trying to publish.

Preparing Your Manifest

The first step to preparing your code to be published is to make sure that your AndroidManifest file is in order. There are three key pieces of information that your AndroidManifest must have to be able to be published. These key pieces of information are

- versionCode
- versionName
- android:icon

Open your AndroidManfest file to the XML view. The information that you must have in your manifest is bolded as follows:

```
<?xml version="1.0" encoding="utf-8"?>
<manifest xmlns:android="http://schemas.android.com/apk/res/android"
   package="com.proandroidgames"
   android:versionCode="1"
   android:versionName="1.0">
  <uses-sdk android:minSdkVersion="10" />

  <application android:label="@string/app_name" android:icon="@drawable/sficon">
    <activity android:name=".StarfighterActivity"
        android:label="@string/app_name" android:screenOrientation="portrait">
      <intent-filter>
        <action android:name="android.intent.action.MAIN" />
        <category android:name="android.intent.category.LAUNCHER" />
      </intent-filter>
    </activity>
    <activity android:name="sfmainmenu" android:screenOrientation="portrait"></activity>
    <service android:name="sfmusic"></service>
    <activity android:name="sfgame" android:screenOrientation="portrait"></activity>

  </application>
</manifest>
```

If your AndroidManifest file does not have this information, you must add it before you continue. The versionCode and versionName are used primarily by the Marketplace to track what version of your game is being uploaded. This is helpful if you are publishing upgraded version of your game.

Another key element in the preceding code is the specification of the icon. Your game must have an icon to be displayed on the Android UI. The icon does not need to be elaborate; it can even be the stock Android icon, but you do need one.

This information should already be in your manifest however, especially if you used Eclipse to create your project. The next step is to sign, release compile, and align your code.

Preparing to Sign, Align, and Release

All apps that are published to the Android Marketplace must be code signed. This allows the Marketplace to identify you, and your game will not be accepted unless it is signed. If you do not have a certificate from a certificate authority (CA), you can self-sign one. The Android Marketplace will accept self-signed apps.

After signing your code, you need to align it. Aligning your code simply makes sure that it is set at 4-bit boundaries. Having 4-bit boundaries is optimal for downloading on mobile devices.

Luckily, if you are using Eclipse as your Android IDE, an easy wizard will take care of both of these tasks at once. With your project open, go to File ➤ Export, as shown in Figure 9–1. This will open the Export Wizard.

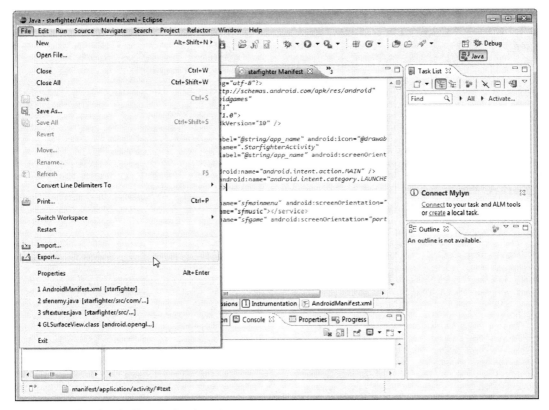

Figure 9–1. *Opening the Export wizard*

With the wizard open, select the Export Android Application option from the Android destination, as shown in Figure 9–2.

Figure 9–2. *Selecting the Export Android Application destination*

> **TIP:** Alternatively, you can get directly to this step by right-clicking the project in Eclipse and choosing Export.

After making your selection, click the Next button. Eclipse will now test your project's AndroidManifest file to make sure that it meets the requirement discussed earlier—to be signed and released. From the Project Checks screen shown in Figure 9–3, click the Browse button.

Figure 9–3. *The Project Checks window*

You can now let the wizard check your project for errors in the manifest that would prevent it from being able to be signed.

Checking the Readiness of AndroidManifest

When you click the Browse button, a smaller window will open that lists all of your loaded projects. Select your project from this list, as shown in Figure 9–4.

Figure 9–4. *Selecting the starfighter project*

The export wizard will now check your code to make sure it is ready to be signed. Assuming you have met the requirements, which include having an icon, a version code, and a version name, then you should see the message "No errors found," as shown in Figure 9–5.

Figure 9–5. *A successful check*

When the check is finished, click the Next button to begin the signing process.

Creating the Keystore

The next screen of the wizard is the keystore selection, shown in Figure 9–6. If you have an existing certificate keystore created—perhaps from a previous app that you uploaded or a certificate that you purchased—select the "Use existing keystore option" to import it.

However, if you are self-signing, you should select the "Create new keystore" option. Selecting this option will walk you through the process of creating a new keystore.

Figure 9–6. *The "Keystore selection" window*

Select a valid location for your keystore file, and enter a password.

> **CAUTION:** You should choose a location for your keystore that is both secure and backed up. You must use the same keystore every time you update a game or app. Therefore, if you lose your keystore, you will no longer be able to upload updates to this game.

Click the Next button to enter the Key Creation window, which is shown in Figure 9–7. Here, you must enter all of the information that identifies you to the Marketplace.

Figure 9–7. *The Key Creation window*

Click the Next button after you have entered the information required for your keystore. Eclipse will now generate a keystore for you that will be used in the next step of the process to sign your app. On the next and final screen of the wizard, the "Destination and key/certificate checks" window (see Figure 9–8), you will select your .apk file to be signed.

Selecting the .apk file before it has really been created may seem a bit confusing, but just follow along. Click the Browse button, and you should see starfighter.apk.

Figure 9–8. *The final screen of the wizard*

Click the Finish button to compile and sign your final game. During this process, the code will be aligned into 4-bit boundaries, making it much easier for mobile devices to download.

You are now ready to upload your creation to the Android Marketplace—much to envy of your friends and colleagues. If your game development tastes extend more toward the next gen rather than the retro, the remaining chapters of this book are what you need. The last four chapters of this book will build on the skills that you've learned to this point and add to them the ability to use OpenGL in a 3-D gaming environment.

Summary

In this chapter, you learned how to prepare your code for upload to the Android Marketplace. You also used the Eclipse Export wizard to create a keystore and sign and align your game as required by the Marketplace. In the next chapter, you will begin to use the same skills that you learned in the preceding eight chapters to create a 3-D game.

Part II

Creating 3D Games

In Part 1 of this book you created your first 2D game for the Android platform. In Part 2 (Chapters 10-12) you will learn how these same skills can be used to create a 3D game. While you won't create the entire 3D game in Chapters 10-12, you will learn how the skills you learned in Chapters 1-9 can be used to create a compelling 3D game. Finally, at the end of Chapter 12, as at the end of Chapter 8, you will again be presented with the source code for the key files of this part of the book. This will help you check your work and strengthen your skills as a game developer.

Blob Hunter: Creating 3-D Games

In the first half of this book, you spent a good amount of time building your OpenGL ES skills creating *Star Fighter*. Admittedly, *Star Fighter* is not going to have gamers beating down your door to play it. However, what this game has done for you is far more important. The skills that you honed while creating a 2-D, top-down, shooter game can easily be translated in to the skills needed to create some stunning 3-D games.

For the remainder of this book, you will put together a 3-D environment that could be used to create any number of compelling 3-D games. Let's start by discussing what differentiates a 2-D game from a 3-D game.

Comparing 2-D and 3-D Games

Visually, we all can tell the different between a 2-D game and a 3-D one. A 2-D game looks flat, much like an animated cartoon, whereas a 3-D game will have the appearance of multifaceted objects in a dynamic space. Are 2-D games irrelevant? Of course not. With the advent of addictive mobile games, such as *Angry Birds*, and a dizzying array of other iPhone, Android, and Facebook games, the 2-D game market is still alive and quite well. You could continue to expand your 2-D games skills and create some amazing games. However, if more-complex 3-D games are more to your liking, you will need to begin by learning what is explained in the remaining chapters of this book.

When you were creating your 2-D game, *Star Fighter*, you created flat squares (out of flat triangles). You then mapped a sprite onto the surface of that square to create your characters. However, hold up a sheet of paper, and look at it. Even though it is flat, it is still three-dimensional in your hand. You can turn it, rotate it, or bend it. Take six pieces of paper, and create a cube. Now, the 3-D shape is much more defined, but all you really changed was the number of flat pieces of paper and how they were arranged.

This is a very basic explanation of simple transition between the skills you learned in *Star Fighter* and what you will need to begin building a new 3-D game—*Blob Hunter*. You see, without even realizing it, you have been working in 3-D all along. You just flattened out everything by neglecting any values for the z axis and telling OpenGL to render your scene in 2-D.

As far as OpenGL is concerned, 2-D or 3-D, the games are the same in space. The difference is in how you treat objects and how you tell OpenGL to render them. Rather than creating flat squares that have sprites mapped to them, you need to create more convincing complex polygons that become your characters and environments.

In this chapter, you are going to create a new Android project to hold *Blob Hunter*, which will be a sandbox for you to learn some vital 3-D game development skills. You will also set up the few files needed to begin your 3-D development.

Creating Your 3-D Project

In this section, you will begin creating the project that will be used through the rest of this book. The process to create the 3-D project will mirror the one you used to create the *Star Fighter* game project.

Following the same steps that you used in Chapter 2, create a new project named blobhunter. This project will hold all of the examples from the remainder of this book. You are not going to create another project as complete as *Star Fighter*, and you are going to learn the secrets to converting your knowledge of working in 2-D into a 3-D environment.

Once your new blobhunter project is created, fill it with some starter files. Although this project is not going to have all the flash and menus of *Star Fighter*, you still some basic files to launch your game.

You learned how to make menus and splash screens earlier in this book. Truth is, the processes used to create those key parts of a game are going to remain the same whether the game play is in 2-D or 3-D. Therefore, it does not warrant being covered again here.

However, in the following sections, you will be adding four basic files to your project that create and display the renderer. That is all that you will be making here. You will not have any menus, or any graceful code killing routines as you did in *Star Fighter*.

BlobhunterActivity.java

The first file that you will need to create in your new blobhunter project is BlobhunterActivity.java. In the *Star Fighter* project, StarfighterActivity.java launched the splash screen, which, in turn, launched the main menu. However, since you will not have those components here, BlobhunterActivity can simply launch gameview.

> **TIP:** The majority of the code that you are going to see in this chapter should look very familiar to you. Essentially, it is all taken from the *Star Fighter* project. The differences are that it has been severely stripped down and renamed.

```
package com.proandroidgames;

import android.app.Activity;
import android.os.Bundle;

public class BlobhunterActivity extends Activity {
        /** Called when the activity is first created. */

        private BHGameView gameView;

        @Override
        public void onCreate(Bundle savedInstanceState) {
                super.onCreate(savedInstanceState);
                gameView = new BHGameView(this);
                setContentView(gameView);
                BHEngine.context = this;
        }
        @Override
        protected void onResume() {
                super.onResume();
                gameView.onResume();
        }

        @Override
        protected void onPause() {
                super.onPause();
                gameView.onPause();
        }
}
```

Notice, in the highlighted sections, that this code references a class called BHGameView. The BHGameView class extends GLSurfaceView and serves the same purpose as the SFGameView in *Star Fighter*. The previous code will not compile until the BHGameView is created in the next section.

BHGameView

The code to create the BHGameView class is very simple and should look like this:

```
package com.proandroidgames;

import android.content.Context;
import android.opengl.GLSurfaceView;

public class BHGameView extends GLSurfaceView {
        private BHGameRenderer renderer;

        public BHGameView(Context context) {
```

```
                         super(context);

                         renderer = new BHGameRenderer();

                         this.setRenderer(renderer);

              }

     }
```

Once again, notice that, in the highlighted sections, you are referencing another class. BHGameRenderer is the game loop for this project and will hold the majority of the code.

BHGameRenderer

Now, create a new file class named BHGameRenderer.

```
package com.proandroidgames;

import javax.microedition.khronos.egl.EGLConfig;
import javax.microedition.khronos.opengles.GL10;

import android.opengl.GLSurfaceView.Renderer;


public class BHGameRenderer implements Renderer{

        private long loopStart = 0;
        private long loopEnd = 0;
        private long loopRunTime = 0 ;

        @Override
        public void onDrawFrame(GL10 gl) {
                loopStart = System.currentTimeMillis();
                try {
                        if (loopRunTime < BHEngine.GAME_THREAD_FPS_SLEEP){
                                Thread.sleep(BHEngine.GAME_THREAD_FPS_SLEEP -
loopRunTime);
                        }
                } catch (InterruptedException e) {
                        e.printStackTrace();
                }
                gl.glClear(GL10.GL_COLOR_BUFFER_BIT | GL10.GL_DEPTH_BUFFER_BIT);
                gl.glLoadIdentity();

                loopEnd = System.currentTimeMillis();
                loopRunTime = ((loopEnd - loopStart));

        }

        @Override
        public void onSurfaceChanged(GL10 gl, int width, int height) {

                gl.glViewport(0, 0, width,height);
                gl.glMatrixMode(GL10.GL_PROJECTION);
                gl.glLoadIdentity();
```

```
            gl.glMatrixMode(GL10.GL_MODELVIEW);
            gl.glLoadIdentity();
      }

      @Override
      public void onSurfaceCreated(GL10 gl, EGLConfig config) {

            gl.glEnable(GL10.GL_TEXTURE_2D);
            gl.glClearDepthf(1.0f);
            gl.glEnable(GL10.GL_DEPTH_TEST);
            gl.glDepthFunc(GL10.GL_LEQUAL);
            gl.glHint(GL10.GL_PERSPECTIVE_CORRECTION_HINT, GL10.GL_NICEST);
            gl.glDisable(GL10.GL_DITHER);
      }

}
```

Again, if you look at the code for the BHGameRenderer, you will notice that it is just a stripped down version of what you used for *Star Fighter*. This is going to be just enough code to really get you going in 3-D game development.

BHEngine

The last file that you need to create to establish your project is BHEngine. In the *Star Fighter* project, you created the SFEngine file that held all of the global constants, variables, and methods for your game. The same file needs to be created in the *Blob Hunter* project to hold any game-engine-related code.

```
package com.proandroidgames;
import android.content.Context;
import android.view.Display;

public class BHEngine {
        /*Constants that will be used in the game*/
        public static final int GAME_THREAD_DELAY = 4000;
        public static final int GAME_THREAD_FPS_SLEEP = (1000/60);
        /*Game Variables*/

        public static Context context;
}
```

That is it. You should now have enough code to get your project off the code. However, the code—and the project it is contained within—does not really do anything yet. Let's create a small 3-D test to show off what this new project can do.

Creating a 3-D Object Test

In this section, you are going to take the *Blob Hunter* project that you set up in the previous section and add some code to it to generate a 3-D test. You are going to use one of the sprite images from *Star Fighter* to create a quick image that will rotate around the player.

Start by taking the image of the scout, shown in Figure 10–1, and adding it to the `drawable-nodpi` folder in *Blob Hunter*'s project.

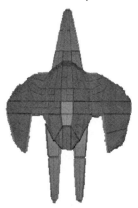

Figure 10–1. *The Scout image*

With the image added to your project, create a constant for it in the `BHEngine` class.

> **NOTE:** The steps to create this 3-D test should be very familiar to you and fairly fresh in your mind from being in the previous chapters. Therefore, there will not be as much explanation of some of the basic (previously covered) technologies. However, if something does not make sense, try going back to the previous chapters.

Creating a Constant

Open the `BHEngine.java` file, and add the following highlighted line of code:

```
package com.proandroidgames;

import android.content.Context;
import android.view.Display;

public class BHEngine {
        /*Constants that will be used in the game*/
        public static final int GAME_THREAD_DELAY = 4000;
        public static final int GAME_THREAD_FPS_SLEEP = (1000/60);
        public static final int BACKGROUND = R.drawable.scout;
        /*Game Variables*/

        public static Context context;
        public static Display display;
}
```

You are now going to create a flat square, exactly like you did for *Star Fighter* and then map this scout image to it as a texture.

Creating the BHWalls Class

Create a new class in your project called BHWalls. The BHWalls class is going to be used in future chapters to create walls, but it will serve here as a way to create a flat square. All of the code for the BHWalls class is from the SFBackground class that you created for *Star Fighter*; nothing has changed.

```java
package com.proandroidgames;

import java.io.IOException;
import java.io.InputStream;
import java.nio.ByteBuffer;
import java.nio.ByteOrder;
import java.nio.FloatBuffer;

import javax.microedition.khronos.opengles.GL10;

import android.content.Context;
import android.graphics.Bitmap;
import android.graphics.BitmapFactory;
import android.opengl.GLUtils;

public class BHWalls {

        private FloatBuffer vertexBuffer;
        private FloatBuffer textureBuffer;
        private ByteBuffer indexBuffer;

        private int[] textures = new int[1];

        private float vertices[] = {
                0.0f, 0.0f, 0.0f,
                1.0f, 0.0f, 0.0f,
                1.0f, 1.0f, 0.0f,
                 0.0f, 1.0f, 0.0f,
        };

        private float texture[] = {
                0.0f, 0.0f,
                1.0f, 0f,
                1f, 1.0f,
                0f, 1f,
        };

        private byte indices[] = {
                0,1,2,
                0,2,3,
        };

        public BHWalls() {
                ByteBuffer byteBuf = ByteBuffer.allocateDirect(vertices.length * 4);
                byteBuf.order(ByteOrder.nativeOrder());
                vertexBuffer = byteBuf.asFloatBuffer();
                vertexBuffer.put(vertices);
                vertexBuffer.position(0);
```

```
                        byteBuf = ByteBuffer.allocateDirect(texture.length * 4);
                        byteBuf.order(ByteOrder.nativeOrder());
                        textureBuffer = byteBuf.asFloatBuffer();
                        textureBuffer.put(texture);
                        textureBuffer.position(0);

                        indexBuffer = ByteBuffer.allocateDirect(indices.length);
                        indexBuffer.put(indices);
                        indexBuffer.position(0);
                }

        public void draw(GL10 gl) {
                        gl.glBindTexture(GL10.GL_TEXTURE_2D, textures[0]);

                        gl.glFrontFace(GL10.GL_CCW);

                        gl.glEnableClientState(GL10.GL_VERTEX_ARRAY);
                        gl.glEnableClientState(GL10.GL_TEXTURE_COORD_ARRAY);

                        gl.glVertexPointer(3, GL10.GL_FLOAT, 0, vertexBuffer);
                        gl.glTexCoordPointer(2, GL10.GL_FLOAT, 0, textureBuffer);

                        gl.glDrawElements(GL10.GL_TRIANGLES, indices.length,
        GL10.GL_UNSIGNED_BYTE, indexBuffer);

                        gl.glDisableClientState(GL10.GL_VERTEX_ARRAY);
                        gl.glDisableClientState(GL10.GL_TEXTURE_COORD_ARRAY);
                        gl.glDisable(GL10.GL_CULL_FACE);
                }


        public void loadTexture(GL10 gl,int texture, Context context) {
                        InputStream imagestream =
        context.getResources().openRawResource(texture);
                        Bitmap bitmap = null;
                        try {
                                bitmap = BitmapFactory.decodeStream(imagestream);
                        }catch(Exception e){

                        }finally {
                                try {
                                        imagestream.close();
                                        imagestream = null;
                                } catch (IOException e) {
                        }
                }

        gl.glGenTextures(1, textures, 0);
        gl.glBindTexture(GL10.GL_TEXTURE_2D, textures[0]);

        gl.glTexParameterf(GL10.GL_TEXTURE_2D, GL10.GL_TEXTURE_MIN_FILTER,
GL10.GL_NEAREST);
        gl.glTexParameterf(GL10.GL_TEXTURE_2D, GL10.GL_TEXTURE_MAG_FILTER,
GL10.GL_LINEAR);

        gl.glTexParameterf(GL10.GL_TEXTURE_2D, GL10.GL_TEXTURE_WRAP_S, GL10.GL_REPEAT);
        gl.glTexParameterf(GL10.GL_TEXTURE_2D, GL10.GL_TEXTURE_WRAP_T, GL10.GL_REPEAT);
```

```
        GLUtils.texImage2D(GL10.GL_TEXTURE_2D, 0, bitmap, 0);

        bitmap.recycle();
        }
}
```

Now that you have a class created to build your object, you are going to instantiate it in the game loop.

Instantiating the BHWalls Class

As you are creating the instantiation of the BHWalls, you will also create two floats. These are going to be used to move the image of the ship around in the 3-D space.

> **NOTE:** Just to be clear, you are not creating a 3-D ship with this code. You will only be taking one of the images from the last project and rotating it through 3-D space—something that could not have been done in *Star Fighter*.

```
package com.proandroidgames;

import javax.microedition.khronos.egl.EGLConfig;
import javax.microedition.khronos.opengles.GL10;

import android.opengl.GLSurfaceView.Renderer;

public class BHGameRenderer implements Renderer{
        private BHWalls background = new BHWalls();
        private float rotateAngle = .25f;
        private float rotateIncrement = .25f;


        private long loopStart = 0;
        private long loopEnd = 0;
        private long loopRunTime = 0 ;

        @Override
        public void onDrawFrame(GL10 gl) {
                loopStart = System.currentTimeMillis();
                try {
                        if (loopRunTime < BHEngine.GAME_THREAD_FPS_SLEEP){
                                Thread.sleep(BHEngine.GAME_THREAD_FPS_SLEEP -
loopRunTime);
                        }
                } catch (InterruptedException e) {
                        e.printStackTrace();
                }
                gl.glClear(GL10.GL_COLOR_BUFFER_BIT | GL10.GL_DEPTH_BUFFER_BIT);
                gl.glLoadIdentity();

                loopEnd = System.currentTimeMillis();
                loopRunTime = ((loopEnd - loopStart));
```

```
        }

        @Override
        public void onSurfaceChanged(GL10 gl, int width, int height) {

                gl.glViewport(0, 0, width,height);
                gl.glMatrixMode(GL10.GL_PROJECTION);
                gl.glLoadIdentity();

                gl.glMatrixMode(GL10.GL_MODELVIEW);
                gl.glLoadIdentity();
        }

        @Override
        public void onSurfaceCreated(GL10 gl, EGLConfig config) {

                gl.glEnable(GL10.GL_TEXTURE_2D);
                gl.glClearDepthf(1.0f);
                gl.glEnable(GL10.GL_DEPTH_TEST);
                gl.glDepthFunc(GL10.GL_LEQUAL);
                gl.glHint(GL10.GL_PERSPECTIVE_CORRECTION_HINT, GL10.GL_NICEST);
                gl.glDisable(GL10.GL_DITHER);
        }

}
```

The BHWalls class has been instantiated, and it is time to call the loadTexture() method.

Mapping the Image

In this section, you will use the loadTexture() method, which was introduced in the *Star Fighter* game. Recall that the loadTexture() method will map the image onto the vertices of the BHWalls.

```
package com.proandroidgames;

import javax.microedition.khronos.egl.EGLConfig;
import javax.microedition.khronos.opengles.GL10;

import android.opengl.GLSurfaceView.Renderer;

public class BHGameRenderer implements Renderer{
        private BHWalls background = new BHWalls();
        private float rotateAngle = .25f;
        private float rotateIncrement = .25f;

        private long loopStart = 0;
        private long loopEnd = 0;
        private long loopRunTime = 0 ;

        @Override
        public void onDrawFrame(GL10 gl) {
                loopStart = System.currentTimeMillis();
                try {
                        if (loopRunTime < BHEngine.GAME_THREAD_FPS_SLEEP){
```

```
                                Thread.sleep(BHEngine.GAME_THREAD_FPS_SLEEP -
loopRunTime);
                        }
                } catch (InterruptedException e) {
                        e.printStackTrace();
                }
                gl.glClear(GL10.GL_COLOR_BUFFER_BIT | GL10.GL_DEPTH_BUFFER_BIT);
                gl.glLoadIdentity();

                loopEnd = System.currentTimeMillis();
                loopRunTime = ((loopEnd - loopStart));

        }

        @Override
        public void onSurfaceChanged(GL10 gl, int width, int height) {

                gl.glViewport(0, 0, width,height);
                gl.glMatrixMode(GL10.GL_PROJECTION);
                gl.glLoadIdentity();

                gl.glMatrixMode(GL10.GL_MODELVIEW);
                gl.glLoadIdentity();
        }

        @Override
        public void onSurfaceCreated(GL10 gl, EGLConfig config) {

                gl.glEnable(GL10.GL_TEXTURE_2D);
                gl.glClearDepthf(1.0f);
                gl.glEnable(GL10.GL_DEPTH_TEST);
                gl.glDepthFunc(GL10.GL_LEQUAL);
                gl.glHint(GL10.GL_PERSPECTIVE_CORRECTION_HINT, GL10.GL_NICEST);
                gl.glDisable(GL10.GL_DITHER);
                background.loadTexture(gl,BHEngine.BACKGROUND, BHEngine.context);
        }

}
```

At this point, you are probably wondering where the big differences are between using OpenGL ES for 2-D and 3-D, because so far, all of the code that you have used has been from the 2-D *Star Fighter* project.

The major difference between how OpenGL deals with 2-D and how it deals with 3-D boils down to how you tell the system to render your world. In the *Star Fighter* game, you told Open GL to render your world as a flattened 2-D environment using the glOrthof() method.

The glOrthof() method discards the meaning of the z axis value. That is, when you're using glOrthof(), everything is rendered the same size, regardless of its distance from the player.

To render your objects in 3-D, you are going to use gluPerspective(), which is discussed next.

Using gluPerspective()

The gluPerspective() method will take into account the object's distance from the player on the z axis and then render the object with the correct size and perspective relative to its position.

The parameters for the gluPerspective() method are slightly different from those of glOrthof(). To call gluPerspective(), you need to pass it a valid instance of GL10, a viewing angle, an aspect, and a near and a far z axis clipping plane.

```
gluPerspective(gl10, angle, aspect, nearz, farz)
```

The angle that is passed to gluPerspective() specifies the viewing angle that you want OpenGL to render; anything that falls outside that viewing angle will not be seen. The aspect parameter is a float of width / height. Finally, the near and far z clipping planes tell OpenGL where to stop rendering. Anything closer than the near z plane or farther away than the far z plane will be clipped from the rendering.

In the onSurfaceChanged() method of BHGameRender, you are going to add the call to gluPerspective().

```
package com.proandroidgames;

import javax.microedition.khronos.egl.EGLConfig;
import javax.microedition.khronos.opengles.GL10;

import android.opengl.GLSurfaceView.Renderer;

public class BHGameRenderer implements Renderer{
        private BHWalls background = new BHWalls();
        private float rotateAngle = .25f;
        private float rotateIncrement = .25f;

        private long loopStart = 0;
        private long loopEnd = 0;
        private long loopRunTime = 0 ;

        @Override
        public void onDrawFrame(GL10 gl) {
                loopStart = System.currentTimeMillis();
                try {
                        if (loopRunTime < BHEngine.GAME_THREAD_FPS_SLEEP){
                                Thread.sleep(BHEngine.GAME_THREAD_FPS_SLEEP -
loopRunTime);
                        }
                } catch (InterruptedException e) {
                        e.printStackTrace();
                }
                gl.glClear(GL10.GL_COLOR_BUFFER_BIT | GL10.GL_DEPTH_BUFFER_BIT);
                gl.glLoadIdentity();

                loopEnd = System.currentTimeMillis();
                loopRunTime = ((loopEnd - loopStart));

        }
```

```
@Override
public void onSurfaceChanged(GL10 gl, int width, int height) {

        gl.glViewport(0, 0, width,height);
        gl.glMatrixMode(GL10.GL_PROJECTION);
        gl.glLoadIdentity();

         GLU.gluPerspective(gl, 45.0f, (float) width / height, .1f, 100.f);

        gl.glMatrixMode(GL10.GL_MODELVIEW);
        gl.glLoadIdentity();
}

@Override
public void onSurfaceCreated(GL10 gl, EGLConfig config) {

        gl.glEnable(GL10.GL_TEXTURE_2D);
        gl.glClearDepthf(1.0f);
        gl.glEnable(GL10.GL_DEPTH_TEST);
        gl.glDepthFunc(GL10.GL_LEQUAL);
        gl.glHint(GL10.GL_PERSPECTIVE_CORRECTION_HINT, GL10.GL_NICEST);
        gl.glDisable(GL10.GL_DITHER);
        background.loadTexture(gl,BHEngine.BACKGROUND, BHEngine.context);
}
}
```

In the next section, you will draw the background plane using a method called
drawBackground().

Creating the drawBackground() Method

You need a new method that will draw the BHWalls vertices to the screen and move
them around to show off the 3-D rendering of OpenGL. Now, create a drawBackground()
method that will use the glRotatef() method to rotate the image of the scout around
the player on the z axis.

The OpenGL method glRotatef() takes four parameters. The first specifies the angle of
rotation. The second, third, and fourth parameters are flags for the x, y, and z axes,
indicating to which axis you want to apply the angle of rotation.

The following code shows the drawBackground() method in context:

```
package com.proandroidgames;

import javax.microedition.khronos.egl.EGLConfig;
import javax.microedition.khronos.opengles.GL10;

import android.opengl.GLSurfaceView.Renderer;

public class BHGameRenderer implements Renderer{
        private BHWalls background = new BHWalls();
        private float rotateAngle = .25f;
        private float rotateIncrement = .25f;

        private long loopStart = 0;
```

```java
        private long loopEnd = 0;
        private long loopRunTime = 0 ;

        @Override
        public void onDrawFrame(GL10 gl) {
                loopStart = System.currentTimeMillis();
                try {
                        if (loopRunTime < BHEngine.GAME_THREAD_FPS_SLEEP){
                                Thread.sleep(BHEngine.GAME_THREAD_FPS_SLEEP -
loopRunTime);
                        }
                } catch (InterruptedException e) {
                        e.printStackTrace();
                }
                gl.glClear(GL10.GL_COLOR_BUFFER_BIT | GL10.GL_DEPTH_BUFFER_BIT);
                gl.glLoadIdentity();

                loopEnd = System.currentTimeMillis();
                loopRunTime = ((loopEnd - loopStart));

        }

        private void drawBackground(GL10 gl){

                GLU.gluLookAt(gl, 0f, 0f, 5f, 0f, 0f, 0f, 0f, 1f, 0f);
                gl.glRotatef(rotateAngle, 0.0f, 1.0f, 0.0f);
                gl.glTranslatef(0.0f, 0.0f, -3f);

                background.draw(gl);
                rotateAngle += rotateIncrement;

        }


        @Override
        public void onSurfaceChanged(GL10 gl, int width, int height) {

                gl.glViewport(0, 0, width,height);
                gl.glMatrixMode(GL10.GL_PROJECTION);
                gl.glLoadIdentity();

                 GLU.gluPerspective(gl, 45.0f, (float) width / height, .1f, 100.f);

                gl.glMatrixMode(GL10.GL_MODELVIEW);
                gl.glLoadIdentity();
        }

        @Override
        public void onSurfaceCreated(GL10 gl, EGLConfig config) {

                gl.glEnable(GL10.GL_TEXTURE_2D);
                gl.glClearDepthf(1.0f);
                gl.glEnable(GL10.GL_DEPTH_TEST);
                gl.glDepthFunc(GL10.GL_LEQUAL);
                gl.glHint(GL10.GL_PERSPECTIVE_CORRECTION_HINT, GL10.GL_NICEST);
                gl.glDisable(GL10.GL_DITHER);
                background.loadTexture(gl,BHEngine.BACKGROUND, BHEngine.context);
        }
}
```

Notice that there is a new method call in this example. The `gluLookAt()` call tells the "camera" where to look in the world. If you have ever worked with 3-D rendering software such as Maya or 3-D Studio Max, you may be familiar with the concept having a camera that acts as the viewer of the scene when it is rendered. OpenGL does not really have a camera as a separate object. However, the `gluLookAt()` method serves as a way to point the rendering to look at a specific location in the world.

The `gluLookAt()` method takes a valid `GL10` object plus three sets of three parameters. These three sets of three parameters are the x, y, and z values for the eye (where the renderer is looking); the x, y, and z values for the center of "camera" (where the renderer is located in the world); and the x, y, and z positions indicating which axis is up. As written in this example, you are telling the "camera" to look at a point that is located at 0x, 0y, and 5z, to center itself on the 0x, 0y, and 0z point, and that the direction up is toward 1y.

Adding the Finishing Touches

Now, just call the `drawBackground()` method, and compile your game. You should see an image of a scout ship rotate in front of and then behind you in perspective.

```
package com.proandroidgames;

import javax.microedition.khronos.egl.EGLConfig;
import javax.microedition.khronos.opengles.GL10;

import android.opengl.GLSurfaceView.Renderer;

public class BHGameRenderer implements Renderer{
        private BHWalls background = new BHWalls();
        private float rotateAngle = .25f;
        private float rotateIncrement = .25f;

        private long loopStart = 0;
        private long loopEnd = 0;
        private long loopRunTime = 0 ;

        @Override
        public void onDrawFrame(GL10 gl) {
                loopStart = System.currentTimeMillis();
                try {
                        if (loopRunTime < BHEngine.GAME_THREAD_FPS_SLEEP){
                                Thread.sleep(BHEngine.GAME_THREAD_FPS_SLEEP -
loopRunTime);
                        }
                } catch (InterruptedException e) {
                        e.printStackTrace();
                }
                gl.glClear(GL10.GL_COLOR_BUFFER_BIT | GL10.GL_DEPTH_BUFFER_BIT);
                gl.glLoadIdentity();

                drawBackground(gl);

                loopEnd = System.currentTimeMillis();
```

```
                    loopRunTime = ((loopEnd - loopStart));
        }

        private void drawBackground(GL10 gl){

                GLU.gluLookAt(gl, 0f, 0f, 5f, 0f, 0f, 0f, 0f, 1f, 0f);
                gl.glRotatef(rotateAngle, 0.0f, 1.0f, 0.0f);
                gl.glTranslatef(0.0f, 0.0f, -3f);

                background.draw(gl);
                rotateAngle += rotateIncrement;

        }

        @Override
        public void onSurfaceChanged(GL10 gl, int width, int height) {

                gl.glViewport(0, 0, width,height);
                gl.glMatrixMode(GL10.GL_PROJECTION);
                gl.glLoadIdentity();

                 GLU.gluPerspective(gl, 45.0f, (float) width / height, .1f, 100.f);

                gl.glMatrixMode(GL10.GL_MODELVIEW);
                gl.glLoadIdentity();
        }

        @Override
        public void onSurfaceCreated(GL10 gl, EGLConfig config) {

                gl.glEnable(GL10.GL_TEXTURE_2D);
                gl.glClearDepthf(1.0f);
                gl.glEnable(GL10.GL_DEPTH_TEST);
                gl.glDepthFunc(GL10.GL_LEQUAL);
                gl.glHint(GL10.GL_PERSPECTIVE_CORRECTION_HINT, GL10.GL_NICEST);
                gl.glDisable(GL10.GL_DITHER);
                background.loadTexture(gl,BHEngine.BACKGROUND, BHEngine.context);
        }
}
```

In the next chapter, you are going to create the 3-D environment for *Blob Hunter*. It will be a corridor-based environment, much like the early *Doom* and *Quake* FPS games.

Summary

In this chapter, you created the project for the *Blob Hunter* 3-D game. You also learned the differences in how OpenGL ES renders 2-D versus 3-D environments. The key to creating a 3-D environment from a 2-D one is all in the way you tell OpenGL to render your objects. OpenGL make the process of moving from 2-D to 3-D gaming very easy for you by allowing you to use the same vertices and textures and only change a few lines of code. This process was clarified when you created the quick demonstration of an object rotating in 3-D space.

Creating an Immersive Environment

In the previous chapter, you learned how to take some of your new 2-D game development skills and apply them to a 3-D game. You learned how OpenGL ES renders objects in 3-D and how to move these objects around to get a 3-D effect.

In this chapter, you are going to build an environment for your 3-D game. Because this is a primer on 3-D development, you will learn how to create the standard of all FPS games—the corridor. You will use the techniques you learned in earlier chapters to create an L-shaped corridor for your player to navigate.

Finally, in the last chapter of this book, you will learn how your players can navigate through this corridor and implement some collision detection to keep them from going through the walls.

Let's start with the BHWalls class that you created in the Chapter 10.

Using the BHWalls class

In the previous chapter, you created a small 3-D test. As part of this test, you created a BHWalls class that creates a square wall shape and applies a texture to it. How does this apply to the 3-D game that you are going to create? Let's examine a 3-D world to find out. In this section, you will learn how to move from the small BHWalls test in the last chapter to a 3-D corridor.

Look around you right now; what do you see? Step outside; look up, and look down.

Chances are, if you were indoors when you looked around, you saw some walls. You could not see into the rooms or environments beyond those walls because the structure of the walls blocked your view. You may know that you are in a house or large building, but your eyes are only seeing the unobstructed portions of the environment.

The same applies if you move outside; yes, the environment is much larger and you can see much more, but what you see is still a finite space. Something always ends up restricting your view—be it a house, trees, or even the ground you are standing on.

Move your attention now to a computer environment. Until you place objects into your environment, your players will have an unobstructed 360-degree view of the world. It is up to you to restrict that view to the specific area that you want them to experience. In *Star Fighter*, the 2-D game you created earlier in this book, it was easy to control the player's view of the world. You created a single, static view of a scene. All of the action of the game took place in this one view.

With 3-D games, controlling what the players see is a little harder, because the players are in control of their view of the world. Therefore, you must place objects and create environments in such a way that you control what the players have access to see, even though they will be in control of how the see it.

In the early days of 3-D first-person gaming, this control over the play's environmental view was accomplished using corridors. Think back to some of the most popular early first-person shooters like *Doom*, *Quake*, and *Castle Wolfenstein*. They all used rooms and corridors to guide you where you to where you needed to go, yet let you feel as though you were in a much larger, free-roaming environment.

You already have all of the skills needed to create an effective 3-D corridor. No matter how long any single corridor is, it can be built from a series of walls. In Chapter 10, you built a wall and moved it around the player. You could simply build 5, 10, or 15 more of these walls and place them in specific locations to create a long corridor with turns.

Creating a Corridor from Multiple BHWalls Instances

Let's take a look at what exactly BHWalls creates.

...

```
private float vertices[] = {
        0.0f, 0.0f, 0.0f,
        1.0f, 0.0f, 0.0f,
        1.0f, 1.0f, 0.0f,
        0.0f, 1.0f, 0.0f,
        };
```

...

This code segment is a piece of the BHWalls class—a very important piece that you should remember from *Star Fighter*. This array represents one square that can be rendered out to the screen. While this square could theoretically represent anything, for you, it is a wall.

You can render multiple walls, and then using glTranslatef(), you can move each wall into place. The code would look something like this:

...

```
gl.glTranslatef(0.0f, 0.0f, 0f);
gl.glRotatef( 45.0f, 0.0f,1.0f, 0.0f);
corridor.draw(gl);

gl.glTranslatef(0.0f, 0.0f, 1f);
gl.glRotatef( 45.0f, 0.0f,1.0f, 0.0f);
corridor.draw(gl);

gl.glTranslatef(-1.0f, 0.0f, 0f);
gl.glRotatef( 45.0f, 0.0f,1.0f, 0.0f);
corridor.draw(gl);

gl.glTranslatef(-1.0f, 0.0f, 1f);
gl.glRotatef( 45.0f, 0.0f,1.0f, 0.0f);
corridor.draw(gl);

gl.glTranslatef(0.0f, 0.0f, 0f);
gl.glRotatef( 0.0f, 0.0f,0.0f, 0.0f);
corridor.draw(gl);
```

. . .

While this is more psudeocode than anything you could use directly in your game, you can see how it would be possible to create a corridor by rendering several walls and using OpenGL to translate and rotate them; you could piece together a corridor.

However, this method has its drawbacks. First, it is time consuming. It would take a long time to create all the walls needed to build a corridor of any substantial size. Second, with that many separate objects to keep track of, messing up something would be very easy. You could lose track of which wall goes where and turn something the wrong way. Finally, with that many objects for OpenGL to create, move, and render, your game would not be as efficient as it could be.

There is a better way to create the game environment. You could build the entire corridor at one time, with one object.

Using the BHCorridor Class

In this section, you are going to create a new class, BHCorridor. The BHCorridor class will be responsible for creating a single corridor from multiple polygons. You will then be able to treat this corridor as a single object.

Being able to treat the corridor as a single object will come in very handy in the next, and final, chapter, where you will allow the player to navigate the corridor. This will require moving objects around, which is much easier when you have fewer objects to keep track of.

Let's build the BHCorridor class. We are going to walk through the full class, because there will be some differences between BHCorridor and the BHWalls class that you used in the previous chapter.

Building the BHCorridor Class

In this section, you will begin to build the BHCorridor class. This class will be used to create a full 3-D corridor at once, rather than piecing one together from a number of separate walls. To begin, create a new class in your *Blob Hunter* project called BHCorridor.

```
package com.proandroidgames;

public class BHCorridor {

}
```

Next, you need to set up your arrays.

```
package com.proandroidgames;

import java.nio.FloatBuffer;


public class BHCorridor {
        private FloatBuffer vertexBuffer;
        private FloatBuffer textureBuffer;

        private int[] textures = new int[1];

        private float vertices[] = {

        };

        private float texture[] = {

        };


}
```

In the BHWalls class, and even in SFBackground from earlier in this book, the vertices[] array would hold 12 values, something like this:

```
private float vertices[] = {
        0.0f, 0.0f, 0.0f,
        1.0f, 0.0f, 0.0f,
        1.0f, 1.0f, 0.0f,
        0.0f, 1.0f, 0.0f,
        };
```

These values represent the x, y, and z axes coordinates of the corners of the square (more precisely, the corners of two triangles that form a square).

You are going to build on this logic by feeding into the array all of the coordinates needed to build the entire corridor at one time (rather than instantiating multiple wall objects and pasting them together). The corridor that you are going to build will be L shaped, as shown in Figure 11–1.

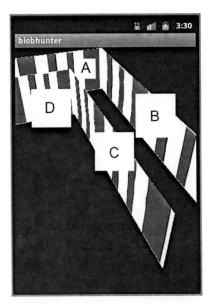

Figure 11–1. *The finished corridor shape*

The image in Figure 11–1 illustrates the shape of the corridor that you will be creating. An arbitrary texture has been added in this image to help you see the shape. Notice that the corridor is L shaped with a bend to the left and is built from four main wall sections. These sections have been labeled A, B, C, and D, and we will be referring to these segment letters as we build the walls.

Building Multiple Walls with the vertices[] Array

Let's set up the vertices[] array to create multiple walls. You can start with wall segment A. This is a flat wall that is facing a player standing at the end of the corridor.

```
private float vertices[] = {
        -2.0f, 0.0f, 0.0f,
        1.0f, 0.0f, 0.0f,
        -2.0f, 1.0f, 0.0f,
        1.0f, 1.0f, 0.0f,
```

Next, you will add the vertex for wall segment B. This segment connects with A on the right-hand side and extends toward the player on the z axis.

```
private float vertices[] = {
        -2.0f, 0.0f, 0.0f,
        1.0f, 0.0f, 0.0f,
        -2.0f, 1.0f, 0.0f,
        1.0f, 1.0f, 0.0f,

        1.0f, 0.0f, 0.0f,
        1.0f, 0.0f, 5.0f,
        1.0f, 1.0f, 0.0f,
        1.0f, 1.0f, 5.0f,
```

Now, add the vertex for wall segment C. This wall segment is opposite segment B and also extends toward the player.

```
private float vertices[] = {
        -2.0f, 0.0f, 0.0f,
        1.0f, 0.0f, 0.0f,
        -2.0f, 1.0f, 0.0f,
        1.0f, 1.0f, 0.0f,

        1.0f, 0.0f, 0.0f,
        1.0f, 0.0f, 5.0f,
        1.0f, 1.0f, 0.0f,
        1.0f, 1.0f, 5.0f,

        0.0f, 0.0f, 1.0f,
        0.0f, 0.0f, 5.0f,
        0.0f, 1.0f, 1.0f,
        0.0f, 1.0f, 5.0f,
```

Finally, add the vertex for wall segment D. This is the segment that is opposite segment A and extends from the end to segment C toward the left-hand side of the screen.

```
private float vertices[] = {
        -2.0f, 0.0f, 0.0f,
        1.0f, 0.0f, 0.0f,
        -2.0f, 1.0f, 0.0f,
        1.0f, 1.0f, 0.0f,

        1.0f, 0.0f, 0.0f,
        1.0f, 0.0f, 5.0f,
        1.0f, 1.0f, 0.0f,
        1.0f, 1.0f, 5.0f,

        0.0f, 0.0f, 1.0f,
        0.0f, 0.0f, 5.0f,
        0.0f, 1.0f, 1.0f,
        0.0f, 1.0f, 5.0f,

        -2.0f, 0.0f, 1.0f,
        0.0f, 0.0f, 1.0f,
        -2.0f, 1.0f, 1.0f,
        0.0f, 1.0f, 1.0f,
};
```

That is it. Those are all of the vertices needed to build the corridor.

> **NOTE:** Because you are working in Java, it is not outside the realm of possibility to store large arrays of data like this in other `.java` files. You can then load these file and read the arrays out of them.

With the `vertices[]` array complete, you can create the `texture[]` array. Like the `vertices[]` array, the `texture[]` array will require some minor tweaking before it can be used to apply a texture to the corridor.

Creating the texture[] Array

In the previous chapters, you built a texture[] array that looked something like this:

```
private float texture[] = {
        -1.0f, 0.0f,
        1.0f, 0f,
        -1f, 1f,
        1f, 1.0f,
};
```

The texture[] array contains the mapping points that tell OpenGL how the texture fits on the vertices. Since you have created a new vertices[] array with four distinct sets of vertices, you also need a texture[] array that will contain for sets of mapping points: one for each set of vertices.

Try not to get caught up in figuring out how to map the texture to the corridor walls without a z axis coordinate. The mapping points in the texture[] array correspond to the corners of the texture not the wall vertices. Therefore, since you will be mapping the entire texture to each wall, the four sets of texture mapping points will be identical.

```
private float texture[] = {
        -1.0f, 0.0f,
        1.0f, 0f,
        -1f, 1f,
        1f, 1.0f,

        -1.0f, 0.0f,
        1.0f, 0f,
        -1f, 1f,
        1f, 1.0f,

        -1.0f, 0.0f,
        1.0f, 0f,
        -1f, 1f,
        1f, 1.0f,

        -1.0f, 0.0f,
        1.0f, 0f,
        -1f, 1f,
        1f, 1.0f,

};
```

Now, your BHCorridor class should look like this:

```
package com.proandroidgames;

import java.nio.FloatBuffer;

public class BHCorridor {
        private FloatBuffer vertexBuffer;
        private FloatBuffer textureBuffer;

        private int[] textures = new int[1];
```

```
private float vertices[] = {

        -2.0f, 0.0f, 0.0f,
        1.0f, 0.0f, 0.0f,
        -2.0f, 1.0f, 0.0f,
        1.0f, 1.0f, 0.0f,

        1.0f, 0.0f, 0.0f,
        1.0f, 0.0f, 5.0f,
        1.0f, 1.0f, 0.0f,
        1.0f, 1.0f, 5.0f,

        0.0f, 0.0f, 1.0f,
        0.0f, 0.0f, 5.0f,
        0.0f, 1.0f, 1.0f,
        0.0f, 1.0f, 5.0f,

        -2.0f, 0.0f, 1.0f,
        0.0f, 0.0f, 1.0f,
        -2.0f, 1.0f, 1.0f,
        0.0f, 1.0f, 1.0f,

};

private float texture[] = {

        -1.0f, 0.0f,
        1.0f, 0f,
        -1f, 1f,
        1f, 1.0f,

        -1.0f, 0.0f,
        1.0f, 0f,
        -1f, 1f,
        1f, 1.0f,

        -1.0f, 0.0f,
        1.0f, 0f,
        -1f, 1f,
        1f, 1.0f,

        -1.0f, 0.0f,
        1.0f, 0f,
        -1f, 1f,
        1f, 1.0f,

};

}
```

Next, add a constructor that will create your buffers, just like you did for BHWalls and SFBackground.

```
public BHCorridor() {
        ByteBuffer byteBuf = ByteBuffer.allocateDirect(vertices.length * 4);
        byteBuf.order(ByteOrder.nativeOrder());
        vertexBuffer = byteBuf.asFloatBuffer();
        vertexBuffer.put(vertices);
        vertexBuffer.position(0);

        byteBuf = ByteBuffer.allocateDirect(texture.length * 4);
        byteBuf.order(ByteOrder.nativeOrder());
        textureBuffer = byteBuf.asFloatBuffer();
        textureBuffer.put(texture);
        textureBuffer.position(0);
}
```

After that, add the loadTexture() method. There are no major changes here either, so
no further explanation should be needed (if you are unsure how the loadTexture()
method works, check back in Chapter 4 for a detailed explanation).

```
public void loadTexture(GL10 gl,int texture, Context context) {
        InputStream imagestream = context.getResources().openRawResource(texture);
        Bitmap bitmap = null;
        try {

                bitmap = BitmapFactory.decodeStream(imagestream);

        }catch(Exception e){

        }finally {

                try {
                        imagestream.close();
                        imagestream = null;
                } catch (IOException e) {
                }
        }

        gl.glGenTextures(1, textures, 0);
        gl.glBindTexture(GL10.GL_TEXTURE_2D, textures[0]);

        gl.glTexParameterf(GL10.GL_TEXTURE_2D, GL10.GL_TEXTURE_MIN_FILTER,
GL10.GL_NEAREST);
        gl.glTexParameterf(GL10.GL_TEXTURE_2D, GL10.GL_TEXTURE_MAG_FILTER,
GL10.GL_LINEAR);

        gl.glTexParameterf(GL10.GL_TEXTURE_2D, GL10.GL_TEXTURE_WRAP_S, GL10.GL_REPEAT);
        gl.glTexParameterf(GL10.GL_TEXTURE_2D, GL10.GL_TEXTURE_WRAP_T, GL10.GL_REPEAT);

        GLUtils.texImage2D(GL10.GL_TEXTURE_2D, 0, bitmap, 0);

        bitmap.recycle();
}
```

Finally, in the next section, you'll create the draw() method. Remember, the draw()
method is called by the renderer to draw out the corridor. There are some changes in
the BHCorridor.draw() to account for the multiple sets of vertices in the vertices[]
array.

Creating the draw() Method

You are going to use the glDrawArrays() method with pointers to the wall segment vertices. Take a look at your vertices[] array. The array is visually broken up into four sets of four vertices—one for each corner of a wall segment. You need to tell OpenGL where each wall segment begins and ends. Therefore, you will pass into glDrawArrays() the start point and the number of vertices for each wall segment.

The glDrawArrays() call for wall segment A will look like this:

```
gl.glDrawArrays(GL10.GL_TRIANGLE_STRIP, 0,4);
```

This line tells OpenGL to start at position 0 in the array and read four vertices. By this logic, wall segment two would start at position 4 in the array and extend for another four vertices, and so on.

With the call to glDrawArrays() being the only difference in the draw() method for the BHCorridor, your method should look like this:

```java
public void draw(GL10 gl) {

        gl.glBindTexture(GL10.GL_TEXTURE_2D, textures[0]);
        gl.glFrontFace(GL10.GL_CCW);

        gl.glVertexPointer(3, GL10.GL_FLOAT, 0, vertexBuffer);
        gl.glTexCoordPointer(2, GL10.GL_FLOAT, 0, textureBuffer);

        gl.glEnableClientState(GL10.GL_VERTEX_ARRAY);
        gl.glEnableClientState(GL10.GL_TEXTURE_COORD_ARRAY);

        gl.glDrawArrays(GL10.GL_TRIANGLE_STRIP, 0,4);

        gl.glDrawArrays(GL10.GL_TRIANGLE_STRIP, 4,4);

        gl.glDrawArrays(GL10.GL_TRIANGLE_STRIP, 8,4);

        gl.glDrawArrays(GL10.GL_TRIANGLE_STRIP, 12,4);

        gl.glDisableClientState(GL10.GL_VERTEX_ARRAY);
        gl.glDisableClientState(GL10.GL_TEXTURE_COORD_ARRAY);
        gl.glDisable(GL10.GL_CULL_FACE);

}
```

Your finished BHCorridor class is shown in Listing 11–1.

Listing 11–1. *BHCorridor.java*

```java
package com.proandroidgames;

import java.io.IOException;
import java.io.InputStream;
import java.nio.ByteBuffer;
import java.nio.ByteOrder;
import java.nio.FloatBuffer;
```

```java
import javax.microedition.khronos.opengles.GL10;

import android.content.Context;
import android.graphics.Bitmap;
import android.graphics.BitmapFactory;
import android.opengl.GLUtils;

public class BHCorridor {
        private FloatBuffer vertexBuffer;
        private FloatBuffer textureBuffer;

        private int[] textures = new int[1];

        private float vertices[] = {

                -2.0f, 0.0f, 0.0f,
                1.0f, 0.0f, 0.0f,
                -2.0f, 1.0f, 0.0f,
                1.0f, 1.0f, 0.0f,

                1.0f, 0.0f, 0.0f,
                1.0f, 0.0f, 5.0f,
                1.0f, 1.0f, 0.0f,
                1.0f, 1.0f, 5.0f,

                0.0f, 0.0f, 1.0f,
                0.0f, 0.0f, 5.0f,
                0.0f, 1.0f, 1.0f,
                0.0f, 1.0f, 5.0f,

                -2.0f, 0.0f, 1.0f,
                0.0f, 0.0f, 1.0f,
                -2.0f, 1.0f, 1.0f,
                0.0f, 1.0f, 1.0f,

        };

        private float texture[] = {

                -1.0f, 0.0f,
                1.0f, 0f,
                -1f, 1f,
                1f, 1.0f,

                -1.0f, 0.0f,
                1.0f, 0f,
                -1f, 1f,
                1f, 1.0f,

                -1.0f, 0.0f,
                1.0f, 0f,
                -1f, 1f,
                1f, 1.0f,

                -1.0f, 0.0f,
                1.0f, 0f,
                -1f, 1f,
```

```
                    1f, 1.0f,

        };

        public BHCorridor() {
                ByteBuffer byteBuf = ByteBuffer.allocateDirect(vertices.length * 4);
                byteBuf.order(ByteOrder.nativeOrder());
                vertexBuffer = byteBuf.asFloatBuffer();
                vertexBuffer.put(vertices);
                vertexBuffer.position(0);

                byteBuf = ByteBuffer.allocateDirect(texture.length * 4);
                byteBuf.order(ByteOrder.nativeOrder());
                textureBuffer = byteBuf.asFloatBuffer();
                textureBuffer.put(texture);
                textureBuffer.position(0);
        }

        public void draw(GL10 gl) {

                gl.glBindTexture(GL10.GL_TEXTURE_2D, textures[0]);
                gl.glFrontFace(GL10.GL_CCW);

                gl.glVertexPointer(3, GL10.GL_FLOAT, 0, vertexBuffer);
                gl.glTexCoordPointer(2, GL10.GL_FLOAT, 0, textureBuffer);

                gl.glEnableClientState(GL10.GL_VERTEX_ARRAY);
                gl.glEnableClientState(GL10.GL_TEXTURE_COORD_ARRAY);

                gl.glDrawArrays(GL10.GL_TRIANGLE_STRIP, 0,4);

                gl.glDrawArrays(GL10.GL_TRIANGLE_STRIP, 4,4);

                gl.glDrawArrays(GL10.GL_TRIANGLE_STRIP, 8,4);

                gl.glDrawArrays(GL10.GL_TRIANGLE_STRIP, 12,4);

                gl.glDisableClientState(GL10.GL_VERTEX_ARRAY);
                gl.glDisableClientState(GL10.GL_TEXTURE_COORD_ARRAY);
                gl.glDisable(GL10.GL_CULL_FACE);

        }

        public void loadTexture(GL10 gl,int texture, Context context) {
                InputStream imagestream =
        context.getResources().openRawResource(texture);
                Bitmap bitmap = null;
                try {

                        bitmap = BitmapFactory.decodeStream(imagestream);

                }catch(Exception e){

                }finally {

                        try {
                                imagestream.close();
```

```
                        imagestream = null;
                    } catch (IOException e) {
                    }
            }

            gl.glGenTextures(1, textures, 0);
            gl.glBindTexture(GL10.GL_TEXTURE_2D, textures[0]);

            gl.glTexParameterf(GL10.GL_TEXTURE_2D, GL10.GL_TEXTURE_MIN_FILTER,
GL10.GL_NEAREST);
            gl.glTexParameterf(GL10.GL_TEXTURE_2D, GL10.GL_TEXTURE_MAG_FILTER,
GL10.GL_LINEAR);

            gl.glTexParameterf(GL10.GL_TEXTURE_2D, GL10.GL_TEXTURE_WRAP_S,
GL10.GL_REPEAT);
            gl.glTexParameterf(GL10.GL_TEXTURE_2D, GL10.GL_TEXTURE_WRAP_T,
GL10.GL_REPEAT);

            GLUtils.texImage2D(GL10.GL_TEXTURE_2D, 0, bitmap, 0);

            bitmap.recycle();
        }

}
```

Adding a Wall Texture

With the BHCorridor class created and able to map a texture to the walls, it is time to
add a nice wall texture to replace the temporary one shown in Figure 11–1. Figure 11–2
illustrates the wall texture that you are going to map to the walls of your corridor.

Figure 11–2. *The wall texture*

Begin by adding this image to your drawable.nodpi folder. Then, add a reference to it in
BHEngine as follows:

```
public static final int BACK_WALL = R.drawable.walltexture256;
```

Your finished walls will appear as shown in Figure 11–3 when this new texture is applied.

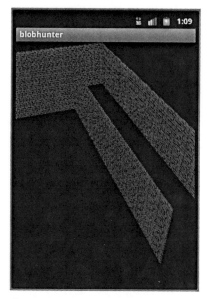

Figure 11–3. *The textured walls*

In the next section, you are going to instantiate a copy of the BHCorridor class and draw it to the screen with the new texture that you just added to *Blob Hunter*.

Calling BHCorridor

As in the *Star Fighter* project from earlier in this book, all of *Blob Hunter*'s rendering is performed in the game rendering class. In Chapter 10, you created this class, BHGameRenderer. In this section, you are going to add a drawCorridor() method that will be called during the game loop. Open the BHGameRenderer.java file, and add a new instance of the BHCorridor, as follows:

```
private BHCorridor corridor = new BHCorridor();
```

Now, you can create a drawCorridor() method. The method is going to set up the gluLookAt() (see Chapter 10 for a description of how this works), and it is going to rotate the corridor on its x and y axes to appear as in Figure 11–3.

```
private void drawCorridor(GL10 gl){

        GLU.gluLookAt(gl, 0f, 0f, 5f, 0f, 0f, 0, 0, 1, 0);
        gl.glRotatef( 40.0f, 1.0f,0.0f, 0.0f);
        gl.glRotatef( 20.0f, 0.0f,1.0f, 0.0f);
        gl.glTranslatef(0.0f, 0.0f, -3f);

        corridor.draw(gl);

}
```

Again, all of this code should look very familiar. By this point in this book, there should be very little new code. You are just taking the code and skills that you learned in created 2-D games and adapting them to a 3-D environment.

Summary

In this chapter, you learned how to create a multipolygon object—the corridor—in a single call. Then, you added a texture to the corridor and rendered it to the screen using BHGamerRenderer. This is a sharp peak in your learning curve, because it teaches you how to manage some very complex objects. Almost any 3-D environment that you can think of, from a vast cityscape to a complex maze, can be built using this technique.

In the final chapter of this book, Chapter 12, you'll create the controls needed to navigate through this 3-D corridor, including collision detection to ensure the player does not walk though your walls.

Navigating the 3-D Environment

You have reached the final chapter of your adventures in learning Android game development. In this book, you started from nothing and created a 2-D scrolling shooter. From the skills learned in creating that game, you were able to create the environment for a 3-D game. Although this book does not cover using all of the skills you have acquired or step you through creating an entire 3-D game, you will learn enough of the basics that hopefully to use that logic to finish the game. In this chapter, you will learn what differences await you when you are trying to create a control system to navigate the 3-D corridor.

When you created a control system for the 2-D *Star Fighter* game, the movement was simple. The player could only move left or right. In *Blob Hunter*, the player should have the freedom to move 360 degrees on the z plane. Let's take a look at what kind of challenges that will pose for you.

At the end of this chapter, I have provided a listing of the key files for the 3D project. These files were chosen because of their complexity, number of changes, or proclivity for causing a problem when you compile your project. If you are having trouble running your 3D project at the end of this chapter, please check you files against those listed after the Summary.

Creating the Control Interface

In this section, you are going to create the control interface, the means by which your player interacts with your game.

In *Star Fighter*, the control interface was a simple left and right motion. However, in a 3-D game, the player will expect to be able to move left, right, forward, backward, and possibly look up or down. While these are many more controls to keep track of, the basic concepts that you learned for *Star Fighter* still apply.

Let's borrow some code for *Star Fighter* and quickly adapt it to move the player forward through the corridor.

Currently, your `BlobhunterActivity` should appear as follows:

```
package com.proandroidgames;

import android.app.Activity;
import android.content.Context;
import android.os.Bundle;

public class BlobhunterActivity extends Activity {
        private BHGameView gameView;

        @Override
        public void onCreate(Bundle savedInstanceState) {

                super.onCreate(savedInstanceState);
                gameView = new BHGameView(this);
                setContentView(gameView);
                BHEngine.context = this;
        }
        @Override
        protected void onResume() {
                super.onResume();
                gameView.onResume();
        }

        @Override
        protected void onPause() {
                super.onPause();
                gameView.onPause();
        }

}
```

You are going to adapt the `onTouchEvent()` method that you created in *Star Fighter* to handle a forward motion as well.

> **NOTE:** In this chapter, you will only add the forward motion control. However, you can easily adapt the control to also handle backward motion.

Before you add in your `onTouchEvent()` method, you need to add a few constants to `BHEngine`.

Editing BHEngine

The goal here is to help you track what the player is trying to do and where the player is in the environment. To do so, add the following lines to your `BHEngine.java` file:

```
public static final int PLAYER_FORWARD = 1;
public static final int PLAYER_RIGHT = 2;
public static final int PLAYER_LEFT = 3;
```

```
public static final float PLAYER_ROTATE_SPEED = 1f;
public static final float PLAYER_WALK_SPEED = 0.1f;
public static int playerMovementAction = 0;
```

The PLAYER_FORWARD, PLAYER_RIGHT, and PLAYER_LEFT constants will be used to track what control the player touched, indicating where the player wants to move in the environment. The PLAYER_ROTATE_SPEED and PLAYER_WALK_SPEED constants indicate how quickly the view of the player rotates on the y axis and how quickly the player walks in the environment, respectively. Finally, playerMovementAction tracks which action (PLAYER_FORWARD, PLAYER_RIGHT, or PLAYER_LEFT) is the current one.

Now that your constants are in place, you can create the control interface in BlobhunterActivity.java.

Editing BlobhunterActivity

The first code you need to add to BlobhunterActivity is a call to the BHEngine.display method. You need to initialize the display variable so that the control interface can call it to determine where on the screen the player has touched.

```
...

@Override
public void onCreate(Bundle savedInstanceState) {

BHEngine.display = ((WindowManager)
getSystemService(Context.WINDOW_SERVICE)).getDefaultDisplay();

        super.onCreate(savedInstanceState);
        gameView = new BHGameView(this);
        setContentView(gameView);
        BHEngine.context = this;
}
...
```

With the display initialized, add an onTouchEvent() method to the BlobhunterActivity class:

```
...

@Override
public boolean onTouchEvent(MotionEvent event) {
        return false;
}
...
```

If you still have the *Star Fighter* project, you can copy and paste the following code directly from its control interface into the new onTouchEvent() method of *Blob Hunter*. In the event that you no longer have the code for the *Star Fighter* project, feel free to download the completed project from the Apress web site.

> **CAUTION:** If you are going to copy and paste from the *Star Fighter* project, be sure to rename the proper constants and variables to correspond to those in the *Blob Hunter* project.

```
...

@Override
public boolean onTouchEvent(MotionEvent event) {
        float x = event.getX();
        float y = event.getY();

        int height = BHEngine.display.getHeight() / 4;
        int playableArea = BHEngine.display.getHeight() - height;

        if (y > playableArea){
                switch (event.getAction()){
                        case MotionEvent.ACTION_DOWN:
                                if(x < BHEngine.display.getWidth() / 2){
                                        BHEngine.playerMovementAction =
BHEngine.PLAYER_LEFT;
                                }else{
                                        BHEngine.playerMovementAction =
BHEngine.PLAYER_RIGHT;
                                }
                                break;
                        case MotionEvent.ACTION_UP:
                                BHEngine.playerMovementAction = 0;
                                break;
                }
        }

        return false;
}

...
```

Next, let's add the control for detecting forward motion.

Letting Your Player Move Forward

Right now, the onTouchEvent() uses the y >playableAreacondition to detect if the player has touched the lower portion of the screen. Add an else statement to detect a touch to the upper portion of the screen. You will use this touch to the upper portion of the screen to determine that the user wants to move forward.

```
...

@Override
public boolean onTouchEvent(MotionEvent event) {
        float x = event.getX();
        float y = event.getY();
```

```
        int height = BHEngine.display.getHeight() / 4;
        int playableArea = BHEngine.display.getHeight() - height;

    if (y > playableArea){
            switch (event.getAction()){
                    case MotionEvent.ACTION_DOWN:
                            if(x < BHEngine.display.getWidth() / 2){
                                    BHEngine.playerMovementAction =
BHEngine.PLAYER_LEFT;
                            }else{
                                    BHEngine.playerMovementAction =
BHEngine.PLAYER_RIGHT;
                            }
                            break;
                    case MotionEvent.ACTION_UP:
                            BHEngine.playerMovementAction = 0;
                            break;
            }
    }else{
            switch (event.getAction()){
                    case MotionEvent.ACTION_DOWN:
                            BHEngine.playerMovementAction = BHEngine.PLAYER_FORWARD;
                            break;
                    case MotionEvent.ACTION_UP:
                            BHEngine.playerMovementAction = 0;
                            break;
            }
    }


    return false;
}
```

...

All you are doing in this new code is detecting if the player has touched the upper portion of the screen, and if so, you set the playerMovementAction to PLAYER_FORWARD.

Keep in mind, when you are creating a full game, that you will want to tweak this slightly to also account for a backward touch control, and possibly some panning up or down controls. In the next section, you are going to react to these controls in the BHGameRenderer class and move the player accordingly through the corridor.

Moving Through the Corridor

Moving through the corridor is a little tricky, but with some practice, you can create a control system that is smooth and stable. Admittedly, you would be able to optimize a great camera system if you were adept enough at OpenGL to create your own matrices and perform your own matrix multiplication. However, from the beginning of this book, the goal has been to let you use OpenGL's built-in tools as a substitute for the learning curve of manual processes.

Open `BHGameRenderer.java`, which is where your game loop code is stored. The first thing you will need to do is add a couple of variables to help track the player's location.

...

```
public class BHGameRenderer implements Renderer{
private BHCorridor corridor = new BHCorridor();
private float corridorZPosition = -5f;

        private float playerRotate = 0f;

        private long loopStart = 0;
        private long loopEnd = 0;
        private long loopRunTime = 0 ;
```

...

The `corridorZPosition` variable is initially set to –5. This represents the initial location of the player in the corridor. The value of –5 should set the player at the end of the corridor, because the corridor, as you have set it in the `BDCorridor` class, extends toward the 4 units on the z axis. Therefore, starting the play at –5 (or 5 units toward the player/screen) will give the appearance that the player is standing at the entrance of the corridor.

Next, locate the `drawCorridor()` method that you created in the previous chapter, and erase all of its contents except for the call to the corridor's `draw()` method, as follows:

```
private void drawCorridor(GL10 gl){

corridor.draw(gl);

}
```

Using a `switch…case` statement, similar to the one in *Star Fighter*, you will detect which action the player is trying to take. However, how do you react to a forward motion if that is what the player wants to do?

In the *Star Fighter* project, you had to move the player only left or right. Both movements were accomplished by a positive or negative value on the x axis. However, in a 3-D environment adding or subtracting on the x axis would result is a sideways, or strafing, motion, and that is not what you are going for here. You want to move the player forward and let them turn their head to the left or right. These are vastly different motions from those you used in *Star Fighter*.

To move the player forward, you are going to add values to the z axis. Recall that you are looking at the corridor along the z axis, and the 0 value for the z axis of the corridor is at the far wall. Therefore, you are starting at –5 (see the `corridorZPosition` variable) and moving to 0.

To simulate turning the player's head, you will need to rotate, not translate, along the y axis: you do not actually want to move along the y or x axis; rather, just like turning your head in real life, you want to rotate on the axis.

Add a `switch` . . . case statement to adjust the `corridorZPositon` and `playerRotate`values accordingly. This is the same process used in *Star Fighter*, so it will not be discussed in detail. If it does not look familiar, check back trough the *Star Fighter* code in Chapter 5.

```
private void drawCorridor(GL10 gl){

        switch(BHEngine.playerMovementAction){
                case BHEngine.PLAYER_FORWARD:
                        corridorZPosition += BHEngine.PLAYER_WALK_SPEED;
                        break;
                case BHEngine.PLAYER_LEFT:
                        playerRotate -= BHEngine.PLAYER_ROTATE_SPEED;
                        break;
                case BHEngine.PLAYER_RIGHT:
                        playerRotate += BHEngine.PLAYER_ROTATE_SPEED;
                        break;
                default:
                        break;
        }


        corridor.draw(gl);

}
```

In the next section, you will adjust the player's position, or view, while moving down the corridor.

Adjusting the View of the Player

As discussed earlier, OpenGL has no concept of a camera like some 3-D systems do. Rather, you are tricking your way through making the environment look a certain way to the player, so to speak.

The same translations and rotations that you used in *Star Fighter* to move 2-D models in the scene will also be used to rotate and translate the corridor so that the player will believe he or she is walking through it.

Add a translate to the drawCorridor() method that will move the model along the z axis, and add a rotate that will turn the model corresponding to where the player is looking.

```
private void drawCorridor(GL10 gl){

        switch(BHEngine.playerMovementAction){
                case BHEngine.PLAYER_FORWARD:
                        corridorZPosition += BHEngine.PLAYER_WALK_SPEED;
                        break;
                case BHEngine.PLAYER_LEFT:
                        playerRotate -= BHEngine.PLAYER_ROTATE_SPEED;
                        break;
                case BHEngine.PLAYER_RIGHT:
                        playerRotate += BHEngine.PLAYER_ROTATE_SPEED;
                        break;
                default:
```

```
                            break;
            }

            GLU.gluLookAt(gl, 0f, 0f, 0.5f, 0f, 0f, 0f, 0f, 1f, 0f);
            gl.glTranslatef(-0.5f, -0.5f, corridorZPosition);
            gl.glRotatef( playerRotate, 0.0f,1.0f, 0.0f);


            corridor.draw(gl);

    }
```

Compile and run your code; you should now have a rudimentary navigation system to move forward and turn left and right. With a little work using the skills you have already learned, you can easily add some collision detection to keep the player from walking through the walls. Try these examples on your own:

- Add a navigation control to allow the player to backup through the corridor. Here's a hint for doing this: create a touch even on the screen that will subtract a given integer value from the current z axis position when touched.

- Create collision detection system to keep the player from walking through the walls. Here's your hint on this one: track the player's current axis positions and test them against the known positions of the corridor walls. Remember that the corridor walls will not move. Something like this might help you:

```
if corridorZPosition <= -5f){
        corridorZPosition = -5f;
}
if corridorZPosition >= 0f){
        corridorZPosition = 0f;
}
```

- Create a navigation system to let the player look up and down in the environment. As a hint on this task, consider that it sounds more difficult than it is. Simply add a touch event that will either add or subtract values from a new rotation on the x axis. This will pivot the player's field of view up or down.

You have the skills needed to create a fully functional 3-D game, and surprisingly enough, they were the same skills you used to create a fully functional 2-D game; you've just added more details.

Summary

I hope you enjoyed this primer into the basic skills required to create some enjoyable casual games and that you continue to practice and expand on those skills. There is so much more to OpenGL ES and Android Ice Cream Sandwich than what was covered in this book, but you now have a great base of knowledge that will help you plot your course further into the world of Android game development.

Reviewing the Key 3-D Code

The listings that follow contain all of the code needed to double check your work in the event that you are having a problem getting Blob Hunter to run correctly. I have selected the BHEngine.java, BHCorridor.java, and BHGameRenderer.java. These files either touch the most code—like the BHEngine, contain complicated concepts—like the BHCorridor, or perform the most functionality—like the BHGameRenderer.

The first file that you can check is the BHEngine.java, shown in Listing 12–1. BHEngine is the key settings file and it contains the settings used throughout the project. Because this file is used so extensively in the Blob Hunter project, it has the greatest likelihood to cause problems when you compile.

Listing 12–1. *BHEngine.java*

```
package com.proandroidgames;

import android.content.Context;
import android.view.Display;


public class BHEngine {
        /*Constants that will be used in the game*/
        public static final int GAME_THREAD_DELAY = 4000;
        public static final int GAME_THREAD_FPS_SLEEP = (1000/60);
        public static final int BACK_WALL = R.drawable.walltexture256;
        public static final int PLAYER_FORWARD = 1;
        public static final int PLAYER_RIGHT = 2;
        public static final int PLAYER_LEFT = 3;
        public static final float PLAYER_ROTATE_SPEED = 1f;
        public static final float PLAYER_WALK_SPEED = 0.1f;
        /*Game Variables*/
        public static int playerMovementAction = 0;
        public static Context context;
        public static Display display;
}
```

Listing 12–2 shows the BHCorridor.java file. This file could cause you problem because it contains a code concept that is not only abstract, but was not covered previously in Part 1 of this book. The structure of the vertices[] and texture array is key to the functionality of the entire project. If the arrays are not setup correctly, the project will not run as expected, if at all. When checking this file, pay close attention to the arrays and the array definitions.

Listing 12–2. *BHCorridor.java*

```
import java.io.IOException;
import java.io.InputStream;
import java.nio.ByteBuffer;
import java.nio.ByteOrder;
import java.nio.FloatBuffer;
```

```java
import javax.microedition.khronos.opengles.GL10;

import android.content.Context;
import android.graphics.Bitmap;
import android.graphics.BitmapFactory;
import android.opengl.GLUtils;

public class BHCorridor {

        private FloatBuffer vertexBuffer;
        private FloatBuffer textureBuffer;

        private int[] textures = new int[1];

        private float vertices[] = {
                        -2.0f, 0.0f, 0.0f,
                        1.0f, 0.0f, 0.0f,
                        -2.0f, 1.0f, 0.0f,
                        1.0f, 1.0f, 0.0f,

                        1.0f, 0.0f, 0.0f,
                        1.0f, 0.0f, 5.0f,
                        1.0f, 1.0f, 0.0f,
                        1.0f, 1.0f, 5.0f,

                        0.0f, 0.0f, 1.0f,
                        0.0f, 0.0f, 5.0f,
                        0.0f, 1.0f, 1.0f,
                        0.0f, 1.0f, 5.0f,

                        -2.0f, 0.0f, 1.0f,
                        0.0f, 0.0f, 1.0f,
                        -2.0f, 1.0f, 1.0f,
                        0.0f, 1.0f, 1.0f,
                        };
        private float texture[] = {
            -1.0f, 0.0f,
            1.0f, 0f,
            -1f, 1f,
            1f, 1.0f,

            -1.0f, 0.0f,
            1.0f, 0f,
            -1f, 1f,
            1f, 1.0f,

            -1.0f, 0.0f,
            1.0f, 0f,
            -1f, 1f,
            1f, 1.0f,

            -1.0f, 0.0f,
            1.0f, 0f,
            -1f, 1f,
            1f, 1.0f,
```

```java
        };
    public BHCorridor() {
        ByteBuffer byteBuf = ByteBuffer.allocateDirect(vertices.length * 4);
        byteBuf.order(ByteOrder.nativeOrder());
        vertexBuffer = byteBuf.asFloatBuffer();
        vertexBuffer.put(vertices);
        vertexBuffer.position(0);

        byteBuf = ByteBuffer.allocateDirect(texture.length * 4);
        byteBuf.order(ByteOrder.nativeOrder());
        textureBuffer = byteBuf.asFloatBuffer();
        textureBuffer.put(texture);
        textureBuffer.position(0);
    }
    public void draw(GL10 gl) {

        gl.glBindTexture(GL10.GL_TEXTURE_2D, textures[0]);
        gl.glFrontFace(GL10.GL_CCW);

        gl.glVertexPointer(3, GL10.GL_FLOAT, 0, vertexBuffer);
        gl.glTexCoordPointer(2, GL10.GL_FLOAT, 0, textureBuffer);

        gl.glEnableClientState(GL10.GL_VERTEX_ARRAY);
        gl.glEnableClientState(GL10.GL_TEXTURE_COORD_ARRAY);

        gl.glDrawArrays(GL10.GL_TRIANGLE_STRIP, 0,4);

        gl.glDrawArrays(GL10.GL_TRIANGLE_STRIP, 4,4);

        gl.glDrawArrays(GL10.GL_TRIANGLE_STRIP, 8,4);

        gl.glDrawArrays(GL10.GL_TRIANGLE_STRIP, 12,4);

        gl.glDisableClientState(GL10.GL_VERTEX_ARRAY);
        gl.glDisableClientState(GL10.GL_TEXTURE_COORD_ARRAY);
        gl.glDisable(GL10.GL_CULL_FACE);
    }

    public void loadTexture(GL10 gl,int texture, Context context) {
            InputStream imagestream =
context.getResources().openRawResource(texture);
            Bitmap bitmap = null;
            try {

                    bitmap = BitmapFactory.decodeStream(imagestream);

            }catch(Exception e){

            }finally {
              try {
                    imagestream.close();
                    imagestream = null;
                } catch (IOException e) {
```

```
                                      }
                                }

                        gl.glGenTextures(1, textures, 0);
                        gl.glBindTexture(GL10.GL_TEXTURE_2D, textures[0]);

                        gl.glTexParameterf(GL10.GL_TEXTURE_2D, GL10.GL_TEXTURE_MIN_FILTER,
GL10.GL_NEAREST);
                        gl.glTexParameterf(GL10.GL_TEXTURE_2D, GL10.GL_TEXTURE_MAG_FILTER,
GL10.GL_LINEAR);

                        gl.glTexParameterf(GL10.GL_TEXTURE_2D, GL10.GL_TEXTURE_WRAP_S,
GL10.GL_REPEAT);
                        gl.glTexParameterf(GL10.GL_TEXTURE_2D, GL10.GL_TEXTURE_WRAP_T,
GL10.GL_REPEAT);

                        GLUtils.texImage2D(GL10.GL_TEXTURE_2D, 0, bitmap, 0);

                        bitmap.recycle();
                }
        }
```

The final key file in the Blob Hunter is the BHGameRenderer.java. This file contains the game loop for the Blob Hunter game. Just as with Star Fighter, the game loop is the most likely place for a code problem because it has the most code of any file in the project. Listing 12–3 provides the source for the BHGameRenderer.java.

Listing 12–3. *BHGameRenderer.java*

```
 package com.proandroidgames;


import javax.microedition.khronos.egl.EGLConfig;
import javax.microedition.khronos.opengles.GL10;

import android.opengl.GLSurfaceView.Renderer;
import android.opengl.GLU;

public class BHGameRenderer implements Renderer{
        private BHCorridor corridor = new BHCorridor();
        private float corridorZPosition = -5f;
        private float playerRotate = 0f;

        private long loopStart = 0;
        private long loopEnd = 0;
        private long loopRunTime = 0 ;

        @Override
        public void onDrawFrame(GL10 gl) {
                loopStart = System.currentTimeMillis();
                // TODO Auto-generated method stub
                try {
                        if (loopRunTime < BHEngine.GAME_THREAD_FPS_SLEEP){
                                Thread.sleep(BHEngine.GAME_THREAD_FPS_SLEEP -
loopRunTime);
                        }
                } catch (InterruptedException e) {
                        // TODO Auto-generated catch block
```

```java
                        e.printStackTrace();
            }
        gl.glClear(GL10.GL_COLOR_BUFFER_BIT | GL10.GL_DEPTH_BUFFER_BIT);
        gl.glLoadIdentity();

        drawCorridor(gl);

        loopEnd = System.currentTimeMillis();
    loopRunTime = ((loopEnd - loopStart));

}



private void drawCorridor(GL10 gl){

        if (corridorZPosition <= -5f){
                corridorZPosition = -5f;
        }
        if (corridorZPosition >= 0f){
                corridorZPosition = 0f;
        }

        switch(BHEngine.playerMovementAction){
        case BHEngine.PLAYER_FORWARD:
                corridorZPosition += BHEngine.PLAYER_WALK_SPEED;
                break;
        case BHEngine.PLAYER_LEFT:
                playerRotate -= BHEngine.PLAYER_ROTATE_SPEED;
                break;
        case BHEngine.PLAYER_RIGHT:
                playerRotate += BHEngine.PLAYER_ROTATE_SPEED;
                break;
        default:
                        break;
        }

        GLU.gluLookAt(gl, 0f, 0f, 0.5f, 0f, 0f, 0f, 0f, 1f, 0f);
        gl.glTranslatef(-0.5f, -0.5f, corridorZPosition);
        gl.glRotatef( playerRotate, 0.0f,1.0f, 0.0f);

        corridor.draw(gl);

}

@Override
public void onSurfaceChanged(GL10 gl, int width, int height) {
        // TODO Auto-generated method stub

        gl.glViewport(0, 0, width,height);
        gl.glMatrixMode(GL10.GL_PROJECTION);
        gl.glLoadIdentity();

        GLU.gluPerspective(gl, 45.0f, (float) width / height, .1f, 100.f);
        gl.glMatrixMode(GL10.GL_MODELVIEW);
    gl.glLoadIdentity();
```

```
        }

        @Override
        public void onSurfaceCreated(GL10 gl, EGLConfig config) {
                // TODO Auto-generated method stub

                gl.glEnable(GL10.GL_TEXTURE_2D);
                gl.glClearDepthf(1.0f);
                gl.glEnable(GL10.GL_DEPTH_TEST);
                gl.glDepthFunc(GL10.GL_LEQUAL);
                gl.glHint(GL10.GL_PERSPECTIVE_CORRECTION_HINT, GL10.GL_NICEST);
                gl.glDisable(GL10.GL_DITHER);

                corridor.loadTexture(gl, BHEngine.BACK_WALL, BHEngine.context);

        }

}
```

Index

CPSIA information can be obtained at www.ICGtesting.com
Printed in the USA
LVOW050548110412

277098LV00004BA/1/P